MY OH MY

The Dave Niehaus Story

AB's		POS	219 SINGLES		AVE	HR	RBI		1/1	13 2 30
9RUNS			256		371	8	60	7 #257		#258
TS 111 353		9	ICHRO			78 MULTI		3rd 3		
					285	14	80			

SAVE-

								E	0	0
								LOB	2 / 2	1 / 3

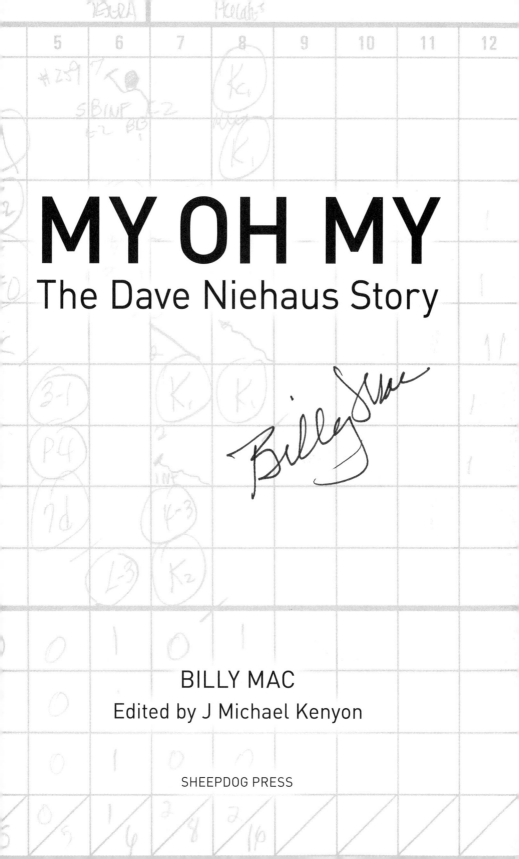

MY OH MY
The Dave Niehaus Story

BILLY MAC

Edited by J Michael Kenyon

SHEEPDOG PRESS

Publisher: Sheepdog Press
Editor: J Michael Kenyon
Additional editing: Connie Lehmen
Indexer: Craig Smith
Cover & text design: Jennifer Shontz, www.redshoedesign.com
Printer: Sheridan Books
Publicity: Connie Lehmen
Production management: Kent Sturgis Publishing Services, LLC

All photos courtesy of Niehaus Family Collection unless otherwise credited.
Photos courtesy of National Baseball Hall of Fame Library: pp. 12, 15, 19, 21,
    22, 157, 268, 269, 320, 322, 325, 331.
 Photos courtesy of Author: pp. 26 (bottom), 30, 50, 53, 55, 119, 123, 146, 147,
    154 (bottom), 159, 263, 270, 272 (bottom), 278, 279.
Photos courtesy of Princeton Library: pp. 54, 56.
Photo courtesy of Gary Osborne: page 64.
Photos courtesy of Al and Dorothy Clausen: pp. 157 (bottom), 184 and 271 (top).
Photo courtesy of Dave Valle: page 193.
Photo courtesy of Ken Levine: page 204.
Photos courtesy of Connie Lehmen: pp. 268 (bottom), 271 (bottom), 272 (top).
Photo courtesy of Dave and Bonnie Grosby: page 329.

Cover photograph: *Dave Niehaus*
Frontispiece: *Dave and Rick in the broadcast booth at Safeco Field.*

Library of Congress Control Number: 2017900932
ISBN 978-0-578-18546-0
ISBN 978-0-578-18547-7 (HB)

Printed in the United States of America
10 9 8 7 6 5 4 3 2 1

Contents

Dave and Marilyn Niehaus.

Dedication

THIS BOOK IS RESPECTFULLY DEDICATED to Marilyn Niehaus, who unfailingly supported the broadcasting career of her husband, David. Her enduring love and constant commitment fashioned a baseball life and a baseball family.

The work also is dedicated to the Niehaus children: Andy, Matt, Greta. It is further dedicated to their children: Zach, Steven, Madeline, Alexa, Audrey and Spencer.

To Rick Rizzs and Kevin Cremin, who worked beside Dave Niehaus and will carry him in their hearts always.

To Ken Wilson, Joe Simpson, Ron Fairly, Ken Levine, Chip Caray, Dave Sims, Mike Blowers, Dick Enberg, Gary Hill, Dave Valle, Kevin Calabro, Wes Stock, Bill Freehan, Ken Brett, Jay Buhner, and other broadcasters who worked with Dave, and to all voices of the game.

Finally, to the baseball writers: J Michael Kenyon, Tracy Ringolsby, Larry Stone, Emmett Watson, Ryan Divish, Bob Sherwin, Blaine Newnham, Shannon Drayer, Bob Finnegan, Steve Rudman, Kirby Arnold, Jim Street, Craig Smith, and Steve Kelley, whose contributions are greatly appreciated.

Acknowledgments

MANY DESERVE TO SHARE the credit for this work:

Marilyn Niehaus who trusted me with the story of her husband's life.

Rick Rizzs and Kevin Cremin, who made me believe I was worthy of the assignment.

Publicist Connie Lehmen, who was always there for me and who is one of the great joys of my life.

My friend Eric Manegold, who challenged me to take on the task.

Bob Simeone and the Seattle Mariners RBI Club, who believed in me all the way.

My wife, Merrilee, whose love and unshakeable confidence in me carried me through to the end.

But there is one person, J Michael Kenyon, without whom this work would never have taken shape. His editorial acumen was instrumental far beyond the thicket of grammatical errors and punctuation omissions he rooted out. It was he who counseled me in the first place to write more than a biography—to write a *baseball* book. He wisely urged me to follow every digression, to introduce all of the baseball people who shaped Dave Niehaus' youth and who led Dave toward his career. It was he who suggested I begin and end the story in Cooperstown.

J Michael possesses the most voluminous mind I know and yet he brought to this effort far more than just an astounding knowledge of the history of the game. His wit and his sense of humor, his veteran scribe's devotion to detail and respect for the game, and his lifetime of anecdotes and musings: I was the beneficiary of it all.

There is no way this work could have been done without him. Without his collaborative efforts there would be nothing more than a wandering narrative lost in the landscape of a well-intentioned but second-rate manuscript. To you, J Michael, and to your bride Joan, a tip of the cap as I cross the third-base line on the way back to the dugout.

The Billy Mac Roster

This special group of people gave both encouragement and financial support to launch this book. They patiently supported me through what turned out to be a very long process.

They share a love and regard for Dave Niehaus and his work and they were there from the beginning, always reminding me how important he was to them. Their love for the game of baseball and for Dave's legacy deserves both my thanks and my enduring acknowledgement.

Thank you to:

John Pat & Barbara Bourassa	Dan McCarty & Lynn Ludeman
Alan Deright	Seattle Mariners RBI Club
Ellen D. Duernberger	Bob Melsheimer
Martha Elliott	Randy & Linda Ritualo
Barbara Evans	Rick Rizzs
David & Kathy Hope	Bob & Linda Simeone
Stuart Jacobson	Tony Simeone
Eric & Susan Manegold	Mel Weipert

Special Thanks

I am completely indebted to the writers and publications whose work I relied upon in constructing this manuscript. Because, in particular, so many newspaper articles were sourced and elements of them interspersed throughout the book, I elected to create a simple bibliography as opposed to the perhaps more scholarly use of footnotes throughout. I strongly urge the readers to peruse the bibliography and become aware of the many bright lights who were the source of so many of the quotations referenced herein.

These columnists, reporters, beat writers and magazine writers have my thanks and my enduring regard for their work.

Foreword

EVERY SO OFTEN, A MAJOR LEAGUE play-by-play announcer comes along and turns your radio from an audio medium to a visual medium. Dave Niehaus was that broadcaster.

Through his eyes and then the tenor of his voice, Dave took us on a nightly journey through the American League from Seattle to Boston and every point in between. With his words and vivid description he made us not only "see" but feel the emotion of a baseball game and feel what it would be like to sit in the front-row seat at the Kingdome or Safeco Field and every ballpark in baseball!

I know. I had the pleasure and privilege to sit next to the man for twenty-five seasons and was truly amazed by his talent and artistry. I can still hear David's call of Edgar's double in game five of the Division Series vs. the Yankees, the biggest hit in the history of the Mariners and I smile every time I do. My Oh My.

No one captured the moment like he did.

Billy Mac, through your writing, research and knowing the man like you did…you took us along on David's journey from a small town in Princeton, Indiana to Seattle, Washington. You opened the eyes and hearts of the fans to get to know a loving, caring husband, father and grand-father and friend to millions of listeners in the Pacific Northwest. You also reminded us why he was one of the greatest broadcasters of all time with his induction into the Baseball Hall of Fame in Cooperstown. Dave made baseball on the radio what it should be—FUN!

Dave Niehaus was a great storyteller. Billy Mac…thank you for telling his story. My Oh My!

—Rick Rizzs

DAVID ARNOLD NIEHAUS. I just love the name and the man. The best radio play-by-play man in the business, ever. No one could draw you into the action like David because he, too, was drawn into the drama as much, or more so than you. Better than being there. One of a kind, one in a million, forever known as The Voice.

He saw something in me in Kansas City in 1982, when I was assisting in the Mariner radio booth for both series with the Royals. When Dave called that winter, asking if I would be interested in being the producer-engineer of the Mariner broadcasts, it was a gift from the heavens; thirty-four years later, I am forever grateful.

Billy Mac knew Dave, loved him like we all did and in this book you will feel that. You'll get to know Dave better than you did and learn a few things along the way about a young man from Princeton, Indiana who, by way of Armed Forces Radio, the Los Angeles Angels and the Seattle Mariners, became the Ford Frick Award recipient in 2008.

That was a day when he was rightly honored, and the place where he gave the speech of a lifetime at baseball's hallowed Hall of Fame in Cooperstown, New York. Concluding his acceptance, he shared how he felt: "No one will ever be more appreciative," he said.

Well, David, there never will be anyone more appreciative of you than we, the fans, the people who worked with you and all of us who loved you.

—Kevin Cremin

Top, from left: In 1936, Ty Cobb, Walter Johnson, Babe Ruth, Honus Wagner and Christy Mathewson became the first inductees into the Baseball Hall of Fame and Museum. Bottom Three years later, the newly built Hall of Fame was dedicated in 1939.

Homeward Bound:
25 Main Street

When you get here, you know that there is only one place like it,
no other place in the world, like Cooperstown. If you are a baseball fan,
you're in heaven…Anything you ever want to know about baseball,
about the history of the game, right between those doors…
—Dave Niehaus

STATE ROUTE 80 IS ONE OF THE ROADS you take to get here. The two-lane highway with a 50-mile per hour limit rolls gently southward along the western shore of Otsego Lake. From the south, just northeast of Oneonta on Interstate 88, State Route 28 carries you through the rolling hills of north central New York state toward the object of your pilgrimage.

A mix of birch, willow and alder trees adorn the routes, co-mingling with the hickory nuts and the American beeches. The chestnut trees that were commonplace are now gone, victims of an early twentieth-century blight; so, too, the elms, decimated by invading pests in the 1960s. It's now the sugar maple trees with their rich spring greens and autumnal reds and golds that will primarily catch the eye as the roads gently ascend above valleys still rustic enough to inspire old colonial musings.

In the heart of what was once the great Mohawk Nation, you will find this town named for Judge William Cooper, father of American novelist James Fenimore Cooper.

As Cooperstown lies just below and in between Albany and Schenectady, it's a bit out of the way no matter where you are coming from. So, while there are a lot of ways to get here, you've got to *want* to get here. Yet, as many and varied as these ways are, they are far fewer than the number of roads taken by those whose destination is Cooperstown, the shrine.

Before June 12,1939, the chief link between Cooperstown and baseball was forged by former National League President Abraham G. Mills. His 1905 Mills Commission, a panel appointed by sporting goods entrepreneur and sports publisher Albert Spalding, had sanctioned the much-disputed and now disregarded claim that West Point graduate and Civil War hero Andrew Doubleday invented the game at Cooperstown in 1839. Despite its lack of authenticity, the claim was widely believed to be true, much to the delight of Stephen Carlton Clark, owner of the local Otesaga Resort Hotel. Clark knew the charm of the myth far exceeded the details of the reality and set about to render the fine print irrelevant. Like a 3-2 pitch just off the corner, it was too good to take and the baseball world just couldn't lay off it.

Yale graduate Clark and his brother, Edward, were grandsons of Edward Clark, founder of the Singer Sewing Machine Company. They built the Otesaga in 1909 and it thrived until Prohibition devastated the region's hops industry and the Depression decimated the local tourist trade. Clark decided to parlay the Doubleday myth into his new great bet on how to revive the town. As one who would later serve as both a director of the Metropolitan Museum of Art and as chairman of the board of trustees of the Museum of Modern Art, he had the expertise and the connections to make it happen.

Before too long, Stephen Clark's great marketing dream for Cooperstown would become a reality: a national shrine to the game of baseball—a tourist attraction tied to the Doubleday myth and an idea that would make this out-of-the-way town a singular destination. On that twelfth day of June, 1939, "the shrine" officially opened and 25 Main Street became every ballplayer's favorite address—the National Baseball Hall of Fame.

Its bronze busts and burnished plaques immortalize a gathering of men whose exploits became the stuff of legend, whose excellence and accomplishments made them iconic. They were inextricably linked to a uniform and a number, so much so that their mighty deeds were measured against not only contemporaries and predecessors but also against the other members of this revered company who wore that same uniform and even the same number.

Built in 1909 with its grand portico and lakeside veranda well-preserved for more than a century, the Otesaga Resort Hotel prospered from construction of the Baseball Hall of Fame and Museum in 1939.

Richie Ashburn and Ozzie Smith, Nellie Fox and Red Schoendienst, Lefty Gomez and Carl Hubbell . . . on it goes past Frank Robinson and Mike Schmidt, Steve Carlton and Sandy Koufax. Those whose names are carved here are compared and contrasted, ranked and judged by many criteria, objective and subjective. Such is their greatness that only the likes of Ruth and Musial and Gehrig and Mays attain a perch from which they are untouched by the trivialities of era and position and number and are, literally, beyond compare.

For many, the road to Cooperstown took them through dusty hamlets and rural sandlots, towns whose entire populations wouldn't fill the bleachers at Sportsman's Park or Briggs Stadium. Their road was painted with baselines and lit by klieg lights on stanchions, foul poles on either side. They were already travelers on this highway by the time they were in high school and for most that is precisely what they left behind for a dirt-paying, bus-riding, semi-nomadic job in any one of dozens of minor-league towns. Few viewed it as a job; everyone saw it as a shot. It was the gateway, the portal and the unavoidable crucible—the arena in which one might prove worthy of "the call."

Almost no one puts on his first minor-league uniform without putting on the dream cloak as well. The game is played with a solitary goal in sight—The Show. Even those with complete self-awareness of their limitations still dream the dream, however briefly. And for those who realize that dream of playing in the big leagues, there is yet another image that dances in their slumbers.

They all dream that dream, too. Cooperstown. The Hall.

From the call to the Hall is a road traveled by only a few. Their journeys singular, their destination common, they come this way. For decades, the daytime was their sole time slot and trains their only means of travel. The more recently arrived logged untold airline miles to spend cloudless afternoons battling the sun and bulb-lit evenings picking line drives out of the banks of electric lamps, enduring rainy, wind-blown days in April trying to keep dry and chilly fog-filled nights in September trying to keep warm.

These few came here never to leave, to place a piece of their soul, a replica of their image, here forever. To dust they would eventually return, but their bronze visage remains for all to see. Preserved in their youth and in their prime and in their glory, they beckon us to reminisce and remember, to replay and to revisit. There is baseball immortality to be found here in Otsego County in upstate New York.

And not just for players.

As few as they are, these baseball brethren, they are enshrined alongside an even smaller coterie, a group every bit as select and every bit as cherished by the fans. This other brethren saw the inside of those same back roads towns and the inside of those same wheezing buses that slept four dozen without a hint of comfort. They shared in the annual march to the season's end, toward the inexorable terminus of that last game of the campaign, embarked toward in April, arrived at in September. They lived the exhilaration and the frustration and the exhaustion produced by the slow, daily grind that is the longest season in major sports.

Their heroics were not recorded in the box scores and their names never appeared among the league leaders in any categories other than sore throats and sharpened pencils.

They may never have thrown a shutout or recorded a save, legged out an infield single or stretched a soft line drive into a double. But without them, neither did we. They never ran through a stop sign to score by a whisker or dug one out of the dirt to nip the runner, but save for them, none of us would have either. They wore no numbers and could not be found in the scorecards. Yet, without them, the numbers would not have been spoken and the scorecards would have remained blank. These were the men who called the game.

Their impact was, at times, even greater than those who toiled between the lines, their reach every bit as far. Into millions of homes they came, down countless highways their voices tumbled from the dashboard. Into crowded, rapturously silent bars and meeting halls they echoed, into the earphones of schoolboys with transistor radios in their pockets. Like an umbilical cord they connected us to the game, to our favorite pastime. Like an outstretched hand, they bade us to grasp on and be connected to "the windup and the pitch."

They gave us the Texas Leaguer and the little blooper, the sharp line drive and the blue darter, the scorching one-hopper that handcuffed the third basemen and the hard, in-between hop that ate him up, the lazy fly ball and the can of corn. From them came the pitches that were down in the dirt and the fifty-nine-footers, the calling card and the chin music. Pitches that danced on the corners and painted the black were gaped at and waved at and "shaken their heads at" and spun on and fanned on and passed on by batters who were all tied up in knots or frozen at the dish or just plain unable to pull the trigger.

They filled our ears and our baseball souls with offerings and deliveries that were blistered and scorched, pounded into the terra firma, chopped off the plate, hammered to left, trickled into right, parachuted into centerfield. Those deliveries might be herky-jerky, all-arms, corkscrew, like a rocking chair and they issued forth seeds and darts and high cheese and rainbows and yellow hammers.

Theirs was a universe in which managers were blowin' their tops and pullin' their hair out or gettin' a little grayer with every pitch as coaches were throwin' up stop signs or wavin' 'em in or on their hands and knees tellin' 'em to get down or, sometimes, just wiping off the previous sign.

Their dialect was a musical mix of Bowery Boys and Shakespeare and Ralph Waldo Emerson, simultaneously regional and universal. Their song sent melodies into the night, sung in a proper New England accent or a Southern twang or a plain old Midwestern directness. Typically these men worked in pairs, the play-by-play announcer and his sidekick, the "color man," the latter most often an ex-player who had toiled in the big leagues and whose charm and appeal was largely based on the particular style with which he "moidered da King's English." Such was the twosome of Buddy Blattner and Dizzy Dean calling St. Louis Browns' games and, later, the CBS television Game of the Week.

One great exception to the broadcaster-player tandem was the subsequent CBS team of Dizzy Dean and Pee Wee Reese. That pairing offered not just the experienced perspective of two great veteran players but, most notably, Dizzy's vocabulary and sentence structure. Ol' Diz simultaneously made fans hoot and holler and English teachers across America shake their heads.

Since 1978 and the inductions of broadcasters Mel Allen and Walter "Red" Barber, State Route 80 to Cooperstown has beckoned these denizens of the broadcast booth to baseball immortality as well. And just as every man who sits down behind a microphone in Amarillo or Des Moines, Redding or Savannah dreams of The Show every bit as much as those whose efforts he chronicles, so, too, the ones who already sit behind a big-league microphone also dream of their name and their life's work being associated with that singular place: Cooperstown.

Including spring training, the baseball broadcaster is a guest in the homes and cars and offices of fans for seven months a year. With the 162-game season and the demise of double-headers, these voices became our daily companions and our conduit to the game twenty-six days a month for more than half of the year.

Long-time broadcaster
Mel Allen won the Ford
C. Frick Award in 1978.
His distinctive voice was
known to millions of New
York Yankee fans in the
1940s, '50s and '60s.

Walter "Red" Barber, who also won a Ford C. Frick Award in 1978, broadcast play-by-play for the Cincinnati Reds, Brooklyn Dodgers and New York Yankees from 1934-1966.

We grow to respond viscerally to the first sound of their voices each evening as we are again transported to the realm of resin bags and chalk lines. They welcome us to that most magical destination, the ballpark. Nightly, daily they summon us to once more see through their eyes and ride up and down and away on the rise and fall of their voices, the tone of their anticipation, their exhilaration, their anguish and the hope that tells us in the end we've got yet another shot at 'em tomorrow night at 7:05.

As the long summer progresses they share with us the plight of the hometown nine. Whether we get out of the gate fast or get off to a slow start, they're with us. When we have a record May or we're going nowhere early, they're giving us a play-by-play account of it all, every starter with great stuff and every reliever who gets shelled. From them we learn whether we're shaping up to be in the race after the All-Star break or whether we'll be out of it by the mid-summer classic.

Even when we're not listening, when we're traveling or working or just forgot it was getaway day with a 12:30 start, they are there—every day, every game. We know no matter how prodigal we are, how forgetful, they are but a button's push, a dial's twist away.

As games routinely became three- and four-hour affairs, we spent more and more time hanging on their every word, on every pitch. The good broadcasters prove a genuine treasure, the delight of children in their beds and old ladies in their chairs, night watchmen at their posts, cabbies behind the wheel, the guy in the big house on the hill and the guy in the rented room downtown.

In this world of the fan, all are truly created equal. It's the broadcaster who shapes our shared experience of the joys and disappointments of the campaign, brings the ballpark to us, expands the stadium to include the listening audience within the sound of his voice. It reminds us what made the ballpark so special: it was the place where the millionaire and the average Joe sat side by side, where the broker sat next to the baker. And when we listened we listened as one, as Phillies fans, or Giants fans—not separated by neighborhoods or income or heritage but joined by this shared love of something we felt represented us, our town, our guys.

For seven months, season after season, year after baseball year, the broadcasters are our shamans, our tellers of the great tales, the poets whose voices give us entrée to the exploits of our heroes. They even give us the chance to feel as if we are the ones diving to our left, chasing one down in the gap or making the barehanded throw to first. We feel we know them because, in a way, we do. The baseball broadcaster cannot help but reveal a great deal of himself. Through the pitching changes and the meetings on the mound and the rain-delays, the anecdotes and the personal references mount up. We become familiar with their upbringing, their baseball memories, their trove of stories about the game and those who have played it.

Like Dante's Beatrice, they are our guides, like Quixote's Sancho we are their companions. They are the ones who welcome us into this universe when the pre-game show begins and safely deposit us back into our world when the post-game show wraps up. No matter how many blown saves and late-inning rallies we suffer, they bid us remain resolute. No matter how many bone-headed plays or kicked groundballs, they help us endure the anguish. Through hot streaks and cold spells, they let us know they're not only bringing us the action, they're cheering or cringing with us as well.

Their passion for the game not only mirrors our own, it informs it, enriches it. Their description of the action becomes inextricably joined to our memories of the events that transpire in between the freshly chalked white lines. When we remember Bobby Thomson's "shot heard 'round the world," we can't help but hear Russ Hodges' voice rebounding in our ears.

Bobby Thomson's three-run, pennant-winning home run for the New York Giants in 1951 was described as "the shot heard 'round the world."

Bill Mazeroski hit the game-winning home run for the Pittsburgh Pirates in the seventh game of the 1960 World Series.

There's a long drive...it's gonna be, I believe...THE GIANTS WIN THE PENNANT!! THE GIANTS WIN THE PENNANT! THE GIANTS WIN THE PENNANT! THE GIANTS WIN THE PENNANT! Bobby Thomson hits into the lower deck of the left-field stands! The Giants win the pennant and they're goin' crazy, they're goin' crazy! HEEEY-OH!

Bill Mazeroski's dramatic game-seven winner in the 1960 World Series, what some have called the greatest home run of all time, always brings to the mind's ear Chuck Thompson's call:

Here's a high fly ball going deep to left...THIS MAY DO IT... BACK TO THE WALL GOES BERRA...IT IS... OVER THE FENCE, HOME RUN, THE PIRATES WIN!

For some of the greats, it is not just their use of words but their remarkable use of silence. When we recall Kirk Gibson's home run in game one of the 1988 World Series, the soundtrack that accompanies the highlight reel in our head is Vin Scully's:

High fly ball to right field...she...is...GONE!

Yet we are more deeply moved by the sixty-eight seconds of silence that followed. For more than a minute, like a jazz virtuoso who knows the spaces are as meaningful as the notes, Scully allows us to take in the sounds of jubilant Dodger players and ecstatic Los Angeles fans until he played the final stanza:

In a year that has been so improbable, the impossible has happened!

Our remembrances of these and so many other great baseball moments are not a reel from a silent movie. The call is an integral part of the experience. There is a reason so many highlights are introduced every night with the words. "Here with the call is..." The enshrinement of the broadcasters alongside the players and managers they helped immortalize is eminently well deserved, and the broadcasters whose likenesses grace Cooperstown are not there by chance or by accident.

Each year all players who garner the requisite number of votes are enshrined. But each year only a single broadcaster makes the annual class at the Hall of Fame, only one voice becomes forever synonymous with the game.

On a sunny Sunday morning, the twenty-seventh day of July in 2008, the thirty-second man to be so honored rose from his bed to find his road had led him to Cooperstown and to the Hall of Fame. Dave Niehaus traversed the 879 miles from southern Indiana to north central New York in a mere fifty-one years. Yet, on this day, every one of those three thousand flights he took to get there and every one of those millions of miles he covered on the way seemed to have been headed expressly to this place.

Along the way, Niehaus had become not just one of the best, but one of the very best. His love affair with the game was akin to his love affair with the English language. The offspring of the two was his complete intoxication with the language of baseball. His work was testimony to his regard for the lexicon of the game, its native tongue of similes and metaphors.

In particular, the homespun images that reflect the small-town roots of the sport were, in his voice, the songs from the hymnal, the nightly selections from the Great Works. As such they were also the threads of continuity stretching from those who had spoken this dialect before him and from whom he learned to speak it to the audience of both the insiders and the uninitiated within the reach of his voice.

Far from just speaking it, Dave Niehaus imbued the language of baseball with more than enthusiasm, indeed, with reverence. With an attribute that would have pleased his Indiana forebears, he was earnest—earnest in a way befitting the small-town American values of the towns that nurtured him and the game. There was nothing ever feigned or self-conscious about his prosaic broadcasts. He was "calling 'em as he saw 'em" when a downpour became a "frog strangler" or a billow of white clouds formed a "popcorn sky."

Dave was equally cognizant of both the linguistic oddities as well as the melodies. He practically sang them. Part of what set him apart and what gave such deep backdrop to his ability to "speak baseball" was his command of the English language. The world of sports broadcasting in general and the realm of baseball broadcasting in particular were not always places in which proper English was spoken.

Dave Niehaus had the ability to move seamlessly between the two languages, making the catch phrases and colloquialisms all the more enjoyable coming from such an eloquent man. He used the *mater lingua* of baseball the way a curator at the Vatican moves in and out of Italian. It was the only language that expressed the nuances of what he saw between the lines, the only one that truly expressed his passion, richly infused with the time-honored catch phrases of the sport he loved so much.

Many revered and storied men have broadcast baseball. I've had the good fortune to hear quite a few of them from Caray to Kalas, from Barber to Scully. Everybody gets to have a favorite and Dave Niehaus was mine. He was a five-tool player: the voice, the vocabulary, the diction, the knowledge of the game and its history, and the remarkable ability to place the listener in the stadium.

He used to say, "You don't have to talk all the time—just be quiet and let the sounds of the stadium come through the radio. Let people know you're at the ballpark."

When you listened to Dave, you were transported from the front seat of your car to the box seats, from behind the plate at your kitchen table to behind the plate at the ballpark. He spoke as directly and as eloquently to the man in the bleachers with the sack of sandwiches for his kids as to the businessman courting his clients in the box seats. He erased all differences in social strata or tax bracket or occupation and replaced them with the common denominator that marked one and all as fans.

The fans were far more than his audience. They were his congregation. He brought them the gospel of the game and spoke from the scripture of its past. He taught them the commandments: "Thou shalt not make the last out at third," and "Thou shalt make him throw you a strike." Even more, the fans were his second family. He lived among them, delighted in their company, traded endless stories with them.

Dave Niehaus' Indiana roots may not have kept him there, but they always kept him connected to some very simple truths. As his long-time friend and initial big-league broadcast partner, Dick Enberg, recalled: "Dave's genius was that he kept it simple. He loved his family and he loved the game of baseball." And he loved the fans.

It didn't happen by accident this son of southern Indiana awoke this summer morning in Cooperstown. There are indeed many ways to get there, but you've really got to *want* to get there. Like his heroes Stan Musial and Jackie Robinson, Harry Caray and Waite Hoyt, Dave Niehaus was emblematic of the most important criteria of all: you have to *deserve* to get there.

Top: Dave with his parents Jack and Delania Niehaus, circa 1944. Bottom: The former Niehaus family home at 625 North West Street, Princeton, Indiana.

Back Home Again in Indiana: Growing Up in Princeton

I'm from Princeton, Indiana, population 7,313.
—Dave Niehaus

IT IS THE CLASSIC, SIMPLE AMERICAN STORY: small-town boy rises to big-time heights.

We were, so many of us, from small places and had been for a very long time. In a landscape now dominated by urban hubs, perhaps we have come to expect the bright lights to shine from the big city and find it quaintly charming when the small-town mystique moves us or touches something in us. Perhaps we like the fact that the story still plays. More likely there are singular stories to be found in both Metropolis and Mayberry. Regardless, those stories inexorably unfold against a backdrop of either urban bustle or semi-rural tranquility.

This story begins as a small-town tale, set in the heartland of the Midwest, a place where simple values and simple stories abound.

David Arnold Niehaus was born February 19, 1935, in Princeton Methodist Hospital at 419 West State Street in Princeton, Indiana, of Patoka Township, the seat of Gibson County. The fifteenth census of the United States, conducted in 1930, listed its population at 7,505. Dave Niehaus' arrival swelled the number to somewhere in excess of 7,600. (When asked where he was from, Dave was known to reply "Princeton, Indiana, population seven-thousand three-hundred thirteen.) Now part of the greater Evansville area, the census of 2010 lists Princeton's current population as 8,644. It was, and still is, a small Midwestern town.

Dave Niehaus would travel far from his place of birth and live to make his mark in distant places. But he never really left here, not fully. Furthermore, that part of himself he left behind was traded for the piece of Princeton he took with him. He was, in part, always the young man from the small town in southern Indiana; always the boy whose background and upbringing were representative of the life lived in the communities dotting the heartland of America. People knew each other in these towns, these boroughs in which decency and common courtesy and the simple willingness to look out for each other were daily practice, not merely desired virtue.

Doors went unlocked in 1940s Princeton. These were the times before suburbs. In what was to become suburban America, people would come to gather in their back yards on patios, around barbecues. Before that, the front porch had been the preferred site of evening communion, not just for individual families, for whole neighborhoods. Greetings were exchanged, porch to porch, especially in the summer when the stoop was also a place of respite from the day's heat and neighbors often shared the evening's baseball broadcast on separate radios tuned to the same spot on the dial.

That meant, on certain summer evenings, whole blocks in Princeton, Indiana might resound with St. Louis Cardinal baseball. You could take your evening stroll through the neighborhood and never miss a pitch. Baseball and specifically baseball on the radio was part of what defined summer in Gibson County.

It is of small wonder, then, this was the scene recalled by Dave Niehaus in his Hall of Fame induction speech. His seminal memories, his fondest recollections of childhood were of summer evenings spent on the front porch. Even on that sunny Sunday in upstate New York some fifty years later, for Dave, the humid Midwest air was still aglow with the light of fireflies and alive with the sound of Cardinals baseball.

There is no knowing David Niehaus without first knowing Princeton, Indiana.

In 1814, Princeton's location halfway between the Evansville and Vincennes stage lines moved four commissioners to name it the seat of Gibson County government. An Irish immigrant named William Prince was one of those commissioners and it was his lot drawn and his name lent to Princeton.

The Wabash and Ohio Rivers nourish the rich farmland of southwestern Indiana and, in the early nineteenth century, the rivers were teeming with barges, flatboats and vessels of all sizes, carrying the commerce of the new West. The Wabash and Erie Canal serviced nearby Port Gibson and Francisco, providing the farmers and tradesmen of Princeton with a gateway for their goods. But the relatively young settlements of the lower-left corner of the Hoosier state were about to undergo another sweeping change to the evolving face of commerce and transportation.

With life on the western frontier of America offering promise to so many and the dreadful nightmare of the Civil War yet unforeseeable, the 1850s was a decade marked by the explosion of a great new technological advance in transportation. This new marvel that would move heretofore unimagined numbers of people and untold tons of freight across the vast and expanding American landscape was the two-railed magic carpet of the railroad. Princeton would prove to be one of the many cities whose status as a railroad town would leave it no longer dependent on the river towns and their barges.

The arrival of the Evansville & Terre Haute Railway in 1852 meant the commerce in many American cities along the canal withered away with the coming of the Iron Horse. Princeton's goods, which had previously found their way to the world via waterway, would seamlessly transition to being hauled away by rail. Long before the construction of the Princeton Depot in 1875, the town had been carried into the future on those twin steel bars. In all, Princeton was emblematic of the emerging American heartland that would, in a very short time, be the Midwest and no longer the West.

Gibson County had been carved out of enormous Knox County and the naming of the new county seat meant a post office would be built in Princeton as early as 1816. Thirty years later, in August of 1846, county auditor William Kurtz published the first edition of the *Democratic Clarion*. The *Princeton Daily Clarion* publishes to this day and was the newspaper of record during Dave's childhood and teenage years. It was the *Daily Clarion* that brought him the box scores each summer morning, along with the tales they told about the St. Louis Cardinals, Brooklyn Dodgers, Cincinnati Reds and the Boston Braves.

Princeton was, in short, the most American of towns, born of the sweeping changes relentless westward migration brought to the American frontier. Like so many places, its location at the edge of expansion toward

A local landmark, the Princeton train station was still the center of commerce during Dave Niehaus' youth.

the Pacific was short-lived. Outposts and forts gave way to communities and towns and those in turn to cities.

At the same time, something else was sweeping across America. It now seemed everywhere there was an open field and a gaggle of youngsters, somehow there was always a bat and a ball. It seemed, wherever America was going, baseball was going as well. The burgeoning Midwest was no exception. By the late 1800s, baseball was the summer sport of choice in Princeton.

The Wednesday, June 29, 1898 edition of the *Daily Clarion* made it clear even the local pastors were guiding their flock at the sametime they were shepherding them around the basepaths. "Church members of Princeton, Indiana have organized a base-ball league, consisting of seven clubs, each club representing a church in that city, and a lively contest for the church baseball championship of Princeton is anticipated. Each pastor will manage his church club. A complete schedule has been arranged and intense rivalry is already manifested."

As with so many Midwest towns spawned by the westward migrations of the 1800s, Princeton's emergence had marked only a temporary stopping point in the exodus from the East. Civilization headed on, further westward, toward further uncharted lands. Soon Princeton went from being somewhere at the end of the territory to a place on the way to somewhere else. Travelers and commerce that initially flowed to the area now flowed through the area to points even farther west.

Princeton became a classic American railroad town. It had been the railroad that set it free from dependence on the Ohio River barges, the railroad that had brought goods and mail and travelers, and the railroad that would carry them on westward. It was the railroad that brought President Theodore Roosevelt to Princeton en route from Louisville to St. Louis on April 4, 1905. To this day, the small and now seemingly quaint railway station still sits on your left as you cross the tracks a few blocks before the courthouse.

When you turn off U.S. 41 and take the old highway into town—the route Dave would have driven in his youth—the tracks meander their way into town with you. The rumble of the freight trains and the roar of their whistles were deeply ingrained in the consciousness of all who lived there. The trains would have echoed through the quiet nights as they approached and then faded away. The downtown station would have filled with the steaming hiss of the brakes and the accompanying scrape of metal on metal, the clank and bang of the hurtling start and gathering momentum for the onward journey. It would have been a regular part of the daily life in Princeton.

A half-century later, when Safeco Field opened in Seattle, it was situated just next to the railroad tracks heading into and out of nearby King Street Station. Those tracks sit just beyond the left-field bleachers. It became routine for the engineers to pull the chain and sound the whistle as they rolled by.

Nearly every time, Dave Niehaus would pause behind the microphone to share that iconic sound with his audience and note the passing train. It is hard to believe it ever happened without evoking a visceral response within him, without him being carried back, transported to a quiet, summer Indiana night pierced by the sound of an approaching train.

Many of the engineers were aware of this and as they passed offered salute to the man whose voice had become part of their daily fabric and become so beloved to baseball fans of the Pacific Northwest. It is why so many of his fans will forever be themselves carried back to the sound of his voice when that train whistle sounds beyond the left-field wall.

With the emergence of the railroad-accessed American West, Princeton became a place from which you dreamed of where you might go. Small-town boys have always dreamed of the big city and in those small towns you are either one of those who stays or one of those who leaves. Dave Niehaus would eventually join the latter, seized with the same spirit of adventure that had marked his ancestors.

The Indiana chapter of the Niehaus family saga began in the 1840s when Dave's great-grandparents emigrated from Germany and settled in Holland, Indiana in DuBois County, due east of Louisville, Kentucky. Later in the century their son, Benjamin, and his wife, Alena Kohler, continued the clan's westward trek, taking residence in Evansville in Vanderburgh County, where they lived until Benjamin's passing in 1934. There, they raised two children, daughter Esther and son Leonard.

Leonard was never very fond of his given name and adopted the name Jack. In his early twenties, he got a job as a baker in Princeton and headed north from Evansville to begin his new career at the Fowler Bakery.

At the time, Princeton was rising from the devastation of a tornado that nearly plucked the town right off the map. The storm of March 18, 1925 left 1,500 homeless and more than one thousand unemployed. Property losses were in excess of a then-staggering $3 million. Mayor Charles A. Neimeier and Farmer's National Bank president Will Blair had overseen nearly a decade of fundraising and rebuilding. Jack's new job was itself one of the small signs of the recovery.

Jack Niehaus liked the work at Fowler's but, over his twenty-two years in the business, he developed an allergy to wheat, a rather calamitous affliction for a baker. Forced to leave the bread and the buns behind, Jack hooked on with Prudential Life Insurance Company and, symmetrically enough, spent his next twenty-two years in insurance.

Delania Grigsby was an Indiana girl, born in Poseyville, Indiana in 1905. After graduating from Poseyville High School and attending Oakland City College, she met Jack Niehaus and became his bride. They moved to Princeton in 1933, settling into a modest but comfortable home at 625 North West Street. She took a job with the phone company as an operator and joined the Telephone Operators Union, Local 1321.

It was into this home, in mid-February of 1935, Jack and Delania welcomed the boy who would be their only child. It was the only home Dave knew for his eighteen years in Princeton. As progress intervened and mobility increased, fewer and fewer families occupied a single residence for the duration of their time together. The sense of continuity provided by that experience makes the notion of home simpler and stronger, all the more wrapped up in the sentiment of identifying one very special place with that idea.

There is a confidence borne of being an only child, especially one with loving, devoted, intelligent parents. Jack and Delania fit the bill. Only children are accustomed to getting their way and the full attention of their parents. From the outset, Dave was a gregarious young man, easily able to make friends. His father's saltiness and his mother's charm fostered a lifelong ability to be endearing to both the boys on the ball field and the girls in the bleachers.

Jack and Delania Niehaus, circa 1938.

In the fall of 1942, the first-grade class of Lowell Elementary School included David among its number. In that era, Indiana public schools were divided between grammar schools with classes from kindergarten through eighth grade and four-year high schools. Accordingly, Dave spent his first eight years of schooling, through the spring of 1949, at Lowell Elementary.

Summers held a special treat for young David beyond baseball. Summers meant seeing his cousin, Ron Greenfield, who lived in nearby Evansville. When Jack Niehaus moved to Princeton, his sister Esther had remained in Evansville where she married James Alexander Greenfield, a World War II artilleryman and founding member of Evansville's VFW Post 1114.

During their school summer vacation, each of the boys spent a month at the other's house, every summer for more than a decade. First came the Niehaus family reunion, annually held in Princeton. It was at those reunions the boys planned their summer adventures, including all that might happen when Dave went to visit Ron.

Even as a boy, Dave performed one of those boyish stunts he'd repeat for a lifetime. Most everybody who ever knew him saw him do it sooner or later. He not only could touch his nose with his tongue, he also could lay the end of his tongue flat on the tip of it. This astonished many of his Indiana cousins and classmates and was his favorite trick to perform at the annual picnic.

"It looked like he had a big hunk of liver in his mouth," cousin Ron recalled.

Among the summer highlights for the Princeton half of their home-and-away series was the Gibson County Fair. Dave was a Boy Scout and it was customary for the county's Boy Scout troops to bivouac on the grounds of the county fair. They were considered sheriff's deputies, but their duties, as you might suspect, were ceremonial. The boys spent many summer nights together in a pitched tent, telling stories beneath a starry Midwestern sky, tales told to the background music of the local frogs and crickets cooling in the summer night. Those two months spent together each summer were all about the truly important things in life: riding bikes and fishing and sleeping out in the backyard. More than anything, though, they were all about *the* most important thing in life—baseball: talking baseball, playing baseball, watching baseball, reading about baseball, listening to baseball on the radio.

On May 24, 1935, fewer than one hundred days after Dave's birth, President Franklin D. Roosevelt sat in the White House and tapped a gold telegraph key, sending a signal to Crosley Field in Cincinnati. There, Larry MacPhail threw a switch to illumine 632 MAZDA lamps, and the new era of night baseball was born. Not only would the game be changed, its impact on American families would be forever altered.

Fathers and sons, mothers and daughters would now spend their evenings together gathered around the box with the glowing dial and the big round sweeping knob to hear the broadcasts of the games. Kids who previously could only catch a few innings after school and parents whose jobs precluded them from tuning in were now able to hear the games in their entirety. In homes and farms across the country chores and homework and dishes were now done in time to hear those magic words, baseball's equivalent of "Open, Sesame"—"Play ball!" When summer arrived, school let out and the weather grew warmer, on porches all across America, evenings were spent beneath a blanket of stars with the crack of the bat and the roar of the crowds.

With the later advent of television, households came to welcome familiar personalities into their homes each evening. Milton Berle, Dinah Shore, and Lucille Ball numbered among those who became part of countless families whose living rooms were centered on the television. But for baseball families of the 1930s and '40s, those nightly guests were the denizens of press boxes and radio booths from Crosley Field to Shibe Park, from Ebbets Field to Comiskey Park. Their nightly stay was no mere half-hour or sixty minutes but nine innings —fifty-four outs' worth of strikes and balls and swings and misses, each evening's drama differing from the night before, each installment one chapter of one hundred fifty-four comprising the great epic of the annual season.

That nightly guest welcomed into America's kitchens and living rooms and onto countless porches was the man behind the microphone —the baseball broadcaster. The relationship between the two parties on either end of the wire belied the miles in between. The voice of the man who called the games for "your team" was the most special of voices. Recognized in an instant as friend and companion, that voice was, most importantly, the vehicle through which the feats and the failures of heroes both revered and unsung were carried—not just into the ears of devoted fans but into their hearts and forever into their memories.

That voice spoke to you in more than words. After a while, every modulation, every inflection offered another glimpse, another clue, another slice of the hope, the tension, the fatigue, the exhilaration, the exasperation, the yearning for one more hit, one more out, one more win—all of the emotions and expectations surrounding each campaign's pursuit of the pennant. The baseball broadcaster's voice communicated with both description and tone, and fans learned to glean information from every nuanced syllable.

For most baseball-crazy boys, the daily ritual of opening the sports page and deciphering the box scores begins in early grammar school. So it was for young Dave Niehaus. The front pages brought home the daily horror of world war raging in two different theaters. The stories found in the sports pages were even greater refuge than normal during the early 1940s, including for those fighting those wars.

As much as he loved those morning forays into the twists and turns of the pennant race, the real enticement of the game was experienced in the afternoons and evenings. The magical, musical call of the game was at that time the sole province of radio. Nearly a century after the railroad came to Princeton, television was a decade away and in most homes the center of attention was to be found on the kitchen table or in the living room. For the Niehaus family, it was the big brown Zenith floor-model radio in the front room, able to be enjoyed equally in the kitchen, in the living room or on the front porch.

The lure of the daily baseball broadcast soon hooked young Dave Niehaus. From the time he could remember, Dave knew the numbers 1340 and 1430 and 1490 on the AM radio dial signified more than mere frequencies; they were, in fact, four-digit combinations. A spin of the dial unlocked the door to a world of magic and mystery, a world in which men larger than life loomed in on-deck circles, strode to the plate, entered the batter's box and dug a toe-hold. In this same world, other giants grabbed a resin bag and tossed it onto the grass, rubbed a new wrinkle into the horsehide, reached back for something extra and took the hitter up the ladder. In this diamond-shaped universe, swift-footed fielders chased 'em down in the gap, took it on one hop off the wall and threw a seed to a waiting third baseman just in time to nip the runner.

For 1340 and 1430 and 1490 on your southern Indiana AM dial were the numbers that accessed separate portals to the common universe of Cardinal baseball, and David's father, Jack Niehaus, was a Cardinals fan. Cardinals' baseball on the radio was a way of life at 625 North West Street.

Dave always reminisced about listening to Harry Caray on KMOX 1120 out of St. Louis. Yet, in fact, while KMOX 1120 AM was the original home of Cardinal broadcasts from 1928 through 1940, it did not broadcast the Redbird games again until 1955. In addition, while Harry would have been Dave's man, Jack would have undoubtedly been a fan of J. Frank "France" Laux, the first full-time voice of St. Louis Cardinal baseball who spent 28 years in the booth.

Because the St. Louis Cardinals and the St. Louis Browns both played in Sportsman's Park, their broadcasts were joined at the hip as well. "PLAY-BY-PLAY NITE AND DAY" was the slogan for the games on WIL 1430 AM and WEW 770 AM by day, and WTMV 1490 AM by night.

On a clear summer night in the 1940s, Jack and his son might well have heard the broadcasts on the 250-watt flagship station, WIL 1430 AM. There was, however, an emerging "farm system" in the broadcast world as well: the radio station network. This meant the magic numbers on the

Niehaus radio dial would have been 1340 AM, WJPF out of Herrin, Illinois some 90 miles south-southwest of Princeton.

The Cardinals of the 1940s were a charismatic bunch. The tradition of colorful characters in "Redbird" uniforms had been etched in baseball lore by the Gashouse Gang of the 1930s, featuring the Dean brothers, MVP Dizzy and sibling Paul, Johnny "Pepper" Martin, Joe "Ducky" Medwick and a young Leo Durocher among their number. They were as good as they were entertaining, fashioning a set of successful summers in 1926, '28, '30 and '31 by winning the National League crown. Like the 1926 and '31 clubs, the Gashouse Gang went on to win the World Series in 1934, this time in seven riotous games over Mickey Cochrane's Detroit Tigers.

As good as those teams were, the Cardinals of the 1940s arguably were even better. Visionary general manager Branch Rickey had conceived of and executed his idea of a "farm system," comprised of minor-league teams affiliated with the parent major league organization. Players would come up through the system under the watchful eye of Cardinal scouts, managers and coaches, eventually graduating to become part of the National League powerhouse. It proved to not only revolutionize baseball, but also to establish a level of excellence in St. Louis that captured the hearts and imaginations of a generation of Cardinal faithful.

By the time a youthful Dave Niehaus was poised to take his place among the legion of Redbird fans, the roster of the 1940s included Red Schoendienst, Enos "Country" Slaughter and one of baseball's legendary hitters and gentlemen, Stan "The Man" Musial. They played great baseball, Cardinal baseball, long on fundamentals and short on mistakes, smart baseball. Under managers Billy Southworth and Eddie Dyer, there was little doubt the product on the field was of genuine quality. Still, there was one more man who played a key role in the Cardinals' success and who would end up playing a key role in the life of David Niehaus.

Harry Christopher Carabina was born of Italian and Romanian parentage in one of the poorest sections of St. Louis. His father died when he was an infant and his mother when he was eight. The young orphan was sent to live with his Aunt Doxie at 1909 LaSalle Street in a tough, working-class neighborhood. Young Carabina grew up to briefly play semi-pro baseball until his life took a crucial turn. At age nineteen, he auditioned for a job at a radio station. The next few years were spent learning the ropes at stations in Joliet, Illinois, and Kalamazoo, Michigan.

Carabina's big break came when WIL Radio in St. Louis teamed him with Charles "Gabby" Street to broadcast games for the National League Cards and the American League St. Louis Browns. Street had managed the Cardinal pennant-winners of both 1930 and '31. (Among the great footnotes of Gabby's career was the notoriety he gained by catching a ball dropped from the Washington Monument. "The Old Sarge," as he was known then, was Walter Johnson's battery mate with the Washington Senators and on August 21, 1908 snagged the thirteenth ball dropped by journalist Preston Gibson from the obelisk 555 feet above.)

So, in 1945 the world came to know Harry Caray. And not just the world, but a Hoosier lad in Princeton, Indiana by the name of Dave Niehaus. The young man would prove to be a keeper of the flame ignited in him by Caray's voice, one who would follow in Caray's footsteps not just to the big leagues but all the way to Cooperstown.

If you have ever had the baseball pleasure of driving through southern Illinois or southwestern Indiana or any of the surrounding environs on a summer evening, you know the hardball feast that pours forth from your radio. On a perfect, clear night you can find yourself at the Skydome in Toronto, Comerica Park in Detroit, the Great American Ballpark in Cincinnati, Comiskey Park or Wrigley Field in Chicago, Jacobs Field in Cleveland, Busch Stadium in St. Louis and even Minute Maid Park in Houston. It is a remarkable journey across the dial and across the baseball landscape, the radio an Encarta of the hardball universe.

Even in the 1940s, there were a half-dozen or more games to be searched out and tuned in, some clear and present, some coated with varying layers of static that, although a nuisance, was not enough to keep the devoted fan from listening intently.

A ten-year old Dave Niehaus could find himself in Wrigley Field in Chicago listening to Jack Brickhouse call the Cubs games on WGN 720 or in old Comiskey Park hearing Bob Elson do the play-by-play for the White Sox on WJJD 1160 by day and WIND 560 by night. He could travel to Crosley Field in Cincinnati by tuning in Waite Hoyt calling the Redlegs' tilts from the Queen City, mostly on WCPO 1230, and, on a clear Midwestern night, maybe even "sit" in Briggs Stadium in Detroit with Harry Heilmann doing the Tigers' broadcast on WXYZ 1270 AM.

But of all these, it was Harry Caray whose "descriptions and accounts of this broadcast" spoke to the soul of the young man from Princeton.

For many of us who would have traded a great deal to have toiled behind the baseball microphone, those childhood memories are more than precious: they are seminal. They spawn a relentless and never-ending "broadcast of the mind." Our youth is spent with an ever-present internal dialogue, describing everything from the games we watch to the games we play to chores like mowing the lawn. In the style and cadence of those epic voices we heard on the radio, the "game" was heard in our heads.

Jim, he's handling that mower with incredible finesse—he spins and turns to the next row, perfectly in line with the previous two, cutting at a rate that's sure to set a new high-water mark for the league. This kid can really handle that Briggs and Stratton.

Whatever the endeavor, the play-by-play is in the mind of the aspiring broadcaster, the monologue always accompanied by the roar of the crowd and the quiet of the approving audience at home. It is the most delightful of afflictions. For a select few, it's the harbinger of a lifetime's vocation. It was just that for young Dave Niehaus, who would lie in bed drifting off to sleep not counting sheep but tallying runs, hits and errors for the Cardinals. His summer nights would end with the replay of the day's results with the emerald expanse of Sportsman's Park below and his broadcast partner Harry Caray at his side. *"Dave, we saw one heck of an effort from St. Louis tonight."*

St. Louis Cardinal fans had plenty to cheer about during the 1940s. That old Zenith radio poured forth 106 wins in 1942, 105 each in '43 and '44. That was good enough for three straight NL gonfalons—a word Dave cherished for a lifetime—and two World Series titles. The Niehaus household was treated to a terrific run of success during the years in which Dave's baseball memories were first formed. And though a high level of success would endure into the 1950s, this decade ended with the heartbreak of three consecutive second-place finishes in 1947, '48 and '49.

Yet, sometimes in baseball there is a year that blurs all others around it, leaving behind the disappointments of near-misses and "almosts." It's the kind of year that lights inextinguishable fires in the souls of fans, fires that warm the chill of lesser seasons, lesser campaigns. As if the fire were not already burning within him, there came for Dave Niehaus and all Cardinal fans, the incredible summer of 1946.

It remains something of a watershed year in baseball history and in the professional history of one of its most remarkable figures. "The Mahatma" as he was known, Branch Rickey had envisioned and created the farm system that changed the way baseball was operated, the way players were developed and, in the process, made a dynasty of the St. Louis Cardinals. His system produced Pepper Martin and the Dean brothers in the 1930s and Musial, Slaughter and Marty Marion in the 1940s.

Some, however, saw Rickey's grand design as a threat to the minor leagues. Commissioner Kenesaw Mountain Landis was among them. In 1938, Landis released seventy-four Redbird farmhands from their ties to the organization. Undaunted, Rickey regrouped. Soon almost every major league team had a farm system and it can be argued this new approach actually saved the minor leagues. It certainly propelled St. Louis to an eleven-year stretch during which the Cardinals finished first or second ten times. The lone exception was their third-place finish in 1940.

Rickey had left for Brooklyn in 1942 to work for Larry MacPhail. The St. Louis team he built finished two games ahead of the Brooklyn team he was now building. In 1946, the Cardinals played one of baseball's storied Fall Classics, a seven-gamer against the Boston Red Sox decided by Slaughter's eighth-inning "mad dash" from first to home on a double by Harry "The Hat" Walker. Played at Sportsman's Park, the tilt remains one of the greatest sporting moments in the history of the Mound City.

What Branch Rickey accomplished with the St. Louis Cardinals was incredible. What he did with the Brooklyn Dodgers was even more so. From 1945 through 1957, Brooklyn won six pennants outright and twice finished tied for first, losing in playoffs each time. During that same skein, they finished second two other times and third on three occasions. As the Dodgers' juggernaut paralleled the Yankees' formidable run, Dave Niehaus came to maturity during a span marked by the overlapping of three of baseball's grandest dynasties.

These were heady days for the baseball fans of southern Indiana and certainly for a young Dave Niehaus. This was the game he fell in love with during those precious innocent years of his boyhood.

At eleven, a boy is about as happy as he will ever be in his life. The world is all bicycles and model airplanes and baseball cards and Westerns, pick-up games and BB guns, frog-catching and fishing. In particular, the perplexing complexities of girls and teen-age peer pressures are still a lifetime away and innocence still reigns. During those sweet summers of late grade school and junior high, the world is all box scores and pennant races and those grey-flannelled heroes are still larger than life, still as legendary as Ulysses or Hopalong Cassidy or Buck Rogers.

A young boy's summers are so inextricably entwined with the fate of his horsehide heroes as to years, even decades later engender specific memories of exactly where you were and whose house you were visiting and what radio or TV you were tuned into at precisely the moment Musial or Berra or Mays homered or threw out a runner or made an impossible catch. For the special few whose lives will be forever stitched to the fabric of the national pastime, those summers are of special import. They're like the memories of a first kiss.

For eleven year-old Dave Niehaus of Princeton, Indiana, his lifelong love affair with baseball surely had a lot to do with the summer of 1946.

The paradox for this boy from Princeton was that despite the fact he thrilled daily and nightly to the Cardinal baseball broadcasts, his heart was some 970 miles north-northeast of the Gateway City. Gibson County's first native son to grace the major leagues played there and starred there. Not a summer morning went without Dave opening the sports page in search of the box scores with the burning question, "What did Hodges do last night?"

Gilbert Ray Hodges was some eleven years Dave's senior, born April 4, 1924, in Princeton. He attended Petersburg High, about 25 miles northeast of Princeton. He was himself a small-town Indiana boy of nineteen when he signed with the Dodgers and saw Brooklyn for the first time. He made his debut on October 3, 1943, at Cincinnati during the last game of the season. When the Dodgers learned from the scoreboard they were assured of a third-place finish, Manager Leo Durocher sent some of the youngsters in to play. In the second inning, Hodges replaced Bobby Bragan at third as Bragan moved behind the plate and Al Campanis replaced Billy Herman at second. Unfortunately for Gil, Eric Tipton's bases-loaded grounder got past him, allowing two runs to score. Fortunately, that misplay would prove an insignificant footnote to a remarkable career.

In a 2008 interview with *The Seattle Times*, Dave recalled his "number one idol" as a kid was Gil Hodges.

"I still think to this day that he should be in the Hall of Fame, and maybe one of these days he will be…" he said. "The Brooklyn Dodgers were my team *because* of Gil Hodges. I grew up in Cardinal territory…I listened to Harry Caray and all the guys in the booth with him, and they probably had as big of an influence as anyone, as far as my broadcasting career. But I was in Cardinal territory and everybody was a Cardinal fan except me. I was one of the *Boys of Summer* guys. You know, Gil Hodges, Jim Gilliam, Duke Snider, Jackie Robinson, Roy Campanella, and Billy Cox—that whole ballclub. They were some of my boys, too, because of Hodges more than anything else."

Gil Hodges went on to become the rock-solid first baseman for one of baseball's most legendary ensembles. The Brooklyn Dodgers, forever named and forever immortalized by Roger Kahn's *The Boys of Summer*, were indeed Dave Niehaus' true baseball allegiance. The Cardinals were the home team and surely had his backing, too, but the Brooklyn Dodgers had his heart. It is, in fact, the earliest of clues that baseball, for Dave, was about more than just pulling for the hometown nine. His early love of the game wasn't rooted solely in cheering for a single squad, it was about the game itself.

The halcyon days of the Trolley Dodgers of Hodges and Campanella and Reese and Robinson would have to wait until after the 1946 season. That special summer Dave Niehaus was in the fold with the Cardinal faithful. There was something ultimately special about this edition of the St. Louis club. For Dave, there was also something special about the way Harry Caray called the game in a way that made those Redbirds larger than life.

"That was prior to the days of television and you couldn't see them," Niehaus said. "Harry had put these guys on such a level. To me it was like listening to God."

Caray and Cardinals baseball influenced his life, even if he didn't know it at the time.

"I never had a burning desire like a lot of kids to be a major-league baseball announcer," Dave said. "But that's the reason I can understand when people write me and say, 'You've become such a member of our family.' Harry certainly was a member of my family and everybody's family in the Midwest, because you listened to him every night. It was the picture that he painted. And his home run calls, 'It might be! It could be! It is! A home run!' I have never ever tried to copy anybody's style, but I guess the first guy you hear has more influence on you than anybody else."

Because of Caray, the players were immense figures in Niehaus' mind and old Sportsman's Park in St. Louis was nothing less than a shrine. Even when he hadn't been back to St. Louis in nearly three decades, his regard had not lessened for what he considered to be one of the two best baseball cities in America.

"Back there, it's a religion, Dave recalled years later, "…the closest thing to it, I think, is Boston—the Red Sox Nation. I think there are better baseball fans in St. Louis and Boston than in New York."

The first time teenager Dave Niehaus stepped inside a major league ballpark was the day in 1949 or '50 his uncle (although Dave often said his father) took him to Sportsman's Park in St. Louis to see the Browns. Curiously enough, his primary recollection of seeing his heroes for the first time was his disappointment. Those rapturous hours spent beside the radio listening to Harry Caray tell of these heroic figures and their larger-than-life exploits had made them seem giants. In his mind, the Cardinals' Stan Musial was eight feet tall and the Browns' Sherm Lollar the size of a statue.

To the young man's surprise, he discovered "they were just regular guys like you and me. That's what radio does with the mind; I had put these guys on such a pedestal that when I went to the game I was disappointed. Kids today will not be so surprised because there's so much television."

However, with that intrusion of reality came a deeper understanding of the role of the shaman played by the baseball broadcaster, a role he himself would take on like no other. The tale told by the play-by-play man was one that indeed made the protagonists seem more than mortal, grand beyond measure. Somewhere in his heart that day, Dave knew a magic spell was cast through that microphone. Those descriptions that came through the wires were like tales that descended from the mountain. Like the signal that sent them, they were amplified again and again until they reached the listener transformed, grown to legend, one night, one inning at a time.

What he could not know that day is he would take his place among the priesthood and he would be the one to send those epistles to the faithful. He would himself play the shaman. He would be the conduit. Through him the chronicles of the players' exploits would transform ordinary men into extraordinary heroes.

Dave with his father, left, and grandfather, circa 1955.

For Dave Niehaus, it was indeed electronic magic Mr. Carabina practiced over those wires. Soon he would practice the same legerdemain.

Still, there was baseball magic to be found right there in Princeton and it was only a bicycle ride away. Six and a half blocks down West Street and a left turn on Broadway, one block to Hart Street and one more to Main. The pickup games at Lafayette Park were never forgotten nor were the bike rides out to Camp Carson on the east end of town. But nothing, nothing remained as clear and as mystical and as memorable in the mind of Dave Niehaus as the Palace Pool Room.

The Palace Pool Room, at 119 West Broadway, was Jack Niehaus' favorite place in Princeton. The first stool at the bar, just to your right upon entering, was "his" seat. If Delania or Dave needed to find him, this was the first place they'd look. Though he always sat at the bar, Jack was never seen having a drink. He was there for the baseball. His boy David followed his lead and it became his favorite summer place to pass the time as well.

The Palace Pool Room was in one of the rows of brick buildings set around the town square and facing the courthouse. It remains there to this day as a restaurant called The Palace.

In Jack Niehaus' day, it had a big bar in the front. The bar didn't serve alcoholic beverages, instead specializing in Coke and Pepsi and RC Cola for the kids. The first table was a snooker table with the smaller pockets and smaller balls. The next four or five tables were regular pocket billiard tables. Dave had a good eye for billiards and was a fine player, perhaps owing to the many hours he spent at the Palace.

The house specialty was an orange soda served cold in a cardboard box container into which a straw was inserted. After pick-up games at Lafayette Park or in between racks of fifteen numbered balls, Princeton kids would sit on the stools of the Palace Pool Room and sip those orange sodas. There young Dave Niehaus would establish a magical, mystical connection to the game.

Though a great deal of time was spent with cue and chalk in hand, the great summer delight involved a different chalk, one reserved for the blackboard. The conjury he witnessed on summer afternoons in the Palace Pool Room forever danced with delight in his memory. Again and again and once more he would tell the story of the magic produced by the thick, white sticks of chalks used to write on the blackboards of the Palace.

Those blackboards were reserved for the baseball line scores, posted inning by inning. The wire on the counter would clack beneath the whirling ceiling fans as the tickertape danced its way out and toward the floor.

As the updates came in, a gentleman by the name of D.A. Keimer would read the tapes and emerge from behind the counter. Next, he would reach into the box for one of the slender white batons. The next move, designed to create a stronger, more resilient marking, was to dunk the chalk into the ever-present pail of water on the floor below the chalkboard. The baptism had another, more magical effect. The numbers would be posted but would remain, for a few seconds, invisible, appearing only as the water dried.

Like symbols called forth from a place as distant and mysterious as the ballparks from which the information on the tickertape came, the numbers would appear. They would reveal themselves as they were written, from the beginning of the digit to its end. Though they had only a moment before been inscribed by the bartender, they now appeared, moments later, as if penned by some invisible hand. They were the missives from the kingdom of baseball.

As each symbol revealed itself, the larger story of the game in progress would unfold. *The Dodgers just got two in the fifth. Spahn's got the Cubs shut out through seven. Musial just reached the seats and the Cardinals have taken the lead.*

Were he Harry Blackstone or Okito the Mystic, the man with the magic chalk could not have amazed the boy from Princeton any more. This was beyond mere sleight of hand, these were invisible rabbits pulled from far-away hats. Jack Niehaus first took his son David there when he was still in elementary school and, unlike the chalk, the memory never faded.

"I used to sit there and be mesmerized by that," Niehaus told *The Seattle Times* columnist Steve Kelley, remembering D. A. Keimer and that scoreboard. "That had as much to do with my baseball love as anything else. Watching those numbers pop up on that blackboard."

No wonder then, in addition to naming Dave Niehaus and Gil Hodges as its favorite sons, Princeton would also lay claim to a man who called himself Charles Criswell King, a self-styled psychic later known to the world as "The Amazing Criswell."

Dave's Uncle James and Aunt Esther were always looking forward to his month at their home in Evansville. Recalled cousin Ron, "He had a great laugh, when something tickled him. My mom and dad liked him very much and he was always respectful of them." Aunt Esther was quite fond of David. She sometimes thought Delania was a little tough on him and consequently made him a welcome guest during his summer stay.

As if that wasn't enough, Dave was especially fond of Aunt Esther, because she was a baseball fan and a devoted follower of the Chicago White Sox. Just so happened she further appealed to Dave's second baseman's heart because her favorite player was Nellie Fox, the scrappy second-sacker for the South Side nine. She made sure for at least a few weeks every summer Dave got a healthy dose of Bob Elson calling the Pale Hose games on WJJD and WIND out of the city with the big shoulders.

The summers spent with cousin Ron also were about watching baseball and the boys did a lot of that. During Ron's annual stay in Princeton, they were inseparable and pick-up baseball games were their daily delight. Even on Sunday after church and chores, the two were off in a cloud of dust, mitts looped onto the handlebars, headed for Lafayette Park—now Gil Hodges Field—to meet the other neighborhood boys.

At Ron's house, they were fairly close to one of Evansville's largest public parks, Garvin Park. In these days preceding organized youth baseball, there were some rough diamonds laid out. The neighborhood kids gathered there to choose sides and play pick-up games.

As Ron recalled in one of our conversations, "This was before Little League, so there was no mom picking up a bunch of kids in the station wagon. The only organized league in town was the 'Y' League, run by the YMCA. We'd all ride our bikes out to what was called East Side Park. David wasn't on those teams, because he wasn't from Evansville, so he had to watch those games from the stands."

Ron recalls Dave being happy to do so and a keen observer even at such a young age. Still, there was more baseball to be seen in Evansville, baseball for both of them to watch together.

Just as those small-town boys dreamed of the big city and just as they root for the big-league teams they followed in the paper and on the radio, they harbored a special and deep-rooted love for their hometown minor league team.

The 1930s and early '40s were hard times for the minor leagues. Doug Feldman in his book, *Dizzy and the Gas House Gang: The St. Louis Cardinals and Depression-Era Baseball*, noted, "More than half the minor-league teams operating in 1929 would fold by 1931."

In *The Business of Baseball*, author Albert T. Powers wrote, "Minor-league baseball was hit especially hard by the Great Depression, with many teams being forced to disband, although popular teams in expanding markets such as Los Angeles and San Francisco enjoyed some success." Powers offered further evidence: "One of the more enduring of baseball's minor leagues, the Western League, closed down shop from 1938 thru 1946. (Cedar Rapids and Waterloo moved to the Three-I League. Sioux City moved to the Nebraska State League. Davenport, Des Moines, and the league itself folded.)"

Despite the Works Progress Administration building ballparks across America, including stadiums as big as Tiger Stadium in Baton Rouge, Louisiana, and as small as Riverview Stadium in Clinton, Iowa, there simply was no capital available to fund teams and even less money for the purchase of tickets by a fan base struggling to afford food. Twenty-five minor leagues finished the 1929 season, only twenty-one remained at the close of the 1930 season and, by the fall of 1932, only sixteen were left. The Arizona-Texas League, the Blue Ridge League, the Cotton States League and the Dixie League were among the many casualties.

Big-league franchises were hurting as well. As *The New York Times* noted in its Jan. 6, 2009 edition: "Despite the immense popularity of baseball in the 1920s, the sixteen teams that made up the major leagues then were not insulated from hard times. Attendance plummeted 40% from 1930 to 1933 and did not return to pre-Depression levels until after World War II, when millions of soldiers returned."

In the 1940s and even more so in the post-World War II years, two factors combined to help restore baseball in small towns: the return of prosperity and the growth of the major-league farm system. Again from Albert Powers: "The principal reason for the solvency of many minor league teams was the growth of the major league farm systems."

As parent clubs developed and stockpiled talent, minor leagues again flourished across America from the Southern Association to the Pacific Coast League. Minor league classifications would run deep below Triple-A and Double-A, all the way down to the D League games played on small, dusty diamonds in remote towns.

Evansville, Indiana was one of the places baseball often left, but continued to return. During the years Dave Niehaus came of age as a young baseball fan, the Class B Evansville Braves were the local champions.

Organized baseball in Evansville could be traced back to even beyond the Evansville River Rats of 1901–1902 who moved to Davenport, Iowa, not to return until their reincarnation as the 1919 Evansville Black Sox.

The Evansville Evas, Little Evas, and Pocketeers of the 1920s gave way to the 1930 Evansville Hubs. The Hubs, like so many other minor-league teams in the Depression era, folded near the end of the 1931 campaign. The entire Three-I League collapsed the following year, made a short-lived comeback in 1935, and went dark again until 1937.

From 1938 to 1942, Evansville made another go of it, but the onset of the war years brought three more silent summers to the ballpark. It was in the late 1940s and on into the 1950s, during the years the two cousins roamed the bleachers at old Bosse Field, the Evansville hometown nine had its most glorious seasons as a farm team in the organization of the Boston Braves (1946–1952) and later the Milwaukee Braves (1953–57).

The Evansville Braves played in a circuit that launched the professional careers of scores of major leaguers, the Three-I League. The league drew its name from the three states in which most of its teams played: Indiana, Illinois and Iowa. Part of Dave's love for the Brooklyn Dodgers came from memories of Carl Erskine's 1943 season in which he won nineteen games as a twenty-year-old hurler for their Danville, Illinois Three-I League farm team.

Evansville was managed by Bob Coleman, the "Hoosier Hotshot," who would one day earn the sobriquet "the grand old man of the minor leagues." Coleman had played in the Three-I League himself as a catcher for the Davenport Blue Sox prior to World War I. His brief big league stints were with the Pirates and then the Senators, for whom he was the battery mate of Hall of Fame-bound Mordecai "Three Fingers" Brown.

Like many of Dave's relatives, Coleman was from Dubois County just two counties over from Gibson County. Specifically he hailed from Huntingburg, Indiana, where two baseball movies were filmed decades later— A League of Their Own, about women's professional baseball, and Field of Honor, about Satchel Paige and Josh Gibson of the Negro leagues.

Coleman's managerial career began at the age of twenty-eight when he was chosen to oversee the Double-A Mobile Bears of the Southern Association. With the exception of 1926, he managed every year through 1957, thirty-nine seasons in all, a remarkable record.

He skippered the Evansville Class B team for twenty seasons across a span of more than four decades. He managed the Hubs for the Detroit Tigers from 1928–1931. He piloted the Bees for the Boston Braves from 1938–1942, managing a twenty-year-old Warren Spahn. His third stint was managing the Braves from 1946–57 for the same parent club, first in

Boston, then when it moved to Milwaukee. This final stretch proved his most successful. During those twelve seasons, Coleman racked up five first-place finishes and four league playoff championships, culminating in back-to-back first-place finishes and league championships in 1956 and 1957. The two cousins saw some pretty good baseball.

Coleman, it may be recalled, was the man tapped by the Boston Braves to skipper the big league club in 1943 when Casey Stengel was sidelined by a broken leg. The injury was sustained when Stengel, while crossing the street, was struck by a cab. The event inspired Boston Daily Record writer "Colonel" Dave Egan to wisecrack that the cabbie who hit Stengel should be awarded a plaque as "the man who has done the most this year for Boston baseball." The great Evansville run under Coleman began with his return from Boston in 1946.

Coleman's teams won 2,496 games. Only Connie Mack, John McGraw, Tony LaRussa and Bobby Cox managed more major-league wins. When he retired after the 1957 season, Coleman was the winningest manager in minor-league history. His record stood until 1985 when Stan Wasiak, a lifelong Dodger organization man, earned the title "King of the Minors." In his thirty-sixth season, he broke Coleman's record for most seasons as a minor-league manager and that same year also broke Coleman's record for career victories, ending up with 2,570.

From 1946 to 1957, Coleman was Evansville's manager every summer, except 1950 when he was asked to nurture his prospects through a summer with the Milwaukee Brewers of the American Association. For a young baseball fan growing up in semi-rural Indiana, he was the stuff of legends. It was Coleman who developed the young talents that ultimately won a World Series in Milwaukee in 1957.

Bosse Field was the home of the Evansville Braves in the 1940s and remains today the third oldest ballpark seeing regular use in America. It first opened its gates on June 17, 1915. Only Fenway Park (April 20, 1912) and Wrigley Field (April 23, 1914) are older.

It was at Bosse Field Dave saw future major-leaguers like Johnny Logan, Eddie Matthews (whom Coleman installed at third base), Felix Mantilla, Wes Covington and, in 1949, a catching prospect named Del Crandall. Little could Dave know that in the distant future he would, for parts of two seasons, spend most every day with a tape recorder in hand interviewing Del Crandall, manager of the 1983 and 1984 Seattle Mariners.

The entrance to Bosse Field, the oldest operating minor league baseball stadium in America. Only big-league venues Fenway Park and Wrigley Field have been open longer.

Among his cousin Ron Greenwood's cherished memories are the countless times they snuck into Bosse Field. Their route and routine evokes similar reveries in all who ferreted their way into the local ballpark:

- Climb up the wall to the third-base side of home plate just down from the box office and the front gates
- Open the first-floor window, slide through and go up to the second floor
- Slither through another window to the top of an eight-foot wall underneath the stands
- Tightrope to the end and shinny down the pole to the sand pit below
- Jump into the sand pit adjacent to the third-base seats and make your way in the dark under the ramp that rose to the first floor
- Go all the way down to the storage area and find the door that served as a back entrance to the men's room
- Dust yourself off in the men's room, make yourself presentable and walk out into the stands

It is hardly surprising that the memory still brings a wistful gleam to Ron's eye and a smile to his face.

That summer of 1946 was a season of unmatched delirium for southern Indiana's fans of the St. Louis Cardinals and of the Evansville Braves. The two youngsters from Princeton and Evansville were captives of their twin loyalties to the boys faraway and the boys there at home. The twin objects of their reverence extended beyond the field and into the radio booth. For just as they had their St. Louis Cardinals and Harry Caray, they also had their Evansville Braves and Dick Shively.

Dick Shively was the voice of the Evansville Braves and that special summer of 1946 was his first year broadcasting their games. In 1941, Shively graduated from Purdue where the Ross-Ade Stadium Pavilion would one day house the Shively Media Center and the Shively Stadium Club. He began his career as an undergraduate, broadcasting Purdue football games on WBAA and went on to call baseball games for the Nashville Volunteers of the Southern Association. He would next direct sports operations for both radio and television at WSM in Nashville before returning to his alma mater. He later served as an officer of the Indiana Sportswriters and Broadcasters Association.

When the Cardinals had a day off or perhaps played at a different time, young Dave Niehaus would tune that Zenith radio in to listen to Dick Shively call the Evansville Braves. Shively broadcast the home games from the press box at Bosse Field but the road games were a different story. Road games were broadcast from the radio station. Dave was about twelve years old when he and cousin Ron first learned how those broadcasts were done and those were the games that most excited Dave Niehaus.

It's a long-gone art now, perhaps no longer done anywhere: the art of re-creation. For road games, Shively received the results from a wire in the studio and then simulated the action for the fans listening. The simulation included sound effects of the crowd noises, sometimes cheering, sometimes booing, sometimes just in the background. The sound effects further included the crack of the bat, the muted sound of the ball hitting the catcher's glove and the umpire bellowing, "Steeeee-rike!" David marveled at Shively's ability to make it sound like the action was unfolding before him and it was from his work Dave first learned the baseball broadcaster's number one job was to "make people *feel* like they're at the park."

These broadcasts had a very real effect on the career of Dave Niehaus. He would one day recreate broadcasts in New York in the 1950s, in Los Angeles in the 1960s, and two final times in Seattle, once in 1981 and again in 1994.

Some years after the glorious summer of 1946, seventeen-year-old Dave Niehaus and his cousin Ron were in the stands at Bosse Field on Sunday night, August 17, 1952 to witness the Evansville Braves game against Cedar Rapids. To be sure, they were there to see the ballgame, but they were also there because it was "Dick Shively Night." Dave thought Harry Caray was special. He thought Dick Shively was pretty special, too.

Yet every childhood summer must end and a new school year begin as the journey from kindergarten to grammar school to high school and college takes shape.

Dave graduated from Lowell Elementary in the spring of 1949. It was in his last couple summers of grammar school he went through every young boy's rite of passage—his first job. It was a decidedly Midwestern occupation.

Decades later he recalled the experience: "I was a corn detasseler in Princeton, Indiana. I must've been twelve or thirteen years old. A corn detasseler is where you take the tassel of the corn and pull it out. You shake that into a paper sack and then turn it upside down and tie it on top of the corn stalk, and the pollen works its way down. The pollen got in the back of your neck and itched like the dickens. That was hard, hard work. I think I was paid fifty cents an hour."

His father Jack had arranged for the job, and the intended lessons were not lost on young David. He said he learned "the value of hard work and the discipline of having to get up in the morning. It was miserable."

With an eye no longer cast toward a career in corn detasseling, Dave entered Princeton High School, home of the Tigers, in the fall of 1949. Soon Dave's favorite joke was that PHS stood for "Pure Horse Shit," but in truth he always recalled his years there fondly.

One of his fellow enrollees at Princeton High was Gary Osborne, whom he had befriended just that summer. The friendship endured for the rest of his days.

"Dave was a good student, particularly in English," Osborne recounted to me. "He was outgoing, just naturally friendly, and so very well spoken. He had a great command of language even as a young man. He really excelled in English class."

Dave's mother, Delania, was always on her son about good manners and insisted that he dress smartly during the winter, including leggings over his trousers. She was on the case if he displayed any sign of bad manners

The former Princeton High School (now a junior high school), which graduated Dave Niehaus in 1953.

and was a tough taskmaster when it came to his schoolwork. Dave learned at an early age to get to the study table and get the job done. His dad was equally demanding when it came to grades. David was their only child and they were committed to him being a successful student.

"To his credit," said cousin Ron, "he really took it, he didn't resist."

His acumen in English class came as no surprise to those who knew him. From his youngest days, Dave was an avid reader and an enthusiastic fan of crossword puzzles. His passion for them would last a lifetime. As a destination in the morning paper, the daily crossword ran a very close second to the box scores. Language and words delighted him and, later in life, if you were ever an overnight guest at the Niehaus home, you'd be hard-pressed to get his attention in the morning until he'd paid an ample measure of it to the day's crossword puzzle.

Dave's father, Jack, former baker and now insurance salesman, had a practical bent. While he also loved baseball and encouraged Dave to play, it was his desire to see his son acquire a profession. Somehow or other he had decided it would be dentistry. As it happened, Dave greatly admired their family dentist and agreed it might make a good vocation.

DAVID A. NIEHAUS
Band 1, 2, 3, 4; Melody Hour 1, 2, 3, 4; Ca
Choir 1; Choir 2, 3, 4; Basketball 1, 2; Ba
ball 1, 2, 3, 4; Intramural Sports 2, 3; St
Solo and Ensemble Contest 2, 3, 4; Stud
Librarian 4; Gibson County Choral Festi
2, 3, 4.

Dave's 1953 Princeton High
School yearbook photo and
extra-curricular activities list.

Freshman and sophomore years went by marked by stability and happiness at 625 North West Street. Gary Osborne recalls Dave learning to drive. "He wasn't very good at it." Osborne said. "He'd drive up to my house and slide to a stop and skid on the edge of the lawn. Somehow he managed to never wreck that '46 Ford."

It was also around that time Dave first took up smoking. Ron Greenwood recalled, "Yes, he loved those cigarettes even in high school, but Jack didn't approve, nor did his mother. He used to hide his smokes in the tree next to his house."

Meanwhile, the Cardinals' fortunes tapered off later in the new decade, but the Bums from Brooklyn were extending their magical streak. Hometown hero Gil Hodges gave David plenty of reason to spend those summers immersed in the box scores and listening for Harry Caray's updates on the Dodgers during his nightly broadcasts.

Throughout his four years at Princeton High, Dave pursued twin loves, the first being sports. Like his cousin Ron, he loved to play baseball and basketball. Southern Indiana was basketball country and Dave played

The Princeton Library was one of Dave's favorite places as a boy.

hoops for the junior varsity in his freshman year and made the varsity as a sophomore. He played guard for the Princeton High cagers and wasn't afraid to put the ball up.

"He and I played in a tournament at Harwood School," Ron remembered. After the game we called him 'Shotgun.' He was a pretty good guard, pretty quick, but he wasn't much for assists."

His teammates those years included brothers Roy and Gary Stoll. Roy went on to star at Tulane University in New Orleans and captain the 1955–56 Green Wave squad. Roy's future wife, Nancy, was one of Dave's tennis partners and Gary's son, Rich, was drafted by the Montreal Expos. For all of them, like so many of their schoolmates, the Teentown Roller Rink was the place to find them on Friday or Saturday nights.

When his mother became ill, Dave chose to spend the late summer and early fall of 1951 caring for her. It meant giving up basketball but it was a clear, albeit difficult choice. Both he and his father were, by then, all too aware their time with Delania was becoming precious.

The 1951-52 Princeton High School baseball team. Dave can be seen in the first row of players, on the far right.

Dave played junior-varsity baseball in his freshman year and the following spring won a spot on Coach Richard Falls' varsity squad. He played the infield, mostly second base, but secretly longed to be a pitcher.

"During the summers," Greenfield said, "we'd play pitch and catch. We'd work on our pitching, giving signals to each other…and we both planned on playing major-league baseball…I didn't make it to the majors, but Dave did." Dave's number one pitch was a knuckleball drop that apparently did not impress Coach Falls enough to let him take the mound in anything other than relief. After hurting his arm in his sophomore year, he stayed at second base.

Despite having played mostly unorganized baseball, Dave earned a roster spot on the varsity baseball team. When they played against Central High of Evansville, he got to face off against his cousin Ron who went on to play for the University of Evansville. But during Dave's sojourn at Princeton High, it became clear his career as a second baseman would not extend into college. Still, he loved the game and played it with an enthusiasm that exceeded his ability, even playing American Legion baseball in the summer.

Dave pursued a second love as well, one that might surprise many who knew him later: music.

Not only did he play, he sang as well. A French horn player, he was in the Princeton High band all four years he attended, even appearing in the Indiana State Ensemble Contest and the Indiana State Solo Contest his sophomore, junior and senior years. After a stint in the freshman Cadet Choir, Dave sang for the varsity choir his last three years as a Tiger, including appearances at the Gibson County Choral Festival in 1950, '51 and '52. More than that, those same three years he was a regular in the PHS Melody Hour, the annual spring variety shows put on by members of the band and the choir.

Throughout his secondary schooling, Dave's love of reading and language never waned. He served as a student librarian his senior year and excelled in his English classes all four years.

For some, high school gives way to an immediate occupation. For others, the road ahead leads to more education.

With the dawn of the 1950s, the American Dream was alive and well in Princeton, Indiana. One of the key components of the credo of upward mobility was the chance to create a better life for one's children. Parents have been sacrificing for that since families first formed and centuries later the drive remained. Jack and Delania Niehaus believed in it, worked for it, dreamed of it for their son—an education, a better life, opportunity.

Dave was fully cognizant of the sacrifices his parents had made for him. He was aware of the dream they dreamed for him. He wasn't going to disappoint. He was headed for college.

Dave was drafted into the U.S. Army in 1958 and soon found himself working behind a microphone for the Armed Forces Radio & Television Service (AFRTS).

Bright Lights, Big City: The Armed Forces Network

*Casey Stengel was one of my idols…He was an unbelievable guy.
You could sit and talk to him for an hour and then leave,
and you would think, what did he say?*
—Dave Niehaus

THREE MONTHS AFTER A JUNE GRADUATION from Princeton High School with the class of 1953, Dave headed off to Bloomington and Indiana University along with his friend Gary Osborne. The state university made college affordable to middle-class students.

As Osborne put it, "We went to IU because we wanted to, but also because the price was right."

Leaving home for college had the usual mix of forward-looking excitement and backward-looking melancholy. For Dave it was made all the more difficult by the necessity of leaving his ill mother behind. Yet, as much as Dave's attentions were focused on his new life as a student at Indiana University, his heart was back in Princeton.

Delania Niehaus had been ill throughout Dave's senior year at Princeton High School. She bravely kept up the good face for her son and her husband. Her brief periods of recovery now served only to mark the time between her relapses. She had been diagnosed with cancer.

There was no greater challenge Jack Niehaus ever faced as a father or a husband to rival the period before and after his wife's passing. He rose squarely to the challenge. With strength and resolve, he steered his son through the turbulent time. Dave always spoke admiringly of how his father was there for him. On Sunday, May 20, 1954, Delania Grigsby Niehaus died. Her funeral was held at her long-time place of worship, the First Methodist Church, and she was buried in Princeton's Park Lawn cemetery.

Dave's goal was to fulfill the dream he had shared with his father and mother, the dream of a higher education and a spot in dental school. As close as he and his father were, it was a challenging freshman year for Dave. He hated the idea of his Dad being alone and was eager to spend the summer of 1954 with him. During that summer, they went to the Pike County Fair where it happened that sixteen-year-old Leah Fisher and her fifteen-year-old cousin were crowned Queen and Princess of the fair.

When Dave introduced himself to Leah, she was immediately struck by two qualities in him. "He was such a gentleman, different from the other boys," she said. "He had a real respect for women. And he was so well spoken, he expressed himself so well."

What Fisher remembers most about the year or so they dated was the ensuing friendship between David and her mother, Ermil.

"David was so lonely for his mother, he really missed her," Fisher said. "He loved Delania very much and he was quite vulnerable, in a state of shock. As it turned out, he and my mother hit it off. There were many times I came home to find that he had come by to talk to my mother. She used to take an afternoon nap downstairs in the room my sister and I shared. Dave would knock, she'd call him in and he'd pull up a chair or lie down on the other bed and just talk to her."

She added, "I'm only sorry my mother never knew of his success. She wouldn't have been surprised. She loved David."

Leah Fisher also recalls Dave's passion for sports and the burgeoning young announcer in him taking hold. She said, "We went to a Princeton High football game and it was packed. We didn't have seats. David got us down to the sidelines, but instead of just watching the game from one spot, he ran up and down the sidelines with many of the plays, calling the action as he went."

Throughout Dave's first two years of general studies, dental school remained his intention. He had befriended both Leah's older sister, DeAnn, and DeAnn's boyfriend, both seniors at Indiana. The family invited Dave and his father to Thanksgiving dinner in the fall of 1954. The youngsters began discussing their futures and when DeAnn, hearing of Dave's dental school plans, blurted out, "David Niehaus, you are much too good-looking to be a dentist. You should be in communications." Something tells me young Dave Niehaus didn't mind having his father hear that.

College offers the opportunity to learn about your intended profession but, even more so, to learn about yourself. There is an adage: if you want to know what your intentions were, look at your results. For Dave Niehaus, the adage would fit like a new Rawlings glove. Soon enough, dentistry's loss would become sports broadcasting's gain.

Both his economic station and his Midwestern work ethic dictated that college summers were meant for working and for saving for the following year. In the spring of 1955, Dave found a notice on a bulletin board at Indiana University—summer jobs were available at Mount Rushmore in South Dakota. They were looking for waiters and Dave had experience working in the campus dining hall. He called his pal Gary Osborne.

Dave and Gary Osborne on a Colorado ski lift, 1955.

The two young men decided this would make for a whale of a summer. They applied immediately and landed those summer jobs working in the restaurant and souvenir stand at Mount Rushmore National Memorial.

The job appealed to far more than his need for employment; it appealed to his love of history, his patriotism and his love for the great expanse of Middle America. Both his cousin and his roommate recall how much he enjoyed his summers in South Dakota, getting to know new people from other schools, including a lot of cute girls.

Fortunately for Dave and Gary, Princeton was still small enough you didn't need a car. Dave's father agreed to let the boys take the family car to South Dakota. He might have reconsidered had he known the two adventurers would detour through Denver so they could see Pike's Peak. Even in early summer it can be a dicey proposition to ascend that gravel roadway, then—as now—used for a hair-raising, 156-turn, high-speed hill climb by Indianapolis 500-type racing cars and motorcycles. Sure enough, the boys picked a blustery day for their ascent.

They had seen their share of snow in Indiana and didn't worry as they drove higher and the storm worsened. The police were closing gates behind them to stop any more drivers from coming up the hill.

Gary Osborne recalled, "Next thing we're sliding around, a couple times way too close to the edge of the roadway and finally we got stuck. A state trooper came along and pushed us so we could turn around. Problem was, the gates closed the roadway to downhill traffic as well and we ended up spending the night in the Niehaus family car on Pike's Peak."

Dave and Gary made it to Mount Rushmore and the summer of 1955 was one they'd replay again and again. They became Saturday night regulars in the nearby town of Deadwood. Each weekend they'd attend "The Days of '76," a recreation of the trial of Jack "Crooked Nose" McCall, the man who shot Wild Bill Hickok. On one of those weekends, both were picked from the audience to be among the twelve jurors. Gary recollects the highlight of that experience as the moment during "deliberations" when each juror was required to take a pull from a bottle of whiskey to "sharpen their judgment." When Jack Niehaus came out to visit in late July, Dave and Gary took him to the show.

"I remember the night vividly, because it was the first time Dave ever drank a beer in front of his father," Osborne.

Carl and Kay Burgess were the owner-operators of the restaurant and souvenir stand at Mount Rushmore and the couple took an immediate liking to Dave. His three summers spent there beneath the towering images of Washington, Jefferson, Roosevelt, and Lincoln were among his most favorite of times and the Burgesses and he became fast friends. Indeed, Dave would later recall them as his first surrogate parents.

That first summer, Dave met one of the park's famous visitors, guiding him to another of his very special friendships. Dave was introduced to World War II flying ace Joe Foss (the "Flying Governor" of South Dakota) by his buddy Gary Osborne. Gary was dating Pricilla Dean, Foss' niece. The governor took a liking to young Mr. Niehaus and their friendship later took on new meaning as Dave's broadcast career coincided with Joe's becoming the first commissioner of the American Football League in late 1959. Carl Burgess would himself serve seven terms in the South Dakota legislature, eventually becoming Speaker of the House before going on to serve in the state Senate.

Larry McKay, Dave's friend and roommate at Indiana University in 1957, recalled Dave's letters from Mount Rushmore as being filled with details about everything from Indians to pristine rivers to the monument itself. Dave delighted in saying he "worked under four presidents." Dave was loved everywhere he went and this national park was no exception. The organizers of the summer buffalo hunt selected Dave to head up the expedition. The task included shooting the buffalo for the annual feast, although whether Dave found it in himself to fire at the creature remains shrouded by the passage of time. Regardless, his sense of wonder at the lands west of Indiana had been enhanced by his South Dakota summers.

One of the job perks for Dave and Gary was visiting behind the scenes at the monument itself. At every possible opportunity, they went up to the workshops where the craftsmen who maintained the monument worked. They saw a side of the structure few ever see. The two young men were fascinated by what they saw and when one of the workmen told them yet another giant sculpture was in the works, they had to see it, too.

As soon as they could, Dave and Gary hopped into the '46 Ford and made the seventeen-mile journey from Mount Rushmore out to nearby Custer County. There, between Custer and Hill City, they found Thunderhead Mountain, site of the Crazy Horse Memorial. Yet unfinished today, the project was begun in 1948 and, in the mid-1950s, was still in its infancy. Dave's ability to talk his way into anywhere somehow got them a meeting with sculptor Korczak Ziolkowski, the man who conceived of and oversaw the project. They would visit often during the summer and Ziolkowski gave the boys an insider's look at that monument as well.

If anything, Dave Niehaus proved the value of a sense of adventure and a curiosity about nearly everything. He loved meeting people and hearing their stories. The chance decision to go meet the Crazy Horse sculptor led to another introduction two summers later that would have a profound impact on his future. Mythologist Joseph Campbell refers to "following your bliss" as the maxim for living a life "according to your gifts." Dave Niehaus followed his bliss to South Dakota and would soon follow it to California.

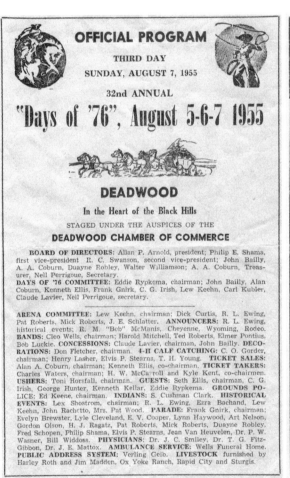

The "Days of '76" brochure.

The boys also befriended a public relations man from Rapid City who was there in association with MGM Studios. Through him, they became regular visitors to the set of *The Last Hunt* that was being filmed on location in nearby Badlands National Park. The movie starred Robert Taylor, Stewart Granger, Russ Tamblyn and Debra Paget. The filming gave the boys a chance to see a big-time Hollywood movie in production. Dave was entranced. He got to see real movie stars up close and the nascent desire to see Los Angeles was born. It was a place he wanted to experience and he was going to find a way to get there.

Dave and Gary Osborne were part of the "Tribe of '55" under the tutelage of Ben Black Elk, the liaison between the native Sioux and the youngsters who came to work during the summers. Their jobs were in the kitchen. They worked mornings and had their afternoons free. They'd return for the dinner shift and be done around ten o'clock. Osborne recalls that among the most memorable moments were the still quiet summer nights after work. They would walk out to the prairie just beyond the encampment. There were still herds of buffalo then, grazing at night.

"We'd sit and talk some but mostly listen to the buffalo rumble around and snort," Osborne said.

Their salary was $42 a month, plus tips. The two Hoosiers did so well they each earned a $150 bonus at season's end. They vowed to return together, but Gary's ROTC obligations took him to Fort Riley, Kansas the following year. As a result, Dave was Princeton's sole representative among the "Tribe of '56."

Dave was openly sentimental about his regard for the grandeur of nature and the splendor of the unspoiled scenery beyond the Mississippi, in stark contrast to the life he lived years later in the bustling urban confines of New York City. His sense of adventure surely served to make him appreciate Gotham and its wonders, but that same wanderlust would one day call him westward once again. Memories of those summer nights on the plains would prove to be a stanza of the song that would call him to the shores of the southern California coast and eventually to the farthest of outposts from Princeton, Indiana—the Pacific Northwest.

Once again, however, summer had to end and a new school year begin.

In 1956, Indiana University had the foresight and the vision to recognize the burgeoning business of radio and television, specifically with respect to careers behind the microphone. Until then, the theatre department had overseen the broadcast curriculum, but the university decided to create a department specifically devoted to the study of broadcasting. The result was a Department of Radio and Television and the establishment of a degree in the field.

Dave Niehaus always claimed he happened to chance upon the offices one day and decided to "inquire within." The truth was Dave had known one thing for quite some time—he really didn't want to be a dentist. He would later describe the epiphany this way: "I just couldn't spend the rest of my life looking down somebody's throat."

How long he actually deliberated or whether he followed an impulse is left for us to guess, but one day in 1956, Dave walked into the office of campus radio station, WFIU. In doing so, he left his former world behind. He was given an audition and was hired to broadcast Indiana Hoosier baseball games.

That night was a sleepless one. Dave tossed and turned, knowing a commitment to the radio and television department meant a commitment to a degree in the field. It also meant he had to call his father and tell him he could no longer dream of his son becoming a dentist.

Dave woke the next morning at 6 a.m. realizing he'd have to call home and break the news. His father had expected him to be a professional person. And now his father wanted to know what Dave was going to do with his life.

"A lot of things have happened to me since I took that turn on campus in Bloomington, Indiana," Dave told Bob Sherwin of *The Seattle Times* in a 2008 interview.

That "lot of things" began in earnest the following spring. The seeds of a new and different harvest took root when Dave began broadcasting those Indiana University baseball games on WFIU from what later would be named Sembower Field, dedicated in 1958 in memory of IU English professor and former Hoosier shortstop, Charles J. Sembower. The "press box" from which Dave worked was actually the top row of the bleachers, but the location only mattered when it would occasionally rain and raincoats and umbrellas were hastily gathered to cover the microphone and transmitter. This was something special, something that resonated with him in a way that told him, from day one, he was where he belonged.

The first game he broadcast on WFIU was a matchup between Indiana and the Ohio State Buckeyes. Prophetically enough, the first "major leaguer" he ever described was on the field that day, a nineteen-year-old Ohio State Buckeye sophomore named Frank Howard. "Hondo," as he became known, would be 1960 National League Rookie of the Year and have a stellar career with the Dodgers and the Senators. The two would ultimately be "reunited" many years later when Howard was hired by Niehaus' long-time friend and then-Mariner manager, Dick Williams, as a coach for the Seattle Mariners in 1987 and 1988.

Larry McKay fondly remembers their year together at the Men's Residence Center. McKay later worked at KMPC and KHJ in Los Angeles and became the voice of "Showtime" as public-address announcer at The Forum for Dr. Jerry Buss and the L.A. Lakers. They both had opted for enrollment in the radio-TV program, Dave one year ahead of McKay, who recalled the joyous and not-always disciplined spirit of his old friend.

"Our day would begin with the ritual of one waking the other, both of us still lying in bed," McKay said. "We'd commonly bemoan our fate with a string of expletives regarding the coming day. Not real expletives but made-up expletives. Dave was the king. This eventually led to the creation of two aliens whom Dave would denounce each morning for the cruel fate bestowed upon the two students: 'Emo Warfang' and 'Zeus Marfax.' Every morning Dave would pronounce that 'Emo Warfang' had cruelly sentenced them to their 8 o'clock class, or that 'Zeus Marfax' was waiting at the lectern in the English building."

Like so many college boys, they had their favorite bar, but theirs was not the one frequented by the occupants of fraternity row. Their shared curiosity led them to Covington's where their nights were spent with the "cutters," the men who worked the southern Indiana limestone mines.

Part of the charm of Covington's was Edna, the head waitress known as "Edny." Large, snaggle-toothed and by legend, cross-eyed, "Edny" was also the bouncer and known to grab many a Hoosier lad by the seat of his trousers with one hand and the scruff of his neck with the other. The youngster from Princeton was spared from enduring such an inglorious exit. Edny liked David and when he asked, it was she who introduced Dave to Harold Fish, the resident piano player and bandleader of the three-piece combo at Covington's. Harold would inaugurate Dave's lifelong appreciation of piano players, one that would extend to my own friendship with him many years later.

A resourceful pair, Niehaus and McKay made odd jobs go a long way. Dave worked as a busboy in the mess hall but the job didn't pay a lot. His love affair with the English language had its own special twist at IU because the *Merriam-Webster's Collegiate Dictionary*, of which he was so fond, was worth five dollars when sold back to the university bookstore. The same price could be fetched for a used, full-length ROTC raincoat. It was amazing how many dictionaries and raincoats were left abandoned in the mess hall and about the campus. Those items made many a circular trip to the bookstore and saw the two young men through many a gap in their finances.

A turning point for twenty-year-old Dave Niehaus came when he took English Composition 103. For his sought-after radio and television degree, he was required to make a C grade. Dave's province was the spoken word, not the written one, and the required twenty-page, typed term paper would devour too much attention and too much time reserved for Covington's and reading the box scores. The resulting "D" in an English class was akin to Einstein's failing a math class.

Forced to retake the class, Dave learned a genuine lesson about application and preparation. He told his roommate he would never again allow himself to be caught unprepared. The shortcoming was never to be repeated and the man who would become known for the work he did before his broadcasts was, in part, born of this episode.

At age twenty-two, with two springs of broadcasting Indiana University baseball under his belt, Dave Niehaus spent the early summer of 1957 taking most of his final classes in Bloomington. He dearly loved the place. He was a genuine Indiana boy, born and raised a Hoosier and schooled at IU. The Midwest was in his blood and in his heart. It shaped his view of the world and of himself.

Still, he had come to know the world was a much bigger place than Indiana. His dreams were now much bigger than the Midwest landscape that shaped them. It was only a matter of finding the way to make those dreams a reality. Broadcasting, and especially, sports broadcasting would change exponentially over the decades to come. A wave of television and radio opportunities was about to roll across the broadcast landscape. Dave Niehaus would be there to ride it—all the way to Cooperstown.

Meanwhile, summertime was approaching and the Dakotas were calling. The tourists were filling the Mount Rushmore National Park, Crazy Horse was being chiseled out of Thunderhead Mountain, and buffalo were grazing amid the cool night breezes. The previous two summers there had been a delight both for him and the Burgesses, who had grown quite fond of him. He decided on one more visit.

Dave had some final classwork to finish for his degree, so he wouldn't be able to stay the full summer. Kay and Carol Burgess told him to come on out anyway, they'd be waiting for him. Fate, as it turned out, was waiting as well.

Upon his return to South Dakota, he reintroduced himself to Korczak Ziolkowski. The Crazy Horse monument sculptor in turn introduced him to David Humphreys Miller, the famed painter whose portraits of the seventy two Indian survivors of Little Big Horn were among his many famous works. Miller had been commissioned to come to Mount Rushmore to paint a mural of a buffalo hunt, a mural that today resides at the Civic Center in Rapid City, South Dakota. His wife Jan Boehm, was taking a break from her job in Los Angeles to be with him.

As it happened, Boehm's job was talent coordinator for one of America's biggest television shows, Ralph Edwards' *This Is Your Life*. When Dave told her he was about to receive his degree in radio and television with an eye towards sports broadcasting, she encouraged him to come to Los Angeles and offered him a job working on the show.

"Well, I'm just waiting around to be drafted. I'll be there," he told her.

Dave Niehaus was graduated from Indiana University with a Radio and Television degree on September 9, 1957. With a job waiting for him in Los Angeles, he decided to head west. His only miscalculation was how long his new job would wait.

He was due promptly in California, but didn't exactly take the direct route. His drive to the Pacific would bring his love of the grand American landscape to the fore. He would take advantage of this chance to soak in the grandeur of the country he loved so much.

So he took his time. Instead of getting to Los Angeles in one week, he took two weeks—"fooling around," as he would later describe it. By the time he crossed the San Gabriel Mountains and descended into the City of Angels, the job no longer awaited him.

"I'd never been west of where I was in South Dakota, which was pretty far west in the Black Hills," he said later. He went to the Grand Canyon, he went to Las Vegas, he went "here and there and so, a week after I was supposed to report, I called her and said, 'Well I'm here.'"

Jan Boehm explained she had to fill the position, but promised to find something else for him. She made some calls and landed Dave a job as a page at NBC Studios.

"I was late getting out to Los Angeles," he said. "That was obviously completely irresponsible on my part. Still, she did get me a job as a page— which is nothing more than a glorified usher—at NBC and I showed people to their seats for all the big TV series and specials."

Nonetheless, he had gone west, made it to Los Angeles and had his first job in "television." He worked at the NBC Studios in Burbank on the sets of the afternoon game shows like *Truth or Consequences*, *The Price Is Right*, and *Queen for a Day*. He liked California and planned to stay a while. Glorified usher or not, the letters NBC were about to look very good on his resume.

Six months later, on March 24, 1958, teen-aged girls all across America wept at the news Elvis Presley had been called to duty in the United States Army. Like most young American boys, Dave Niehaus scratched his head in disbelief at the display. Yet, only days afterward, his own draft notice arrived and, a scant nine weeks later, Dave himself donned the khakis and olive green on the first day of June, 1958. Elvis' hitch would take him away from show business; Dave's would lead him right to it.

Dave was sent to Fort Ord, 350 miles up the California coast from Los Angeles, to begin eight weeks of basic training. Those are anxious weeks for new recruits mostly spent adapting to the regimen of military life and won- dering where deployment would eventually take them. For Dave, it would take him right back to Los Angeles. He did have a degree in Radio and Television and he did work at NBC. Just as important, while working at the NBC studios he had made a good impression on someone who could help.

Robert Seal had been one of Dave's bosses at NBC. While the young Hoosier was learning how to toss hand grenades and properly employ a gas mask, Seal was urging the Army to pay attention to Niehaus' civilian resume. He wrote a letter recommending Dave for assignment to the Armed Forces Radio and Television Service.

The weight of the network executive's endorsement combined with young Niehaus' degree from IU caught the eye of Commander J.R. McK- enzie, then head of the AFRTS. An audition tape was made and his talents confirmed. On July 3, 1958, Commander McKenzie sent his own letter of recommendation and Dave found himself in line for his first professional broadcasting job, even if it was at an enlisted man's pay. Dave was assigned to the AFRTS and immediately sent back to Los Angeles for six weeks

Dave Niehaus meets then Vice-President Richard M. Nixon, circa 1959.

of training at their West Coast offices. With the better part of two years remaining in his hitch, the Army assigned him to work with the East Coast division of its broadcasting arm in New York City.

The odd part of the assignment was that he was not to bivouac in any barracks, meaning the young G.I. had to find an apartment and make his way in pricey Gotham on a soldier's pay. He needed to find a roommate. He found seven. Eight guys shared a flat in Kew Gardens in the heart of Queens, not far from the Interboro Parkway, which later was rechristened the Jackie Robinson Parkway. The apartment was crowded and crazy but affordable.

Even in 1958, New York was a city of more than six million people and the Midwest boy never was truly comfortable there. There were as many people in his neighborhood as there were in his hometown. Still, the fledgling broadcaster knew he was in the land of opportunity. Appreciating his incredible good fortune, he soon developed a reputation for hard work and preparation, just what you would expect for an earnest young man from Indiana.

Dave was an active member of the U.S. Army while broadcasting games on the Armed Forces Network and was justly proud of his military service. He often reminded his friends that during his deployment there, "nobody ever attacked New York." Gotham was indeed safe while the young officer was behind the microphone.

He was designated an official member of the AFRTS broadcast team on October 3, 1958. The Yankees and the Milwaukee Braves were two games deep into their rematch of the 1957 World Series and the AFRTS broadcast lineup for those games was already set. With no baseball to call until the following season, Dave drew a variety of assignments including college basketball, about which he knew plenty, and professional hockey, about which he knew nothing.

His first hockey broadcast was in February of 1959. Trouble was, he learned of the assignment on Saturday and the game was on Sunday. The other thorny issue: he'd never broadcast a hockey game. In truth, there was an even thornier issue: he'd never even seen a hockey game. His first hockey broadcast would be his first hockey game ever. Still, Sunday, February 22, 1959, found him behind the microphone at old Madison Square Garden.

As Dave told Jon Wells of *The Grand Salami* magazine in 1997, "I went to New York and broadcast the first hockey game I ever saw—didn't know a faceoff from a blue line or anything. As a matter of fact, I'll never forget—the game was between the Montreal Canadiens and the New York Rangers and at that time they (the Canadiens) had Maurice 'The Rocket' Richard. Richard a hall of famer, et cetera, but I didn't know anything. I studied at the library there on Forty-Second Street about hockey in the afternoon and went to old Madison Square Garden, which was on Eighth Avenue and broadcast the game. I think the Rangers won that game 6–1 or 6–2 or something like that. (Actually, 5–1.) I think that just about everybody that scored a goal was Maurice 'The Rocket' Richard, didn't matter whether he had a Rangers uniform on or a Montreal Canadiens shirt."

Fortunately for Dave and the stat keepers of the National Hockey League, it was his only broadcast. "I hope nobody taped that broadcast," he joked, "it was terrible." Nonetheless, had Dave done more NHL games,

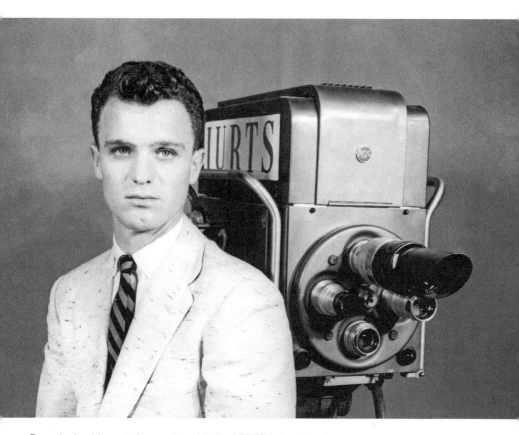

Dave during his post-Army stint with the AFRTS in Los Angeles.

Richard would have scored considerably more than seventeen goals that season. But what really makes that broadcast and Dave's later recollections of it even more priceless: Maurice Richard slammed into the boards at Chicago Stadium on Sunday, January 18, 1959, breaking his ankle. He did not play the rest of the season and was not on the ice that night at Madison Square Garden. The listeners must have been even more puzzled than the announcer.

With the spring of 1959, baseball returned. The Yankees were again world champions, and, with the departures of both the Giants and the Dodgers for the West Coast, the men in pinstripes now had the town all to themselves. Yankee Stadium was one of baseball's greatest shrines and was about to become Dave Niehaus' office.

Despite the fact much of his work was done at old Yankee Stadium in New York, part of his heart must have been back at Bosse Field in Evanston.

Although Mel Allen was in the same press box, surely his thoughts had to have often been with Dick Shively, for most of Dave's job was broadcasting re-creations of games from the tickertape and wire services. Like the earliest practitioners of his art, he was making the game come alive in every detail, all from the green expanse of the playing field of his imagination.

His work went out mostly to soldiers stationed in Europe and elsewhere around the world. Soon he was also broadcasting some American League games live from the house that Ruth built. As a result, he was rubbing elbows with the Yankee beat writers and broadcasters, and with a few legendary guys who worked in the dugout.

Among Dave's many treasured friendships in the game was with Charles Dillon "Casey" Stengel, the Ol' Professor. Stengel to this day remains one of the most colorful and beloved figures the game ever produced. He had been around the game for fifty years, having begun his minor-league career in 1910. He reached the majors in 1912 with the Brooklyn Dodgers and played in three World Series, one with Brooklyn and two with the New York Giants. In 1923, he hit the first World Series home run in what is now old Yankee Stadium. He would become the only man in baseball history to wear the uniform of all four New York franchises—the Dodgers, Giants, Yankees and Mets.

The friendship began as simply as one could imagine. Well after finishing the day's broadcast, Dave, as was his custom, was still at the ballpark taking notes, interviewing players and coaches and the like in the press room. He had seen Stengel there before but had never spoken to him. His decision to do so began a lifelong fellowship with one of twentieth-century baseball's truly storied figures. There was a good deal to talk about. As a young man Stengel, like Niehaus, had designs on becoming a dentist. Like Niehaus, baseball changed that idea. Stengel had once been traded for Billy Southworth, who managed the Cardinals in the mid-1940s. And Stengel managed the Boston Braves when they were the parent club of the Evansville Braves.

As Dave related the story to Mike Gastineau, Seattle sports-radio host and author of *The Great Book of Seattle Sports Lists*, "He'd come in the press room at Yankee Stadium after the game and have a couple drinks. He drank Scotch. As the evening wore on, he had a few scotches and said, 'Where do you live, son?'

" 'I live in Kew Gardens.' I was an E2 at the time. I don't think I even had a stripe. I wasn't even a private first class. He said 'Would you like to

The 1963 AFRTS baseball broadcast team. From the left, Darrell Dreyer, Dick Schad and Dave Niehaus.

come over to my place and have a drink?' I said, 'Are you kidding me?' "

"So his chauffeur took us down to the Essex House where he lived, and we sat there and talked baseball and drank until the sun was coming up. When I told him I was planning on taking the subway home, he went downstairs with me and gave the cabbie a $20 bill, which was like $100 today, and he said, 'Make sure this young man gets home safely.'"

The two men remained friends until Stengel's death in September of 1975 in Glendale, California. Dave would later recall, "He was one of my idols. I went to his funeral, where Billy Martin was one of his pallbearers. He was just an unbelievable guy. You could sit there and talk to him for an hour and leave and you would still say 'What did he say?' It was a celebration more than anything else. They played *Take Me Out to the Ballgame.* It was a happening."

Dave's Army hitch was up in June of 1960 and so was his tenure as a baseball broadcaster for the Armed Services Network. Accordingly, on May 20, 1960, he was relieved of his AFRTS assignment. He beseeched his commanding officers to let him stay on as a civilian and they acceded to his request. But he was tired of New York. The great expanse of the Midwestern summer sky was not to be seen there. The sounds of the buffalo grazing on the South Dakota prairie were not to be heard there. The great American West was calling.

Things had worked out before for Dave Niehaus and they did once again. AFRTS did have a spot for him as a civilian, but it was in Los Angeles. He couldn't have gotten better news.

This quintessentially American young man who had been born in Indiana and spent his summers in the great expanse of the plains of South Dakota had just spent the last two years in the close and crowded city of New York. He was more than ready to go. After a brief stop in Princeton to see his father, he was California bound. This time he didn't tarry.

The AFRTS job didn't pay enough to make ends meet, so Dave also went back to the NBC Studios where he got a job and a promotion to a position in the film department. It turned out to be in the warehouse, stacking and sorting film and sending reels of film to affiliates and clients. Mostly it was moving boxes. Still, it was show business.

As is so often the case in Los Angeles, his co-worker was an aspiring actor and singer. Dave really liked the kind and gentle young man from Sylacauga, Alabama and they quickly became friends. They not only worked together, they lived in the same apartment complex. Among their neighbors was a young actor named Clint Eastwood, who was just breaking into films.

Dave would tell his buddy Jim that he would be a big-league broadcaster someday and his buddy Jim would tell Dave someday he was going to be a professional singer. Dave Niehaus made good on his promise, just as Jim Nabors made good on his. Nabors would go on to achieve considerable success in the recording business and even more renown in television and film.

Dave often accompanied Nabors when Jim performed at open mike nights or audition nights at clubs and coffee houses in Los Angeles. One fateful night in a Santa Monica club, Nabors was doing his bit about a character he created named "Gomer Pyle." Andy Griffith was in the club and was so impressed he offered Jim a guest shot as Gomer on *The Andy Griffith Show*. Griffith later would help him develop his own series around the character.

Nabors' television show, *Gomer Pyle: U.S.M.C.*, became one of the iconic comedies of the Sixties. The selfless Griffith made sure that Jim retained ownership of his character and the show. The two men remained friends forever. For decades, Jim Nabors marked each Memorial Day by singing

Back Home Again in Indiana to the throng attending the Indianapolis 500 and is the only man to have been twice named grand marshal of the Indy 500 parade. Jim got his big break and Dave's was just around the corner.

Dave's job with the AFRTS called for him to do one game a week. The games were not to be broadcast live but were recreated in-studio from a tickertape account of the action. Every detail from the weather to the windup, from the white jerseys of the home team to the white shirts in the stands, was the broadcaster's responsibility to relay to the listener. Dave knew exactly what he would be called on to do. He was born for this job.

Years later, Dave's friend and Mariner broadcast partner, Rick Rizzs, said this to me: "The reason he connected with the fans was that he was such a great storyteller—all the great ones got that from the guys they grew up listening to. He enjoyed painting the pictures, putting people in the front row at the ballpark, making everybody see the game as he saw it. With that comes the knowledge that you're the conduit, the connection."

The baseball fan and the born raconteur in Dave made him a perfect fit for the assignment of translating ticker tape into a baseball broadcast. It was a good job that got better quickly. Armed Forces Radio decided to do a live major league game out of Los Angeles once a week. The brass did not have to look far for someone with talent and big-league experience to man the microphone. Niehaus got the nod.

He began calling a game each weekend, either a Dodgers tilt or an Angels contest. The Dodgers played in the Los Angeles Coliseum and the expansion Angels toiled in L.A.'s old Wrigley Field, not to be confused with the Chicago park of the same name. In 1962, the Dodgers moved into their new home in Chavez Ravine (which is how Angel fans always referred to it) and the two clubs shared that yard until 1966 when Anaheim Stadium, "the Big A," opened for business. It was at Dodger Stadium that Dave first met another of his lifelong comrades, Dodger star first baseman Ron Fairly, who, some three decades later, became Dave's sidekick in the Mariner broadcast booth.

Even on the West Coast, the new frontier of major-league baseball, Dave Niehaus was making his pilgrimage through what are now venues somewhat lost in history. He had managed to find his way back to the baseball broadcast booth. It was the best job he'd ever had and he had missed it. He worked hard at it. He got better at it. He loved it even more.

Only a handful of years before, at Indiana University, he had been looking to the future and seeing himself with a nascent dental practice in

Dave with a plaque honoring him for his work with the AFRTS, circa 1964.

Princeton. Dental school was on the horizon. He might have even convinced himself he could do it.

Sometimes the heart leads us where the head will not.

The young man who had walked into the School of Radio and Television back in Bloomington surely was listening to something his heart was saying. The dream of being the voice coming through that old floor-model

Zenith had been suppressed, but not silenced. A moment comes when you simply can't turn a deaf ear to the call of your true desire.

As hard as it can be to determine what path will make you happy, it may be equally difficult to envision actually getting the chance to travel that path. Sometimes you follow your instincts and let the universe take care of the details. Failure is not a consideration and, even if it is factored into the equation, it would be far better than never trying. He had to have known the moment he opened that door for a radio audition, he was closing it on dental school. Surely, he at least hoped so.

The trains that had put Princeton on the map had given way to automobiles, a transition that returned Princeton to small-town status. When Eisenhower's dream of a nationwide interstate highway was fully realized, the bulk of traffic would flow along four-, and six-, and eight-lane freeways—no longer along two-lane state highways. The new grid of federally financed thoroughfares left places like Princeton and Evansville behind. Before long Princeton would no longer be just off U.S. 41; it would be more than two hours south of east-west I-70 and nearly as far from north-south I-65. There was certainly no going back.

In five years, the baseball field at Indiana University (capacity 2,250) had given way to Yankee Stadium and now to Dodger Stadium and soon to The Big A. Bloomington had given way to Gotham and now to the City of Angels. Not bad so far.

Young Dave Niehaus loved California and he loved his new job. He couldn't imagine loving anything more.

He soon would.

Dave and Marilyn's wedding photo taken in Las Vegas, December 27, 1963.

THE FOURTH INNING

One Great Love:
Dave and Marilyn,
a Lifelong Affair

*When Dave worked up the nerve to walk over and speak to Marilyn
Story, he didn't even say hello. He didn't introduce himself. Dave
merely asked, "Do you like baseball?" Marilyn's reply: "No."*

MARILYN STORY WAS BORN to parents George and Elsie on September 3,
1940, in Salt Lake City, Utah. George spent five years during World War
II working on the railroad and after the war took a job at a Salt Lake City
grocery store. An enterprising man, he soon saved enough money to buy
his own store in nearby Logan. His hard work paid off and the fledgling
business succeeded. Elsie, however, began to weary of the long and difficult
winters.

The winter of 1948–49 was never to be forgotten by any who endured
it. Christmas came and went rather mildly but in the first few days of January
a vicious blizzard hit. Another followed on January 15, still another a
week later. The National Guard airlifted hay to feed snowbound livestock
as temperatures plunged to minus twenty-five in the city and minus forty-
five in surrounding areas. A slight thaw in February provided no relief,
instead bringing the cruel misery of floods. The icy waters had little time
to recede as March and April brought new onslaughts of snow. Even Las
Vegas got seventeen inches. Sears and Roebuck advertised a "completely
assembled" cellar drainer for $42.95, "capacity 3,000 gallons per hour."

Elsie Story had seen enough. When the family visited relatives in California the following summer, her mind was made up. With her oldest

Marilyn and Dave at a friend's wedding in June of 1963.

daughter Shirley turning fifteen and entering senior high, and younger daughter Marilyn now ten, she convinced George southern California was the place to be and this was the time to go.

The lease on George's Logan grocery store was expiring—the timing was perfect. He bought a store in Sepulveda, California, and moved his family west, settling into a home in Northridge. The new store was so prosperous George bought a second one in Chatsworth, where he numbered Lucille Ball and Desi Arnaz among his regular customers

Marilyn was graduated from Reseda High School in the spring of 1958 and that fall enrolled at Pierce College in nearby Woodland Hills. She spent a year and a half there before taking a sabbatical in the spring of 1961 to help out in her dad's store in Sepulveda. Later that year, she and her best friend (and Kappa Beta Phi sorority sister) Lynda Coffin decided to save up for a boat cruise to Hawaii. As it happened, that boat not only carried her off to the islands, it set Marilyn on a course leading her to the man she would love like no other.

Peter Geiger, a vice-president of Bank of America, and two of his friends, a Hollywood attorney and a Los Angeles engineer, were on the same cruise. Peter and Marilyn became friends and remained so for the next five decades. After returning to the mainland, the attorney asked Marilyn out and eventually he and his engineer friend invited Marilyn and best friend Lynda to a party in Van Nuys. Unbeknownst to the attorney and the engineer, that night they were only serving as Cupid's coachmen. Marilyn and Lynda would each meet their future husbands at that party, and neither were the men who brought them.

Marilyn was a striking brunette with a Suzanne Pleshette hairdo and the smile to match. She was the kind of gal a fellow would notice from across the room. In Dave's defense, she was a knockout, enough to make any young man find himself at a loss for the right thing to say. So when the transplanted son of Princeton, Indiana worked up the nerve to walk over and speak to her, he didn't even say hello. He didn't introduce himself. He merely asked, "Do you like baseball?"

"No," Marilyn replied. She later reminisced, "I think that kind of threw him off. It's not that I didn't like baseball. I just thought it was an odd question to ask me."

Marilyn was immediately struck by the handsome young man but playfully offered him no help. Dave said nothing more and walked away, but surely did so planning his next move. Minutes later he returned and asked her to dance. Marilyn Story spoke her second word to Dave Niehaus. "Yes."

Soon enough she would love both baseball and this handsome young man from the Midwest. Over the ensuing two years, they dated more frequently and soon, exclusively. Just as it became increasingly clear to Marilyn that David was the one, Dave knew he couldn't let this very special gal get away.

On Thursday, August 22, 1963, one of the ballplayers Dave Niehaus loved the most was going to play his last game in Los Angeles. The St. Louis Cardinals were in town and one of his heroes, Stan Musial, was to take the field at Dodger Stadium for the final time in his career. Only ten days earlier, Musial had made public his decision to retire at the end of the 1963 season. This was Dave's chance to see one of his favorite franchise's most storied players ever, for the last time.

That evening he picked up the stunning brunette he'd met at that party in Van Nuys twenty-four months earlier for a historic night at the ballpark, a night that would draw a direct line from his seat that night in Chavez Ravine back to his front porch at 625 North West Street in Princeton, Indiana some seventeen years earlier. The young couple headed for a restaurant to grab some dinner before the game.

There is no sabermetric, no rubric for what makes a baseball fan tick. The siren song of the park can make a fan untie himself from the mast of most any obligation, any meeting or appointed round in order to file through the turnstile to see, perchance, baseball history, a play never before seen or an occasion to be recounted years later around the hot stove. For a Cardinals fan from the Midwest, this night was one of those nights. We can only guess the state of anticipation gripping Dave Niehaus as he and Marilyn set out that evening. *Stan Musial would play in Dodger Stadium for the final time that night.*

How can we fully sense the love of the game, of his team and of his hero that enveloped Dave that summer day? Dodger Stadium was in just its second season and arguably the most beautiful place in the big leagues to see a game. When you entered from the parking lot on the third-base side you actually entered the third deck. The sense of awe inspired by the panorama of the field and the way the ground before you literally gave way to the lush green canyon below is among baseball's true wonders. To make that entrance knowing Stan Musial's last game in Los Angeles was about to be played out upon that stage would have been more than any young Cardinals fan could have dreamed back in the summer of 1946.

Those two seats for which Dave Niehaus held tickets remained empty that night. The young couple didn't make it out of the restaurant until long after Sam "Toothpick" Jones struck out Bill "Moose" Skowron, the final Dodger hitter, to nail down a 3–2 Cardinals win. Dave Niehaus had come to the realization there was now a place in his heart even more special than the one held by the St. Louis Cardinals or by Stan Musial. The 48,567 fans in attendance could not have known that fan number 48,568 had, that very evening, proposed to fan number 48,569.

Whether he had intended to propose at the ballpark that night, we'll never know. We do know, whatever charm that evening's game held for him, they were no match for the powers of the grocer's daughter from Salt Lake City. He loved her, then and forever.

Years later, he would miss games for the birth of a child, for his son's graduation, for his induction into Cooperstown. He never missed a game for a better reason than that night in 1963. In typical Dave Niehaus fashion, he had his own way of asking for her hand. At one point in the dinner he turned to Marilyn and asked, "How would you like to be a June bride?"

An ecstatic Marilyn Story moved in with her sister Shirley and brother-in-law Jack to save money. They had two young children, so it was a full household. Yet Marilyn remembers Dave playing with the children nearly every time he came over. "I watched him play with those kids—he'd come over and rile them up—and he loved it," she told me. "I knew right then he was going to be a wonderful father."

As welcome a guest as Marilyn was, it was a small house for five. As Marilyn tells it, "One day Shirley just smiled at me and said, 'Why don't you two get married and get a place of your own?' I realized it was time."

She and Dave decided to move the wedding up to May. May turned out to be too long a wait for these lovebirds, so they decided on February. Marilyn had seen a virtual parade of friends get married and had, in fact, been a bridesmaid six times before. This time she was going to be the bride.

Still, love has its own clock and its own calendar. Time spent together moves all too quickly and time spent waiting is an eternity. Endless hours can be spent together doing almost anything, but no hours are as endless as those spent apart. Fittingly enough, on December 27, 1963, Dave and Marilyn, her parents, and Dave's roommate and soon-to-be best man, Conrad Martin, climbed into Dave's 1962 Pontiac Le Mans and drove through the desert to Las Vegas where the young couple exchanged vows. They would, from that moment, forever be Mr. and Mrs. Dave Niehaus.

Dave moved out of his Burbank apartment and Marilyn out of her sister's house. They rented one side of a duplex in Burbank and spent the next six months there. When Marilyn's sister Shirley and her husband bought a new house, they offered Dave and Marilyn a chance to buy the house they were selling. The delighted newlyweds moved into the residence at 16746 Jersey Street in Granada Hills.

Family was in the plans from the very beginning for these two. On August 22, 1964, their first child, an eight-pound, four-ounce boy, Andy, was born.

The fledgling family soon faced a genuine crisis. Dave's job was about to move a continent away. His experience broadcasting for the Armed Forces Network had landed him the job as sports reporter for the AFRTS Los Angeles-based branch. Now the decision-makers at AFRTS decided to close their West Coast offices and consolidate operations in New York City.

Marilyn, Dave and son Andy, circa 1968.

Dave wasn't about to uproot his young family and head back to Gotham. Besides, the job didn't pay enough to give up their home and the southern California weather they'd grown to love.

As she did so many times, Marilyn provided Dave with wise counsel.

Every Saturday morning, to make a little extra money, Dave rose early and made the lengthy drive into the city to do a five-minute radio show. The round-trip drive was well over twenty times longer than the show. Still, his every Saturday morning was spent on 710 AM, KMPC Radio. It was Marilyn who suggested Dave apply for a full-time position at the station, and her advice turned out to be as solid as her devotion to her husband. Program Director Steve Bailey liked young Mr. Niehaus' drive and his acumen. He especially loved his rich, baritone voice. Soon Dave would be the busiest sports reporter on the KMPC staff.

Two years and nine months later, Christmas brought them a very special gift in the person of their second child, Matthew, born on December 27, 1967. Daughter Greta blessed them with her arrival on May 25, 1970.

Dave Niehaus was a natural born story-teller. His broadcasts painted a picture of the game but, even more, they told the story of the game. Each game was a chapter in the great novel of a season told in 162 installments. One of Marilyn's most delightful memories of just how far Dave's talent went is a broadcast to which only she and her sister were witnesses.

On the morning of February 9, 1971, the alarm clock next to Dave Niehaus rang at 6 a.m. He reached over and punched the button, hoping for a few more minutes of rest. He got exactly forty-one seconds. Centered in nearby Sylmar, an earthquake with a magnitude of 6.6 moved the Olive View Medical Center a full foot off its foundation and destroyed the nearby Veterans Administration hospital. The southbound overpass from Interstate 210 to Interstate 5 collapsed onto the soon-to-be Santa Clara Metrolink tracks.

Only some six or so miles from the epicenter, the Niehaus home in Granada Hills shuddered and shook. Their home remained intact, but the authorities later that day issued an order requiring evacuation. Dave and Marilyn packed up three children, including baby Greta, two dogs, baby bottles and blankets, and headed across town where they took up temporary lodging with Marilyn's sister and brother-in-law in Northridge.

During the following days, one of Dave's assignments was to broadcast reports from the earthquake-damaged areas of Los Angeles. One of those assignments was a "live" report on the condition of the Van Norman Dam. Fear surrounding the possible breach of the dam was what prompted authorities to evacuate the Niehaus' neighborhood. Dave gave a stirring report on the dam, its condition and the possible impending peril represented by the concerns over its ability to hold. It was a detailed and colorful broadcast, live and direct from the living room couch in their temporary residence in Northridge.

Dave had been unable to get to the Van Norman Dam, because police would not allow him to get close to the structure or do his broadcast. So Dave did the next best thing. He got as good a look as he could, went home and did his "live" broadcast there, much to the delight of his giggling wife and sister-in-law who marveled at his passionate and detailed report of what he was seeing there at the dam. As he always said, "It *was* a live broadcast."

Dave and Marilyn out on the town.

This was a piece of cake for a man who had spent countless nights transforming a ticker tape into a tale of an evening at the ballpark. His admiring bride always remembered she and her sister doing their best to stifle their laughter as her husband broadcast "live and direct" from the still-dangerous scene of the earthquake's effects.

There would be more houses and more uprootings. The journey had yet a few more locales in which their love story would unfold. But by this time the Niehauses were a family, one that remained as solid and unshakeable as the love that was the root cause of it all.

Back home in Princeton, his father's life was undergoing changes of its own. Jack's friendship with his friend Hazel Rachel Simmons, herself a widow from rural Gibson County, had blossomed. Jack refused to tie the knot with Hazel until his son was married. Six weeks after Marilyn and Dave made their vows, Jack and Hazel filed a marriage-license application with the Gibson County office of the Indiana State Board of Health and were married on February 7, 1964. They were, by all accounts, a happy couple. As cousin Ron Greenfield tells it, Jack "really picked a winner" in Hazel.

Not only did Dave get along with his new stepmother, Marilyn also formed a close friendship

Dave and Marilyn.

with the second Mrs. Leonard Niehaus. In fact, Marilyn came to love Hazel dearly.

Like so many devoted husbands, Dave had a handful of monikers for his wife. His favorite sobriquet, always accompanied with a smile and a boyish sparkle in his eye, was "The Enemy." When it was time to tell a joke among the boys, Dave would usher his audience aside with the sentence, "Over here, 'The Enemy' is in sight." They were, in reality, each other's best friend whose genuine regard and respect for one another carried them through forty-eight years, forty-two major-league broadcasting seasons, three children, seven grandchildren and more than five thousand ballgames.

Every season they joined in the chase for the ring always knowing the ones they already wore were the most precious of all.

Dave's publicity photo
and business card from
KMPC Radio, Los Angeles,
circa 1964.

California Angels
Los Angeles Rams
U.C.L.A. Bruins

DAVE NIEHAUS
Sports Broadcaster

KMPC

Golden West Broadcasters ⊂\/\/⊃

5858 Sunset Boulevard · Los Angeles · California 90028 · (213) 469-5!

California Dreamin':
The Angels Beckon

The best game I ever saw was one I heard
Dave Niehaus do on the radio.
—Gene Autry

DAVE'S WORKLOAD AT KMPC continued to increase and the station's visibility in the sports marketplace of southern California was on the rise. His work broadcasting recreations of games for AFRTS kept him close to baseball. Previously, the only big-league job in town was with the Los Angeles Dodgers and a fellow named Vin Scully had a deservedly secure spot in that chair. When expansion brought the American League Angels to town and to KMPC, Dave was determined to find a way to get his employers to see the wisdom of tapping him to do the broadcasts.

He eventually found a way that unexpectedly took him to the gridiron and the hardwood as well.

Dave's five-minute Saturday morning sports report took place under the direction of Steve Bailey, who had learned of Dave's experience with AFRTS and gave him a chance. Five minutes on Saturday morning wasn't much, but Dave knew it was a start. He managed to turn five minutes into five years.

Bailey, in charge of all KMPC sportscasts, was impressed with Niehaus' style and his sonorous voice, enough so that when Dave heeded Marilyn's advice and asked for a full-time job, Bailey acquiesced. By the early part of 1965, Dave was working the regular sports beat for 710 AM.

The KMPC roster, by that time, included some very bright lights and the station marketed itself as "The Station of the Stars." Bailey's sports

Sketch of Dave Niehaus, circa 1968.

announcers included Bob Starr, Don Wells, Jim Healy and Joe Torre. The host DJs featured stars Gary Owen, Wink Martindale, Bob Arbogast and Jim Lange. In both sports and entertainment, KMPC was a giant among southern California radio stations. AM 710 was a great place for Dave Niehaus to be.

With each passing season, Bailey grew more confident about his decision to hire Dave. Bailey knew something about sports broadcasting, having teamed with Bob Kelley and Don Wells as third man on the Angel broadcast crew in their inaugural year of 1961. Buddy Blattner replaced Kelley in 1962, with Wells and Bailey remaining in the booth for that season.

Dave's airtime increased dramatically and as the Sixties rolled on, he was among the most-heard voices on the station. People were listening, one person in particular. That one listener turned out to be the man who would give Dave his biggest break of all and turn out to be one of his dearest lifelong friends.

Orvon Grover "Gene" Autry had been one of America's great cowboy matinee idols. Following in the footsteps of Tom Mix, he joined Roy Rogers and Hopalong Cassidy as one of a triumvirate of Western matinee stars and, notably, joined Rogers as one of the two most remembered cowboy crooners. His recording of *Back in the Saddle Again* became the biggest-selling record of its kind, a latter-day anthem for young and old fans of six-shooters and white-hatted heroes who foiled the black-hatted bad guys every Saturday at the movie houses and later on the television screens.

Autry's talent was not limited to acting. Indeed it was every bit as evident in his savvy ability to turn a profit on real estate. As one of show business' highest-grossing artists, he took Will Roger's advice to heart ("Buy land, they ain't makin' any more of it.") and shrewdly invested in large southern California tracts.

Autry was so attuned to his finances that he remembered the smallest of details. Dave loved to tell the story of a flight home from the East Coast on Autry's private plane after a road trip. Winging their way over the immense American heartland, Autry called Dave to the window and bade him look out at the seemingly uninhabited expanse below.

When Dave asked what he was supposed to be seeing, Autry replied, "You're looking at the site of the 1937 Nebraska State Rodeo where they paid me thirteen hundred forty-seven dollars and fifty-two cents to perform." Thirty years later, Autry recalled to the penny what he had made, justifiably proud of how much money that was in those days. He later parlayed his growing fortune into the purchase of radio stations, including KMPC, the flagship of his Golden West chain.

Gene's uncanny sense of what was about to happen in both real estate and broadcasting was further evidenced by his desire to land a contract to broadcast major league baseball on his stations. He loved the radio business and he loved the game. As a result, he journeyed to Palm Springs in early

1961 to attend baseball's annual winter meetings. His intention was to land a radio contract; he instead wound up buying a baseball team, the expansion Los Angeles Angels, the newest addition to the American League.

The entire story is a bit more complex. On November 19, 1960, the Associated Press broke the story that Los Angeles radio executive Kenyon Brown had sold his minority holdings in the Detroit Tigers and joined a syndicate with Gene Autry with the intention of bidding on the new American League franchise. So, while Gene always liked to say he was just looking to buy a radio contract, he, in fact, knew a stake in the ownership was likely to be a part of the deal.

KMPC had broadcast Dodger baseball for two years while the team played in the Coliseum. Walter O'Malley, the Dodgers' powerful owner, had plans for his new stadium in Chavez Ravine already in motion and did not want the AL to expand into his market. O'Malley was pushing a nine-team interlocking 1961 schedule for the junior circuit instead of the ten-team idea being floated. He further made it clear if any team came to southern California, it could play in the Rose Bowl.

Yet another of baseball's storied owners played a role in the proceedings. Charles Finley, whose maverick ways would draw the ire of his counterparts for years to come, was waving around what he called five million dollars of his own money and had been interviewed by the expansion committee. Just as Kenyon Brown went public with his syndicate, "a group of radio and television executives," the league postponed their decision on ownership of the southern California expansion franchise.

Added to this mix was another quite powerful man, U.S. Senator Estes Kefauver of Tennessee. Kefauver, incensed by the departure of the Washington Senators to Minnesota, was making a great deal of noise about baseball "keeping faith with the public." Pressure was mounting to get an expansion deal done.

In the meantime, Kenyon Brown's primary role in the syndicate had been assumed by Bob Reynolds, a Stanford graduate and Autry's partner in the original purchase of KMPC in 1952. On November 3, 1960, the *L.A. Herald-Examiner* reported Autry and Reynolds would bankroll the new entry into the American League. Still, O'Malley stood in the way.

At a Monday, December 5 meeting, O'Malley rose to say Autry's "interested parties" were fine men and he'd have no qualms about them coming to town—as long as it didn't happen until 1962. They all met again the next day and into the night of Tuesday, December 6, finally hammering out the "compromise" to which O'Malley agreed. O'Malley's demands were enough to have people ranging from Chicago White Sox owner Bill Veeck to Los Angeles Mayor Norris Poulson screaming bloody murder, but Autry and Reynolds were happy.

Walter O'Malley's "compromise" left no doubt as to who held the upper hand in the negotiation. The Angels would have no TV broadcasts in 1961, would play all their games in 1961 in the 22,000-seat Wrigley Field, and then become O'Malley's tenant at Chavez Ravine for the next four seasons. Never being one to fail to get the cash as well, O'Malley also negotiated a $400,000 indemnification fee.

The new owners ponied up $2.4 million and the deal was done. Tuesday, December 13 found them in Boston for the expansion draft where they assembled a collection of players, the majority of which had their better days behind them. A month later, Leonard K. Firestone, president of the tire company, joined Autry and Reynolds in the fledgling ownership group. Unfortunately, in early April, Kenyon Brown died of a heart attack next to his swimming pool and never saw the staggering return their investment would bring.

Autry was not just a shrewd businessman; he was a keen judge of talent and the young sports reporter at KMPC caught his eye and his ear. They met occasionally at the station and Mr. Autry was impressed by Dave's ability and his voice. But it took a little old lady to open the door for Dave Niehaus, one who, coincidentally, lived back in St. Louis, Missouri. She remains the unsung heroine of his story. Seems those folks back in the Midwest were always looking out for Dave.

The little old lady was Buddy Blattner's aunt. In 1968, Blattner was part of the California Angels radio broadcast team for KMPC Radio. His aunt took ill that spring. When her condition worsened, Buddy took a leave of absence to be at her side, said absence creating a temporary vacancy on the KMPC team. Steve Bailey tapped Dave Niehaus to fill the spot alongside Don Wells. Autry was listening.

In 1969 followed the "big break" that began the transplanted Hoosier's ascendancy into his chosen calling and on toward the pinnacle of his profession. The American League expanded again, awarding additional franchises to Kansas City and Seattle. The Royals and the Pilots needed announcers, too, and Kansas City chose Buddy Blattner to be their man in the booth.

With the departure of Buddy Blattner, a spot opened up on the Angels' broadcast team. Autry personally selected Dave Niehaus to fill the opening in the lineup alongside Dick Enberg and Don Wells. Gene made a whole lot of smart moves in his life and one of the smartest was tapping Niehaus to fill out that troika. Decades later, "The Cowboy" would freely admit letting Niehaus go to Seattle in 1977 might have been the dumbest thing he ever did.

Autry and Niehaus shared an affinity for baseball and radio and a good joke over a "see-through," their name for a tall vodka and soda with a lime. They popularized it at spring training in Palm Springs, most likely at the Gene Autry Hotel's Sombrero Room (the former Givenchy Hotel and Spa, today popularly referred to as the Parker Palm Springs.) The restaurant to this day serves the cocktail under that name.

Hall of Fame baseball writer Tracy Ringolsby remembers how much Gene Autry loved the game.

"At Angels Park in Palm Springs," Ringolsby recollected, "he'd sit on the bench and the kids would come out of the clubhouse for spring training, the non-roster kids. Every kid that came out, he'd speak to them by name and he'd talk to them about—'yeah, you're from Monroe, Louisiana or you're from Akron, Ohio—you know I played such and such a place in Akron and I had dinner at such-and-such a place in Akron,' and he'd personalize it with all the young players. It was amazing that he could have that recall and know who each of those people were and then make a point of knowing something about their home town so that they could feel like he paid attention to them."

Like Niehaus, Autry was a wonderful storyteller with a great sense of humor. The Angels' owner was a sought-after speaker at baseball banquets across the country.

As Ringolsby tells it, "Autry just had a way with things. He was once speaking at a banquet in Tulsa for A. Ray Smith and was introducing Whitey Herzog, who had just been fired as manager of the Texas Rangers. He said, 'You know, I'd like to introduce a friend of mine that's here with me tonight, Whitey Herzog. He just got fired as the manager of the Texas Rangers, but that's okay, I had gonorrhea once and I didn't deserve that, either.'"

Dave Niehaus told this story as often as any. His ability to impersonate Autry was uncanny and he relished regaling friends and acquaintances who knew them both. No one ever tired of hearing him do the impression.

One of Gene's favorite lines was one he delivered at another Tulsa banquet: "It's great to be here looking out at all the flowers of Tulsa sitting here. Obviously there's a couple weeds mixed in with you—you don't need to look around, you know who you are."

Gene Autry was a loyal man who valued loyalty as much as any quality. Don Goodell was a public-relations man who wrote the first story about Autry after Will Rogers discovered the singing cowboy in 1929, when Autry was working in a Tulsa, Oklahoma railway station. At the age of seventy-seven and well beyond, Goodell remained on Autry's payroll. Gene didn't forget his friends.

Autry's story bears retelling. He worked as a telegrapher on the St. Louis-San Francisco Railway, known as the old Frisco Line. His work took him to various stations and, during the lulls between telegraphs, he strummed his guitar and sang. A 1941 press release names Chelsea, Oklahoma as the site of his big break, but Autry's 1953 book, *Gene Autry and the Lost Dogie*, places it in Sapulpa, sixty miles to the southwest, on the other side of Tulsa.

Autry's story does go something like this: a "tall lean stranger" walks in, hears Gene singing and says "you're pretty good" and advises him to go to New York. He did and was promptly told "go back to Oklahoma." He did that as well and began singing on Tulsa's KVOO Radio as "Oklahoma's Yodeling Cowboy." Despite the success, he didn't quit his day job, continuing to work as relief telegrapher at the Tulsa railway station. There he befriended a brakeman on the Frisco Line named Jimmy Long, who had what Autry called "an ear for music." The two collaborated on a song called, *That Silver-Haired Daddy of Mine* and the rest is history.

The stint as relief telegrapher led to an equally important event for young Autry. He was introduced to Jimmy Long's niece, Ina Mae Spivey, herself a daughter of a railway telegrapher. On Friday, April 1, 1932, she became Mrs. Orvon Grover Autry and remained so until her death in 1980.

The young telegrapher and cowboy crooner went on to become the owner of the expansion Los Angeles Angels. When the Angels headed for Palm Springs in the spring of 1969, Dave Niehaus headed there with them.

There would come a day nearly a decade later the Autry-Niehaus working relationship would end. But both Autry and Niehaus, who treasured their enduring friendship, came to realize it worked out the way the baseball gods intended. No one would or could ever argue that southern California's loss proved to be the Pacific Northwest's greatest gain. The "dumbest" move the Los Angeles Angels ever made proved perhaps the smartest move the Seattle Mariners ever made.

As for that spring of 1969, it would witness the pairing of two quite extraordinary talents.

Dave Niehaus and Dick Enberg first encountered each other in 1964 at the Skandia Restaurant in Los Angeles. In those days, the upscale eatery at 9040 Sunset Strip would have been called "swank." Every Thursday, it played host to a luncheon for local sports broadcasters and writers.

Enberg quite humbly recalls, "Dave would have been there representing the Armed Forces Network. He was at that time doing Dodgers and Angels games once a week for them, a sort of 'Game of the Week' and I, well, I sort of invited myself." Enberg, the young man from Mt. Clemens, Michigan, was soon on the A-list of invitees.

There would have been plenty enough to talk about given that Enberg, like Niehaus, had spent significant time in Bloomington at Indiana University where he earned both a masters and a doctorate in Health Sciences. Little did both men know, they'd soon launch the next stage of their professional careers on the same broadcast. Enberg was teaching and coaching baseball at San Fernando Valley State College and was about to apply for a broadcasting job at KTLA. KTLA just happened to be the television sister station to KMPC radio that was soon to employ young Niehaus.

Gene Autry's broadcast empire would serve as the launching pad for both men with Gene himself instrumental in each of their careers.

For three years, from 1966 through 1968, Enberg did the pre- and post-game shows for the Angels radio team of Bud Blattner and Don Wells, the latter having come from Chicago, where he teamed with Bob Elson. The Seattle Pilots and the Kansas City Royals joined the American League in 1969. When Blattner took the job as lead man for Kansas City and headed for the heartland, Enberg was picked to replace him. Wells was understandably desirous of the number one chair but KTLA's Stan Spiro, the boss man at the station, put Enberg in the lead spot. Steve Bailey then lobbied with Stan Spiro for his go-to guy, Niehaus, to take over Enberg's role and that's what happened.

It was what Gene Autry wanted and he was, after all, the owner. The third spot fell to Dave Niehaus, who, for the first time, had a full-time job announcing big-league ball.

So, at spring training on Friday, March 7, 1969, in Yuma, Arizona, two men who would turn out to be among the very best broadcasters of their generation were paired behind the microphone. It was Dick Enberg's first

Dave interviewing a California Angel during spring training, circa 1970.

professional broadcast of a major league game and Niehaus' first as a civilian on AM radio. The Angels fell to the San Diego Padres, 11 to 5.

Curiously enough, that game was a harbinger of events still four years away. As happened in a number of games that spring, both teams utilized what were called designated "wild card" batters. A direct forerunner of the designated hitter, these "wild cards" were inserted into the lineup to bat for the pitcher without the hurler being removed from the game. Ex-Dodger Al Ferrara collected three hits for the Padres as their wild card and Dick "Dr. Strangeglove" Stuart rapped out a double and a single and drew two walks for the Halos.

Not surprisingly, Stuart remarked, "I like the new rule, I hope it's adopted." On behalf of the pitchers, former Brooklyn Dodger World Series hero, Johnny Podres, whose three-inning relief stint garnered him the win and a leg up on a job with the Padres, lamented the rule, saying it "takes a little of our fun out of the game."

Baseball did not hear Podres. The American League instituted the designated hitter rule in 1973 and never went back.

The Angels had endured their one season at Wrigley Field and the four at Dodger Stadium before moving into their own digs at "The Big A," Anaheim Stadium, in 1966. It was there on April 8, 1969, Dave made his debut as an official member of a major league baseball club's radio team.

The baseball gods have a funny way of weaving threads throughout the careers of their faithful. The opening-night opponent was, of all teams, the Seattle Pilots. Marty Pattin started for the Pilots and went five innings for the win as he bested L.A.'s Jim McGlothlin in a 4–3 Seattle victory. The man who took over for Pattin in the sixth was Diego Segui who, eight years hence, would throw the first pitch in Seattle Mariners' history.

Dave got his first look at a gorgeous, green little city tucked away next to Puget Sound in the state of Washington on April 28–29, 1969. The reason Seattle fans even then were agitating for their own domed stadium was underlined when the Monday night series opener was rained out. So, the Angels and Pilots played just one game, Tuesday afternoon, with Pattin and McGlothlin locking horns again, both going the distance. Pattin prevailed, 1–0, on a scintillating two-hitter.

The game was played at Sicks' Stadium, venerable home of Seattle's beloved Rainiers, one of the Pacific Coast League's more successful and enduring franchises. Author Dan Raley's magical memoir, *Pitchers of Beer: The Story of the Seattle Rainiers*, chronicles their saga. A truly splendid baseball book, its readers will fully appreciate what it meant for Dave Niehaus to work this venue, how beautifully it wove into the tapestry of his career. Dave's broadcast that night is an uncanny and remarkably coincidental link between the storied history of Rainier baseball and the coming of Mariner baseball.

Dave with his Angels' broadcasting partner, the former L.A. Dodger star
pitcher Don Drysdale, circa 1973.

Dave worked from the booth in old Sicks' Stadium, high up, almost directly above home plate and attached, rather vertiginously, to the grandstand roof. From that perch, he called four more games in July and another five in September. The broadcasts of those Angels-Pilots tilts emanated from the very same press box where legendary Seattle baseball broadcaster Leo Lassen had called Rainiers games for nearly thirty seasons.

The summer of 1969 began a stretch during which Dave became one of the busiest sports broadcasters in Los Angeles. Never one to turn down an assignment or shy away from taking on another sport, he literally answered the bell when KTLA Channel 5 approached him to go ringside. Thursday nights his bailiwick became the venerable Olympic Auditorium, home of the legendary ring announcer, Jimmy Lennon. Dave teamed with long-time promoter and matchmaker Mickey Davies to call the action. Los Angeles Rams football and both UCLA football and basketball were about to be added to his list of duties.

Still, it was baseball that had his heart. His biggest joy was that his 1969 "rookie" year authenticated Autry's judgment and Bailey's choice to put him in the Angel booth. Both bosses were so pleased, he won himself a return spot on the 1970 roster and remained in that role through the 1971 and '72 seasons as well.

The timing couldn't have been better for Dave, as a year later, following the 1972 season, Wells was gone and Niehaus was set to move up the ladder. It looked as though the number two slot was his. That, however, lasted only until the decision was made to bring Don Drysdale on board.

Drysdale had been a star pitcher for the L.A. Dodgers during his career and his charisma and good looks had made him a frequent guest on television sitcoms and variety shows. Don had retired from baseball in 1969 and then spent two years in the booth for the Montreal Expos and one for the Texas Rangers. Not even Dave could argue the wisdom of bringing him on board. Dave was back to third on a three-man team.

Dave was realistic about the situation, though he might have felt differently had it not been Drysdale. The two had met a few years earlier and genuinely enjoyed each other's company. They were guys who reveled in what they did and in the after-work camaraderie that was nurtured in watering holes frequented by the players, scouts, management and media throughout the league. One of many practical jokes Dave played on his friend over the years had Drysdale believing his playing days would end north of the border.

As Phil Collier reported in *The San Diego Union-Tribune* on October 23, 1968, Dave had spent the previous evening with San Diego Padre President Buzzie Bavasi on the eve of the expansion draft. The Montreal Expos had just paid ten million dollars to join the National League. Few ballplayers wanted to be selected to play for the first Canadian-based expansion franchise.

With a "devilish grin," Bavasi turned to Dave Niehaus and said, "Dave, call Don Drysdale in Los Angeles—let's have some fun." Within minutes the call was placed.

"Don, this is Dave Niehaus," greeted the broadcaster. "I'm in Montreal for the draft."

"Oh, my Lord, where am I going?" the stunned Drysdale replied.

"They tell me to Montreal, in the first round," Niehaus replied.

There was a long silence before Drysdale heard Bavasi laughing in the background. Only then did the Dodger right-hander catch on to the prank.

The 1973 KMPC broadcast team, from left: Don Drysdale, Dick Enberg and Dave Niehaus.

Throughout the 1972 baseball season, Enberg called the first three innings on television, the middle three on radio and the final three on television. Drysdale did the reverse and Dave partnered with each of them, on radio, covering the lead role when necessary. Drysdale was a welcome addition and as Enberg put it, "really helped with the long grind" of spending more than seven months a year broadcasting baseball. His fun-loving style, especially on the road, meshed perfectly with Dave who, when away from his family, wanted nothing more after the game than the simple pleasure of dinner and drinks along with three or four hours of talking baseball.

The threesome was a big hit with baseball fans and the L.A. market. At that time, Stan Spiro's role as general manager at KMPC meant he oversaw a wide range of programming. Baseball, however, was his baby, his passion. He was a baseball guy who was beyond enthusiastic about the rights KMPC had to broadcast the Angels and with the product his station delivered. That enthusiasm was reflected in his expectations of his radio team.

"Stan Spiro told me," Enberg recalled, "you're going to be on the air more than any other voice in L.A. except maybe Vin Scully (long-time L.A. Dodgers play-by-play man)—almost six hundred hours a year. I want those radios to stay on KMPC so that when those people wake up in the morning their radios are still on KMPC."

The three did their job and then some. Despite some pretty lean years for the Angels, KMPC reigned among the giants of AM radio in the City of Angels.

Enberg was doing a considerable amount of work for NBC, and when those obligations meant a hiatus from the Angel booth, Dave's role would increase accordingly. His stellar work alongside Drysdale during Enberg's June 1973 trip to China with the college basketball all-stars made it apparent that his work was first-chair quality.

One of the next assignments Spiro gave Dave was Los Angeles Rams football. In 1966, three years before their pairing in Yuma, Enberg began doing play-by-play for the Los Angeles Rams and did so through the 1977 season. For five of those years, 1972 through 1976, Dave was the part of that radio team as well, working the pre-game, halftime and post-game shows as well as conducting player interviews, although Drysdale replaced him temporarily in 1973 in an experiment that was short-lived.

Dave handled similar duties for UCLA football with legendary Bruin radio announcer Fred Hessler as the play-by-play man. KMPC had been the flagship station for the Dodgers but lost those rights to KFI after the 1959 season. KMPC president Bob Reynolds set out to acquire the rights to UCLA football to fill the void. UCLA insisted KMPC cover the basketball games as part of the deal and Reynolds reluctantly agreed.

The basketball rights proved valuable beyond anyone's ability to predict. KMPC wound up airing UCLA basketball during the heyday of Coach John Wooden, who engineered college basketball's most incredible run of success ever. Fred Hessler was the radio voice of UCLA basketball during the nine-year period in which they won eight national titles. Bruin basketball was a ratings bonanza.

In the fall of 1973, Dave took on the same role for UCLA basketball games as he had for UCLA football games, doing pre-game, post-game and player interviews. He became one of the legion of men and women touched by John Wooden, the "Wizard of Westwood." Both Dave and Marilyn, whose seats for the games were with the Wooden family, treasured these years and their nights at Pauley Pavilion. Dave considered the chance to work with the beloved and revered Wooden among the special privileges of his career.

After all, the two men shared similar backgrounds. Wooden was, like Dave, an Indiana native. Born in Hall, Indiana, Wooden had been a three-time all-state selection at Martinsville High School, where he helped lead

Dave and his son Matt with Hank Aaron, who played twenty-one seasons for the Milwaukee and Atlanta Braves and for thirty-three years held the major league record for career home runs (755).

his team to the Indiana state championship in 1927. Wooden went on to attend Purdue University in Lafayette, Indiana, playing on the 1932 Boiler-maker team that is today regarded as the *de facto* national champion for that season. To be around Wooden and call UCLA sports with broadcasters of the quality of Hessler and Enberg made for a very special experience both personally and professionally.

Although he could not know it at the time, UCLA's annual jaunt to Clarence S. "Hec" Edmundson Pavilion to play the Huskies in Seattle gave Dave a further look at his future home. He loved his work and he loved southern California. The idea of leaving was still unthinkable.

"What I recall most about Dave was his smile." Enberg reflected. "He was always a happy guy, a happy-go-lucky guy. And he always had a joke to tell you. Even when it wasn't all that funny, you still laughed because his laugh made you laugh. He had a passion for baseball, for family and for good times. And if you loved those three things, it made you a good broadcaster—in fact, an excellent baseball broadcaster—because the baseball broadcaster spends so much time on the air."

As those who knew him will readily attest, Dave also had a bit of his father's Germanic temper, although you'd only see it (and hear it) off microphone. If there was one thing that could make him blow his top, it was bad baseball. The kill switch on his microphone got its share of use by Dave. His was a remarkable ability to calmly and professionally call a botched or bungled or bonehead play, hit the kill switch and explode into a torrent of disdain for the lame exhibition he had just witnessed and then hit the "on" switch once again and return to that smooth Midwestern baritone. It was a delight to watch and testimony to both his passion for the game and for the professional demands of his craft.

On through the end of the 1976 season, Enberg, Drysdale and Niehaus brought the Angel games to the KMPC Halo faithful. Dave was a happy man who had the job he'd always wanted. He adored his wife and loved being a father to his three children (although ask any baseball wife, including Marilyn, and she'll tell you four months away from home every year makes Dad's job a little easier than Mom's.)

There was reason to be content. Yet there were times when Enberg, whose admittedly type-A schedule was full year-round with radio broadcasting as well as television hosting, wondered if perhaps Dave was "too content."

"I saw a great talent, a wonderful talent, but I think he needed the opportunity to have the total stage, or a major portion of the stage, to show all he had," said Enberg, whose resume is as impressive as anyone's. "I began to wonder if he was content to just be a part of the team; maybe he didn't want to take the chance."

The truth is Dave still had plenty of that Princeton boy in him, the one whose talents and natural gift of gab, whose delightful demeanor had charmed everyone who met him. The demands on the number three guy to be completely ready at any moment and at his best at all times were simply not the same as they were for the guy in the lead chair. His passion for the game and his love of calling it had gotten him an awfully long way. The driven, meticulously prepared, big-shouldered Dave Niehaus had not yet fully emerged. But he was about to.

Dave with stage, film and television star Billy Barty, circa 1972.

As Dick Enberg told me, "He was the right guy at the right place at the right time for Seattle. Dave was able to build his own career with a team that was building from page one. He needed to be his own man. I think he had been too satisfied too long being a swing man."

When the call came from the salesman at KVI in Seattle, Enberg was one of those to whom Dave expressed his reservations.

"Dave came to me and said he was having some difficulty with that decision, some trouble with the idea of taking the Seattle job." Enberg recalled. "After all, his life in Los Angeles was a pretty good one. I said, 'Man, you've got to take that job. There are only twenty-six (at that time) jobs like it in the world. This is your chance.'" Besides, as Enberg counseled him, "We were the same age, so the station wasn't going to catapult him past me and there was no way to outshine Drysdale in the L.A. market."

Enberg joyously recalls that moment. He is a genuinely kind man with the same Midwestern sense of decency and comradeship that defined the man from Princeton. The opportunity to urge a colleague on to greater heights happens rarely. He speaks openly of the joy he felt over the years "to recognize and feel his success." In fact, Enberg expresses a small amount of envy of Dave's ability to pace his life according to the rhythms of the baseball season.

"He always kept his life simple," Enberg observed. "That's probably why he had such a successful marriage. Yes, he did some work with basketball and football, but he found the sport he loved to broadcast the most and took it to a level of excellence."

Like so many of Niehaus' comrades-in-arms, Enberg's regard for Dave is palpable and was evident throughout a conversation I had with him at spring training in 2014. Enberg even paid his pal a cinematic tribute. Dick was hired to do the voice of the arena announcer in the 1977 James Caan film, *Rollerball*. If you listen closely to one of the pre-game announcements, you will hear the voice of Dick Enberg saying, "Today's referee: David Arnold Niehaus."

Enberg's only regret is he didn't have had one more chance to tell him, "G*^*&*&^! Quit smoking!" It wouldn't have mattered. Most everybody told Dave that. He would listen eventually when his heart told him in no uncertain terms.

As for Enberg, his love of baseball came full circle when he returned to the booth for the San Diego Padres in 2013. He decided to once again make it his only job.

With a terrific wife, three beautiful children and the job he'd always dreamed of, Dave Niehaus had it going on in southern California. He was part of Angel baseball, UCLA football, UCLA basketball and the KMPC all-star sports team. Still, there was something left to achieve.

Life boils down to chances and choices, the chances you get and the choices you make. Dave Niehaus had his chance and he was about to make his choice. It would prove to be a great chance and an even better choice.

Dave Niehaus and Ken Wilson study the action from the Kingdome broadcast booth. Inset: Ticket to the first Mariner game, April 6, 1977.

Goodbye, City of Angels: The Seattle Mariners Get Their Man

I look at every game as 1/162nd of the season. Each game has a different story. It's the reason people fall in love with baseball. I look forward coming to the ballpark telling a different story every day.
—Dave Niehaus

IN 1969, DAVE NIEHAUS, the amiable and fun-loving sportscaster at KMPC radio, got his first chance to call Angel games. In the ensuing years, thanks to this break and the faith of Gene Autry, his career and his workload remained on the rise. He began as the backup to Dick Enberg and then as part of the team with Enberg and Don Drysdale. His work with UCLA football and basketball led to some choice assignments, including KMPC's broadcast of the 1971 Rose Bowl played between USC and Ohio State.

The additional duties, plus doing on-air sports reports at KMPC, made for a full schedule even without considering the demands of raising three children with Marilyn.

Some baseball fans make a case for the end of the world beginning in 1957 with Walter O'Malley's decision to move the Dodgers west to Los Angeles. However compelling their case, the exodus from Brooklyn and the flight of the Giants from New York to San Francisco coincided with the threat of Branch Rickey's Continental League. The indisputable result was a wave of big-league expansion.

Dave Niehaus' journey mirrored baseball's westward trek and his career was part and parcel of the national pastime's foray into a number of emerging major markets on the sunset side of St. Louis.

The 1961 expansion brought the Angels to Los Angeles, creating the broadcasting job that would eventually become Dave's. The 1969 American League expansion to Kansas City and Seattle opened the door for his ascension to a big-league booth. Still further expansion, in 1977, would play the pivotal role in Niehaus' career.

Long story short: The Seattle Pilots of 1969 left town after one season and moved to Wisconsin, becoming the Milwaukee Brewers. The Brewers themselves replaced a Braves organization that had moved on to Atlanta. Seattle successfully sued baseball over the Pilots' hasty departure and was awarded a new franchise, which entered the American League in 1977 alongside the Toronto Blue Jays. The Pacific Northwest became home to the fledgling Seattle Mariners. Both became home to Dave Niehaus.

In the months following the 1976 season, baseball's annual winter meetings were held in Gene Autry's adopted hometown at the Los Angeles Hilton. The Seattle ownership group made their debut that fall.

Danny Kaye and Lester Smith were two of the original six partners who brought the expansion franchise to Seattle in 1977. Walter Schoenfeld, Stan Golub, Jim Walsh, and Jim Stillwell rounded out the sextet. Kaye, the brilliant actor-writer-comedian, was a southern California resident and a huge baseball fan. He heard Dave Niehaus' work on the Angel broadcasts with Enberg and Drysdale. As it happened, KVI 570 AM in Seattle, a Golden West station and sister station to KMPC, won the rights to carry the Mariners games. This was good news for Dave Niehaus, because Gene Autry owned KVI.

Kaye was convinced Dave was the right choice, a star in the making, needing only to assume the lead role on a broadcast team to make his mark. Kaye and Smith decided to have a KVI salesman feel out the situation with a call to Niehaus. Truthfully, Dave wasn't all that interested in swapping the known of his current situation for the unknown of a job with a fledgling franchise in a town that had already once lost its major-league team to another city. In a 2008 interview, Dave himself told the story of the departure of the Seattle Pilots:

"The truck was headed north out of spring training to play year two on April Fool's Day 1970, only to make a quick right turn to Milwaukee and end up the Milwaukee Brewers. What a slap in the face for this area!"

Kaye's appraisal of Niehaus proved to be an astute assessment. Danny went to work setting up the best package he could to lure Dave northward. He would help him find a home, a car, good schools for the kids, and he would pay him what he deserved to make.

Still, one man stood in the way, especially when it came to the money. Owner or not, Kaye had joined with Smith in creating an organization and knew he had to allow the people he'd already hired to do what they'd been hired to do. The man they had installed as club president was Dick Vertlieb.

What Kaye did not know was that his club president had already hired someone. Bill Schonely, like Dave an AFRTS alumnus, worked at Seattle's KOMO Radio from 1956–59 alongside the legendary Keith Jackson. Schonely called Seattle Totems hockey games as well as Roller Derby for KTNT-TV.

When he moved to KVI radio as sports director, Schonely brought the Totems with him. His many assignments included calling games for the Pacific Coast League baseball games in Seattle alongside Walt Brown during the team's four-year stint as the Seattle Angels, from 1965 through 1968. Like Dick Shively and Dave Niehaus, Schonely recreated games from the tickertape when the team played in far-off reaches such as Little Rock or Honolulu.

In 1967, Don Richman, the general manager of the NBA Seattle Supersonics, wanted Schonely to be the team's play-by-play man. Sponsor Atlantic-Richfield Oil intervened and Bob Blackburn got the job instead. At that time, the Sonics' business manager was Dick Vertlieb, and when he got the GM job with the Mariners, he reached out immediately to Schonely.

Dan Raley's terrific compendium, *How Seattle Became A Big-League Sports Town: From George Wilson to Russell Wilson*, quotes Schonely: "I was going to be the guy... Vertlieb offered me the job, but asked me to keep it quiet for ten days." In the ensuing week and a half, the Seattle sports scene was forever altered.

Dick Vertlieb was a somewhat quirky guy and his eccentric ways were, in part, reflected in his office furnishings.

As Niehaus told *The Seattle Times* M's beat writer Larry Stone in July of 2008, "I'll never forget walking into his office on First Avenue. He had one chair, a barber's chair, the kind you pump up. I sat in the barber's chair, and he's over here, interviewing you. I spent all day interviewing with Dick."

When it came time to talk money, Dave had his guns ready and made it clear to Vertlieb what it would take. Vertlieb's reply was, "You're not going to make more money than me."

Dave didn't back down. He was, after all, quite happy with the life and the career he was carving out in Los Angeles. He was working with Dick Enberg and Don Drysdale on the Angels broadcasts and they were two of the most respected guys in the trade. He was working UCLA basketball with Fred Hessler and football games for the UCLA Bruins and the NFL's Los Angeles Rams. He was in one of the two most visible markets in the sports world, broadcasting all three major sports. In addition, Dave was not just good at broadcasting; he was good at being a husband and a father. Marilyn's parents still lived near Los Angeles and he wasn't going to separate her from her folks or his children from their grandparents unless it was the perfect opportunity.

Still, the taxes on his suburban Northridge home leapt nearly $1,300 in the previous year, and the round-trip between Northridge and the Angels' ballpark in Anaheim was 161 miles. The Seattle job was certainly worth a look.

So that day in Vertlieb's office, he spoke his mind. "Dick, I don't care how much you make. This is what it's going to take to move my family and three kids."

The soon-to-be Mariners lead man later recalled, "I didn't get that good a feeling about it. I went back to L.A. and told my wife, 'It was a fun experience, but I think we're safe.' I get a call three or four days later— 'You've got the job.' "

Caesar crossed the Rubicon, Lewis and Clark crossed the Mississippi and now Dave Niehaus crossed the Columbia.

The delighted Danny Kaye never stopped making sure Dave was happy in Seattle. Ever after, whenever he saw Marilyn, he would look down his always-present cigar and with a twinkling smile ask, "Do you still like it here?"

The first thing Dave did was to find a place to live.

Dave and Marilyn moved into a Northwest contemporary house on a bluff in Bellevue overlooking Lake Sammamish. Newly arrived from southern California, they spent the first night in their new house. It was February 19, 1977, Dave's birthday, and the sun had come up on one of those clear winter days.

"Boxes all over the place, no drapes," Niehaus recalled, "and I opened my eyes and looked from the bed through the window at the snow-capped Cascades sparkling and the lake glimmering. And I saw this bird on top of the tree. I ran out onto the deck and then I ran back in, woke up Marilyn and said, 'Look, look at that bird up there! That's. . .that's. . .an American Bald Eagle!' Then another one flew past the deck and joined the first! I thought I'd died and gone to heaven!"

The next thing he did was to go out and meet the fans.

"I'll never forget," Dave told Stone, "I came up here from California in January of '77, (and) on a caravan went to the eastern part of Washington—Spokane, Yakima, all the little towns over there. It was cold and I was obviously wondering if I'd made the right choice. I always had heard great things about Seattle being a great draw in the Pacific Coast League days and I knew it would be a great draw in the major leagues. Let's not forget that in '77 we set an all-time major-league record for an expansion ballclub in the United States, drawing 1.3 million fans."

At forty-two, he already had more than two decades of experience behind the microphone and had been paired with some great talent. His Seattle sidekick would be no exception. Ken Wilson almost replaced the departing Niehaus with the Angels radio-TV team. It was, in fact, Dick Enberg who had heard Wilson while vacationing in Hawaii and brought him into the mix of candidates to fill Dave's shoes in Anaheim. As it transpired, Wilson became the first of Dave's teammates in the Kingdome booth. Wilson's hiring came with its own share of Dick Vertlieb-inspired drama.

Wilson got a call at his home in Hawaii from Vertlieb that was unusual to say the least.

"He said to me," Wilson recalled, "'I'm a very sick man, but we're getting ready to hire broadcasters and we're considering you for the Seattle Mariners and I'm going to get back to you but I'm very sick and I can't talk to you anymore right now.' I said. 'Okay, thank you.' And that was it."

"So that was a pretty loose conversation, by my judgment," Wilson continued, "I didn't have a lot of details and I don't believe it was offering a job. So I sat there and a short time later, might well have been the same day, I got a call from Stan Spiro who was the general manager of KMPC and he said 'Ken, Dick Enberg speaks very highly of you and we'd like to talk to you about joining Dick and Don Drysdale on the Angels broadcasts.' I said 'Great.' He says, 'Can you come and talk to us?'"

Wilson got on a plane that night, the overnight flight to Los Angeles, and was in Spiro's office at 9 a.m. the next morning.

"We were talking about moving from Honolulu to L.A. to join the Angels broadcast team and he got interrupted. It looked like it was all going to happen. He came back into his office and said, 'Ken I can't talk to you anymore.' I said, 'Why's that?' and he said, 'Well, the Seattle Mariners are going to be on KVI, which is a Golden West, the same Gene Autry stations that we're a part of. And they're very mad and angry.'"

Wilson suddenly found himself tossed into the often-mercurial world of Dick Vertlieb. He asked Spiro what they were angry about. Spiro replied, "They feel they've already hired you...we can't afford to get in an argument with them over you."

There was little for Wilson to do except head back to the airport that same day and head for Seattle.

"Next thing I know I'm sitting in a bar in Pioneer Square next to Dick Vertlieb," said Wilson, "whom I had just spoken to...this all happened in the span of two or three days, and he was angry, he was very angry, and thought that I had somehow misled him, or something...it was very confusing. I was trying to tell him 'Hey, you and I had a minute-and-a-half conversation and you were going to get back to me and you didn't offer me a job or anything.' So I was totally in the wrong in his point of view."

At that point, Vertlieb finally got around to offering the job. As Wilson recalls, "He said, 'Well, I'm going to hire you with Dave Niehaus and you're going to be equal partners. Dave's going to do five innings, you're going to do four and you're both going to be on TV.' Of course I'm thinking at that point maybe I ought to go to L.A., but I knew I couldn't go back to L.A. because that wasn't going to be on the table anymore...so I took the Seattle job. I mean, at that point I'm in my twenties and I was probably happy to go anywhere."

So in his own wacky way, Dick Vertlieb paired Dave Niehaus with Ken Wilson to begin what would be a six-year stint together in the Mariner broadcast booth.

Wilson has a wonderfully smooth delivery and a calm, measured way of calling the game. It was a solid pairing. Those of us fortunate enough to have heard that tandem were not always privy to quality big-league baseball, but we were always privy to quality big-league announcing. The Niehaus-Wilson duo managed to transform a lot of bad baseball into a lot of good broadcasts.

Wilson remembers even more vividly what it was like to work with Dave. He told Larry Stone, "The first thing I realized was that Dave was warm and welcoming.... He'd been in the big leagues; I had never been. We were both really optimistic, very enthusiastic about the entire situation. We were marrying each other. It was a new city, a fresh organization. It doesn't get much higher than that. Probably too high. We got a quick realization—not that we didn't know it—that it would be a long time before we saw a team that won. Neither of us anticipated the problems with the Kingdome. It was such an uninviting facility."

Fortunately for both Niehaus and Wilson, they shared two common traits that would serve their partnership well. They each were committed to making it work and they each had a great sense of humor.

"Dave and I were totally different personalities and had different styles on the air," Wilson remembers. "My goal was and it always has been since…whoever I was put with I was going to make it work, to try to make your partner be as great as he can be because that's just going to help both of you if people like you. I always wanted people to be better with me than they'd ever been with anyone else."

Wilson looks back with genuine fondness.

"Dave and I always got along great…we always did things on the road together…we had a lot of laughs. We took the game very seriously, we always took the game seriously, but at the same time we wanted to have a lot of fun…there were many broadcasts where we had all we could do not to break up totally and turn the mic off and be laughing so hard we could hardly go back on the air…and it happened more than once.

"And it wasn't that we were making fun of the team or the players, we were just making fun of *something*, you know, something we had said or said off the air. And when you're with somebody every day, you get inside jokes and you get laughing and all of a sudden you're both laughing and the mics are off and somebody's gotta talk—it becomes a bit of a challenge…and that happened frequently, but we tried to have fun. We knew we weren't going to see a lot of victories. So we tried to have a good time and I think people gathered that we were serious about the game and we were going to laugh a little bit.

"He and I were so different. He was from the Harry Caray, Bob Prince school where it was excitement and using phrases and nicknames. I grew up listening to Ernie Harwell who was a disciple of Red Barber, as is Vin Scully, so I was kind of in that line. So I didn't use nicknames and such…it was an interesting combination they put together. We had fun; that was the main thing.

"We knew we were going to lose the first year and the next year, we looked like we were going to lose forever…and we weren't far wrong as it turned out. It was almost forever before they won."

Both of these gentlemen were extremely capable announcers. Wilson went on to call baseball for the Cincinnati Reds, St. Louis Cardinals, California Angels, and Oakland Athletics as well as NHL hockey for the Chicago Blackhawks and the St. Louis Blues. But throughout their tenure with the fledgling M's, Seattle remained a distant outpost of the major leagues. The ESPN highlight reels were broadcast and archived by the bottom of the second inning out West and game highlights made the next day's show, if at all. The solid work done by the Niehaus-Wilson duo was known almost exclusively to the listeners of the Pacific Northwest.

There was one rather sizeable caveat: the enduring legend of Leo Lassen. I grew up an aerospace brat in the decades in which space engineers followed the defense contracts wherever they went. I was fortunate enough to hear a good many broadcasters in my life. The experience gave me the background to appreciate just how good the work being done in the Mariner booth was. I had even spent some years in Seattle when my father worked there for The Boeing Company, which meant I had heard Leo Lassen.

For decades in the 1930s and '40s, the Seattle congregation of the horsehide faithful had worshipped at Sicks' Stadium, home of the Pacific Coast League Seattle Rainiers.

Again, Dan Raley's reverent and humorous book, *Pitchers of Beer: A History of the Seattle Rainiers*, is the classic work on the exploits of Seattle's franchise in what West Coast fans thought of as the "third major league."

The voice of the Rainiers belonged to a man named Leo Lassen. Born in Wisconsin, Lassen moved to Seattle as a child, and after graduating from Seattle's Lincoln High School, began his sports-writing career at *The Seattle Star* in 1918. In 1931, he took the job of announcing Seattle's Coast League games and spent twenty-eight summers behind the microphone.

In 1957, KOL Radio, which was paying Lassen an annual salary of $16,500 to do year-round sportscasts and Rainier baseball, offered Lassen $8,500 to do only baseball. Lassen balked. The thankless job of replacing him fell to ex-KOL broadcaster Rod Belcher, who had moved over to Seattle's KING Radio. Belcher recalled those two seasons under skippers "Lefty" O'Doul and Connie Ryan as featuring "some pretty bad teams." Lassen and KOL kissed and made up, allowing for Leo's return for his two final seasons calling the action in 1959 and '60.

The Seattle Times columnist Emmett Watson and Dave, 1998.

Lassen was a local legend, an icon. His staccato "back, back, back, back...it's over" home-run call was mimicked by any and all Northwesterners whose radios, like Niehaus' old Zenith, had been their lifeline to the national pastime. His nasal, choppy delivery was the staple on which Rainiers fans had been raised—not to mention his nightly sign-off, "This is Leo Lassen speaking. Hope you enjoyed it."

Far too many were far too willing to make Dave aware of Lassen's standing in the baseball community of the Northwest. It didn't take long for this to make him crazy. Leo was a beloved regional fixture, but Dave Niehaus was a very special talent. That's no slight to the very talented Mr. Lassen any more than calling Johnny Bench the best ever is an insult to Walker Cooper. It's just how it is.

Emmett Watson, esteemed columnist for *The Seattle Times*, wrote about this in August of 1985:

"In a sense," Watson wrote, "Dave's first job here was to get the fans de-Lassenized, so to speak. Everybody compared him to Leo the Great, whose broadcasting heyday was in the '30s, '40s and '50s. In his long reign,

Leo literally 'raised' three generations of baseball fans, who were hooked on him. Unlike Leo's high-pitched intonations, Dave's voice is a beauty. He has constantly improved his work, trying to avoid the 'homer' stamp, and he experiments with shading and register to lend an air of low-keyed excitement to a game."

Leo Lassen had called games for the Pacific Coast League Seattle Rainiers for nearly thirty years by the time he retired in 1960. That "back-back-back-back-back...it's over!" had been virtually the only home-run call Seattle fans had ever heard and, as Ken Wilson told Watson, "All we heard about was Leo Lassen. It was, essentially, that you guys will never be as good as Leo Lassen. All we could do was shrug our shoulders, do every game and have a good time."

Dave's humility and his Midwestern sense of propriety kept him from ever uttering a public word of complaint. It was, after all, a no-win proposition. But privately, when the subject was broached, he lamented the number of times fans brought up Lassen's name and the equal number of times he'd wonder "Who the *&*#* is this Leo Lassen guy? Won't these people ever let it go? I'm never going to make these people forget this man!"

He would.

In due course it happened, although, for those of us who knew Dave and marveled at his work, it was nowhere near soon enough. Yet, as summers came and summers waned, the cumulative weight of one sparkling broadcast after another began to allow the present its deserved ascendancy over the past. "Swung on and belted" and "fly, fly away" would become the phrases echoed in the voices and replayed in the hearts of Mariner fans everywhere.

No slight to Mr. Lassen, a regional treasure and a competent and distinctive broadcaster. But from the very first "Hello, everybody" on April 6, 1977, it was clear the new voice of Seattle baseball was the real deal, a genuine talent who brought passion and pipes to the airwaves. For Dave, it was a night toward which his entire career had pointed. The moment the red light went on and all the fans tuned into KVI and the Mariner radio network heard his voice, Dave Niehaus became the lead man on a major-league radio broadcast team. He had achieved that most sought-after designation in his profession—the voice of the franchise.

Opening Night of the 1977 season remained one of Dave's cherished Mariner memories. Twenty years later, he told an interviewer:

"There was just incredible excitement. Anticipation. A new baby.

Hopes. I was nervous. The fans were so happy. I'll never forget that night as long as I live."

As late as 2008, Dave still ranked the experience at the top of his Mariners list: "Fifty-eight thousand people showed up. It was Diego Segui against Frank Tanana. We got shut out, 7-0, the first night. Nolan Ryan pitched the next night…shut us out. I was beginning to wonder not only if we were ever going to win a ballgame, but whether we'd ever score a run! We won the third game. It was a fun year because it was new, a bunch of castoffs, (M's manager) Darrell Johnson was two years removed from maybe the greatest World Series ever played, in 1975 between the Boston Red Sox and the Cincinnati Reds.

"To be able to be the man to reintroduce major-league baseball to this area is still my biggest thrill."

There was, however, one last-minute hitch. As Dave told the story to Jon Wells, publisher of Seattle baseball magazine *The Grand Salami*: "I'll never forget, though—I had about a minute to go on the air on opening night and Gene Autry came in with the general manager of KVI and I was concentrating—we'd done about fifteen to twenty exhibition games, but this was still the night, opening night.

"And I got a tap on my shoulder. Gene used to, maybe he still does, have a little drink, have a little vodka and he says, 'David, is there a place in the whole Kingdome that a man can get a drink?' I've got a minute to go on the air, but there was a bar right behind my booth. I said to Gene, 'What do you want to drink?'—out of courtesy more than anything else, because I knew he drank vodka. 'Just a shot of vodka, a big, BIG shot.'

"I got up, ran, and came back with a little vodka in a plastic cup for him. He downed it. I turned the mic on—'Hello, everybody. We'll be back in just a moment with our special guest, Darrell Johnson.'"

What Dave left out of that retelling was Autry's sigh after getting his vodka. Gene took a sip and said "Goddammit, I knew I never should have let you go, I never should have let you come up here." It was more truth than jest. Autry was a keen judge of talent and knew his prize progeny had just flown the nest.

Over the next thirty-four seasons, Dave proved to be far more than just the voice of the Seattle Mariners franchise. He proved to be its beating heart, its unbreakable, unshakable connection to baseball fans throughout the Northwest. Some of the listeners were Mariner fans and some of them just baseball fans, but they were all Dave Niehaus fans.

It was to be five games into the inaugural campaign before a Mariner finally hit a home run—Juan "Moncho" Bernhardt's fifth-inning solo shot off of Angels left-hander Frank Tanana. That would be the first time a Mariner was the beneficiary of what, over time, became one of baseball's singular home run calls. This delightful phrase became music to the ears of Mariner fans, and one day found its way full circle into the musical tributes paid to Niehaus after his death.

The classic Niehaus call began with "Swung on and belted—deep to..." and continued on through the exact location, flight and eventual destiny of the blast. "Swung on and belted deep" was so dear to his heart that it even became part of his e-mail address. When the crack of the bat resulted in a drive deep enough, long enough to clear the fences and reach the seats, Dave' voice became a rising explosion, his baritone climbing in pitch with each syllable. The soaring melody accompanied the lyric "swung on and belted—deep to left-centerfield—to the track, to the wall and it will FLY, FLY AWAY!"

Those three final words were always spoken with consummate joy and with an impact not unlike fireworks on the Fourth of July. Indeed, it was like the Fourth of July to Dave, just like it is to every kid who witnesses a home run. And when he spoke those words, he connected all his listeners to the mix of excitement and joy and downright reverence the game inspired in him and connected them to the child in themselves.

For in truth, at that moment, David was fully and completely connected to his own childhood sense of wonder, connected again to Harry Caray's voice echoing across his porch on a starry Midwestern night, describing a Stan Musial blast, connected again to the inexhaustible reservoir of love he harbored for the game of baseball. Ponce de Leon would have gladly sipped from this well.

The ability to place all who listened in the state of innocence in which they first encountered baseball was among Dave's greatest gifts. When he spoke those words we, at the other end of the wire, would also fly, fly away to that cherished spot in our memories, to that very real realm of recollection of ballgames past and heroic home runs remembered. Unashamedly, his heart flew beyond those fences as well and beckoned us each to ride along and, for that moment, we were all once again transported back to our youth and restored to a momentary innocence.

Dave once told columnist Emmett Watson, "You can almost chant a game."

Those three words, "Fly, fly away" were beyond chant, they were song. It is of little wonder they actually sprang from song. Buried deep in Mariner lore is the story of how it came to be.

The Seattle sports scene, indeed the town itself, has been graced with few larger-than-life characters than the likes of J Michael Kenyon. Among the most voluminous minds you might ever encounter, J Michael was cut in the mold of classic sportswriters, newspaper reporters who happened to have a by-line in the sports section. In other words, sports and art and music and food and life were just elements of the grand design, the big picture to be relished in his writings.

Kenyon and Niehaus met when the reporter interviewed him earlier in the year in Seattle and the pair began hanging out together at spring training in 1977. Their friendship would endure. They were baseball guys who understood the game, covered the game and its players, who were no

Dave Niehaus with J Michael Kenyon and his wife, Joan Stout, 1998.

strangers to an evening spent with a quality beverage and an endless store-house of stories. The two pals were alternately responsible for each other's nicknames, "The Noose" and "The Ol' Scrivener." (Niehaus referred to himself as "The Veteran Spieler.")

That spring was Kenyon's "rookie" year covering the M's for the *Seattle Post-Intelligencer*. As J Michael recounted to me:

"Noose told this story, over and over, for thirty years. And it's true.

"This is spring training, 1977, I'm the rookie baseball reporter for the *P-I*, soon to be, in the parlance of Niehaus, 'The Old Scrivener.' He's already the 'Veteran Spieler,' showing me the ropes around the Cactus League. His second-favorite place for dinner (after the Pink Pony in Scottsdale) was Pinnacle Peak Patio Steakhouse, about a mile or so up on the bluff northeast of Scottsdale...with a sign that read 'NO TIES ALLOWED.' Hundreds, maybe thousands, of them were snipped off and hung from the ceiling.

"It was a dark, gloomy night with a hint of a thunderstorm in the works...in those days, it was nowhere built up out there like it is now...He's driving, just the two of us—Kenny (Wilson) was somewhere else—and we're going out Happy Valley Road, bouncing over the various gulley washes...nothing but sagebrush in sight, save for the looming peak ahead of us...wondering what might happen if we get caught in a flash flood...radio blaring, etc.

"On the return trip, sated by those monster, delicious steaks they served (and plenty of hot beans, another Noose favorite!)...as well as two or three 'see-throughs' (Noose talk for vodka over ice)...we're not talking so much, radio still going...and lo and behold a selection from John Denver's just-released *Greatest Hits, No. 2* comes on. The song originally was from his 1975 *Windsong* album—*Fly Away*.

"If you'll listen to the song, you'll hear where the back-up singers form a sort of choral arrangement for Denver when he gets to the 'Fly away, fly away' part and I said, 'There's an idea.'

"Dave, absently, his thoughts elsewhere, said 'Huh?'

"I pointed at the radio and told him to listen.

"And Denver (and his accompanying vocalists) repeated the refrain... 'Fly away, fly away.'

"The rest is history. I think he used it in an exhibition game a day or two later...My contribution, if you can call it that, to get the Noose headed out on the road to Cooperstown."

It's no wonder to any who have made the acquaintance of these two that they were fast friends from the start.

Long before sports radio became the rather homogeneous, franchised format that it is today (but like everything else distinguished by some of its great practitioners), Kenyon hosted his own show on KVI Radio 570 AM in Seattle that he referred to as "the left-field foul pole on your radio dial." Eclectic to say the least, the show featured daily guests of every pursuit and "bumpers"—recorded promotions—from stars as disparate as Larry King and Marilyn Chambers. The latter, a velvet-voiced adult film star, would whisper, "Whenever I'm in Seattle I have *nothing* on... but the J Michael Kenyon Show."

My first meeting with the estimable scribe aptly illustrates why he and Niehaus were such friends. I was up in the broadcast booth visiting with Dave. It was time to make my exit and just as I did, a Mariner hitter was plunked by a pitch. As my friend Michael Vandermeer and I boarded the Kingdome elevator to return to the 100 level, Michael wondered aloud how nervous that makes a hitter his next time at bat. I replied, "The guy it makes nervous is the guy in the on-deck circle. Makes you wonder who was in the on-deck circle when Tony Conigliaro (Red Sox outfielder seriously injured by a HBP) got hit."

From the back of that Kingdome elevator a voice boomed, "Rico Petrocelli." I turned, dumbstruck, and the gentleman at the back could not conceal his smile of delight.

"Jose Tartabull pinch-ran for him," he continued.

I walked up to him, my hand outstretched, and said, "I don't know who you are but I'd sure like to meet you."

"J Michael Kenyon," he replied.

I couldn't resist. "The left-field foul pole on your radio dial?"

"Indeed." I was soon to learn far more about the history of baseball (and golf and the world) than I could have ever anticipated. J Michael Kenyon and Dave Niehaus may have been born half a continent apart, but they were cut from the same cloth. "Fly, fly away" was more than a small contribution to the road to Cooperstown and one for which both Dave and the Mariner faithful were forever grateful.

I know. I was there. Still, it took me more than two seasons to put aside my Jesuit-instilled sense of decorum. When the 1979 campaign rolled around, I made it my goal to meet Dave Niehaus. In those days, the Kingdome was rarely inhabited by more than ten thousand fans per game. There wasn't the kind of security around the broadcast booths as there is at parks nowadays.

I had, in my childhood, read an article written in *LIFE* magazine by a world-famous event crasher. His secret was simple: always act like you're supposed to be wherever you are. That advice had gotten me into a lot of places and this proved no exception. A sweet little old lady was the only person assigned to the entrance to the broadcast area on the 300 level of the Kingdome. When she asked me what I was doing here, she seemed more surprised than concerned. What would anybody be doing here?

I told her I was there to visit Dave Niehaus in the radio booth. Taking my gate-crashing mentor to heart, I said, "He's expecting me." She politely smiled and replied, "Oh. Well, please, go ahead." Moments later, I was in the *sanctum sanctorum* watching Niehaus and Wilson at work, thrilled to the bone.

I knew the rules and kept quiet. The half-inning ended and as the commercial break ensued, Dave stood up and stretched. As he turned, he looked at me and said, "Hello, can I help you?" His tone was remarkably like the little old lady out front, as if to indicate that someone would enter the booth only by mistake and certainly not by design.

"I'm here to meet you," I replied. I still remember the genuinely incredulous look on his face.

"Seriously?" he asked.

"Seriously." I said. "For two years now I've listened to you and you may be the best I've ever heard. I'm sorry but I just had to meet you."

"No kidding." I introduced myself to Dave Niehaus and Ken Wilson. The commercial break was ending. As I recall it was a pitch for Langendorf Old-Fashioned White Bread, baked the slow old-fashioned way—"There's nothing slower than Langendorf Old-Fashioned Bread." Wilson looked at me with a sly grin and a shake of the head toward the field.

"There's one thing slower than Langendorf Old-Fashioned Bread," he said, "the Seattle Mariners."

I was in heaven. I'd been onstage and backstage with some pretty serious singers, musicians, actors and actresses, but nothing, *nothing* beat this. To be in a major-league broadcast booth during a game was very special. To be in that booth with these two gentlemen, these two genuine pros, was a moment I still treasure.

Those early years were marked by the struggle of both the team to make its mark on the standings and the broadcasters to see their excellence recognized by the fans. Nowhere was it more evidenced than in the "fan mail" Niehaus and Wilson received. Filled with tales of Leo Lassen and "tips" on how to be more like him, the letters were too often misaddressed, incredibly so in Dave's case. The letter-writing public struggled mightily, employing a seemingly infinite number of manglings of his last name. One of them stuck.

Kenyon, who in those days also served as Kingdome official score-keeper, recalled: "One day Niehaus is going through his mail and there's a letter addressed to 'Dave Noose.' 'Dave Noose.' It was perfect, just perfect. We doubled over in laughter and somehow or other it became his new sobriquet. Rechristened, 'Noose' he would be from that day forward."

To this day, those who knew him by that moniker still affectionately refer to him as "The Noose."

It didn't just happen in print. Dave's wife, Marilyn, recalls Dave and Ken Wilson being introduced at a luncheon. The speaker introduced "The Seattle Mariners broadcast team from KVI Radio, Ken Wilson and Dave Nu…er, Nuhausen…er, Noose!" At which point Wilson turned to Marilyn and said, "Did he say 'Noose?'"

Ken Wilson was not spared, either. The overwhelming number of letters he received addressed to "Ken Williams" earned him the moniker "Williams." Dave affectionately called him by that alias and it is, to this day, the cognomen of choice for those who knew them both.

There is no documenting how many southern California youngsters may have heard Dave Niehaus call the Angels' games and began dreaming themselves of being a big-league broadcaster. We do know that on April 6, 1977, he began a skein of unparalleled excellence (and perseverance) that forever placed him front and center in the baseball hearts of kids of all ages. That night, before a sellout crowd—officially 57,762 were in attendance—the Seattle Mariners opened for business. Along with the Toronto Blue Jays, they were the Romulus and Remus of the 1977 American League expansion.

Like royal children of suspect lineage, the M's were looked at indifferently and, for almost two decades, locked outside the gates of the homes of Northwest sports fans. Fortunately, the radio signal floated right past those gates and into the homes of even the only casually interested. And when it did, it carried the voices of Dave Niehaus and his partner, Ken Wilson. Together they called the first six seasons of Mariner baseball from 1977–1982. Talk about laboring in obscurity.

To be certain, there were the loyal five thousand in Seattle who lived and breathed professional baseball summer after summer. But even the personal magnetism of Danny Kaye failed to bring the Husky, Seahawk and Sonic fans through the turnstiles on a regular basis.

Kaye will also forever be remembered by the fans for his delightful display at the 1979 All-Star game. Played at the Kingdome on July 17, the game's ceremonial first pitch was thrown out by Kaye, accompanied to the mound by a cadre of more than two dozen youngsters. Kaye rocked forward and began a convoluted and comic windup. As he came to the plate with his delivery, each one of the children pulled out their hidden baseballs and together tossed a torrent of first pitches to AL starting catcher Darrell Porter of the Kansas City A's.

It was as charming a moment as it was memorable—and fully in the best spirit of a great entertainer who was so proud to have gone from baseball fan to baseball owner. Niehaus thought it the most delightful opening pitch he'd ever seen.

The 1979 All-Star Game was also marked by the appearance of Barry Bremen, the decade's Great Imposter, who achieved some notoriety for his ability to crash a great many high-profile sporting events. Bremen first got everyone's attention by donning a Kansas City Kings uniform and shooting layups in the pre-game drills at the NBA All-Star Game. His was an infectious spirit and his high jinks were in the best of fun.

Bremen made it known that he was going to be at the baseball all-star game that summer and both the Seattle police and Kingdome security were on high alert. Bremen was not going to crash this event and most certainly not after announcing it in advance.

However, Barry Bremen had a very special accomplice that day, one of baseball's greatest players and greatest guys, George Brett of the Kansas City Royals. Brett knew the security was tight and Barry's chances of being arrested were pretty high. He helped keep Bremen hidden in the laundry facility adjacent to the home locker room. When it came time for the team pictures to be taken on a section of portable grandstands set up in the outfield, a strange face was among those in the back row. It wasn't until after the first set of pictures was taken and the players began to turn and shake hands that one of them noticed somebody who most certainly didn't belong in the frame.

Sure enough, thanks to a big-league assist from a future Hall of Famer,

Bremen had managed to elude the Seattle Police Department and the King-dome security and crash yet another major sporting event.

The laughs in those early years were confined mostly to the clubhouse or the team plane—unless you counted the dark humor that played itself out on the field. The darkness would all-too-soon fall over the owners' box as well. Mounting losses and dwindling revenues led to Danny Kaye and Les Smith's decision to sell the club. For Dave, one of the toughest times during those early years was when he learned the news that his friend who had played such an instrumental role in his career would be divesting of his interest in the team.

The first Mariner manager was Darrell Dean "D.J." Johnson, an ami-able Nebraskan and veteran baseball man. He and Niehaus became instant friends and Johnson became the first in a long line of Mariner pilots to forge both a great working relationship and an enduring friendship with Dave. Darrell was a good manager and Dave Niehaus held him in high regard. If that wasn't enough, he smoked Marlboros. That alone was suf-ficient to endear you to Dave.

Johnson literally hailed from two different towns—Horace and Ord, Nebraska. It seems the boundary line between the two communities ran directly though the farmhouse in which DJ was born on August 25th of 1928. Not only did he and Dave share the same Midwest perspectives, Johnson had made his big-league debut with the St. Louis Browns in 1952 and later played for the Cardinals in 1960. Memories of Sportsman's Park were the kind of things that heightened their fondness for one another.

A former major-league catcher who had played behind Yogi Berra, Darrell Johnson was, according to J Michael Kenyon, "a guy who studied at the feet of Casey Stengel, who studied at the feet of the immortal John McGraw." Dave was keenly aware of the lineage and pried more than a few Stengel stories out of the M's manager on the pre-game shows. In addition, Johnson's managerial resume included a 1972 International League pennant-winner in Louisville, a 1973 International League playoff champion in Pawtucket and his 1975 American League pennant with the Boston Red Sox.

Darrell Dean made news early in 1977 when he cut Kurt Bevacqua toward the end of spring training. The promising infielder had hit .477 in the Cactus League but complained to the press he felt "like a rat in a maze." When Dave Niehaus interviewed Johnson after Bevacqua's reassignment, he asked why the move had been made. Replied Johnson, "He wouldn't shut up."

Johnson saw the game with an eye toward its simplicity. He taught the fundamentals of the game with unwavering commitment. His assessment of Bob "Scrap Iron" Stinson, the M's inaugural backstop: "A gutsy guy. But the Dodgers never have taught proper fundamentals to their catchers. Get your body in front of the ball. Simple as that."

Stinson was a genuine favorite of Dave's once he learned how the catcher got his nickname. A 1966 first-round draft pick of the Los Angeles Dodgers, he played his rookie season in Ogden, Utah. Early in the season, he crashed through the left-centerfield fence trying to catch a fly ball and spent the night in the hospital. Despite his injuries, he played the next night and went three for four with a home run and two doubles.

DJ's assessment of the duties of the other half of the battery was equally succinct: "How to pitch? Simple. Throw one out there. Throw one inside. Throw one up in the zone. Throw one down. In and out. Up and down. Simple."

As good a big-league helmsman as he was, Johnson was an equally proficient golfer. He was at home on the diamond and on the links. Kenyon recalled: "The guy could have, should have, been a touring pro. But, in the post-WWII '40s, when he was coming out of Richmond (California) High in the Bay Area, baseball looked like a living, golf looked like a gamble."

The skipper was seriously old-school about the game and its etiquette as well. One night at the old El Gaucho restaurant in Seattle, he drew the disbelieving ire of long-time barkeep and knowledgeable baseball fan Alfred Black.

"Willie Mays could not," intoned Johnson, "would not...have played for me. Not on your life. Man couldn't display his socks." Mays was one of the first players to wear his uniform pants down to his ankles, setting the precedent for the next generation of players who eschewed "showing the sock." Of course, the "Say Hey Kid" would have played for Darrell, but quite possibly with his pant legs a bit higher.

It's a credible argument that game six of the 1975 World Series was the most thrilling ever played in the Fall Classic. It certainly ranks as the most thrilling penultimate contest ever in a seven-game series. The man making out the lineup card for the Bosox that night was Darrell Johnson. He brought savvy aplenty to the expansion Mariners and managed capably and consistently from day one. But the men who are hired to be big-league managers are certain of only one thing: they will, at some point, get fired. With the continued escalation of player salaries, it became more and more the rule: if the club doesn't perform, don't change players, change managers.

In 1977, the Mariners went 64–98 and drew 1.3 million fans, an expansion team record and within 70,000 of the major-league average. In 1978, the 56–104 M's drew 877,000 fans and were nearly 600,000 below the major league average. In 1979, the team went 67–95 and drew only 844,447 fans, nearly 750,000 shy of average attendance throughout the big leagues. Bad baseball and a bad venue were making for some bad numbers for ownership.

Yet, one of the Kingdome's quirky features caused one of Dave's salient memories of that third season. It involved former Tiger slugger Willie Horton, who played his last two years in the bigs with Seattle. Horton arrived in the Northwest just twelve round-trippers shy of joining the 300 home run club. On June 5, against long-time friend and former Tiger teammate John Hiller, Horton sat at 299. Willie then connected with a Hiller fastball and sent a rocket toward the left-field stands. I was in the park that night. We rose as one to the sight and to the sound of Dave Niehaus' "Swung on and belted. DEEP TO LEFT FIELD, WILLIE HORTON HAS... "

His call from above stopped as abruptly as the celebration below when everyone watching saw the baseball collide with one of the speakers hanging above the bleachers and carom back into left-centerfield. If there was a moment that year that seemed to capture the frustrations of Mariner players, fans and broadcasters alike, it was that one.

Mariner outfielder Tom Paciorek recalled the moment vividly. "We couldn't believe it," he said. We were all aware number three hundred was next for Willie... one second we're jumping up and screaming and the next we were just sick to our stomachs. And we all loved Willie. He was a great guy and he was the biggest guy on the team. Every brawl that year I went out and stood right next to Willie because I knew nobody was going to come near him. Fortunately for Willie, the next night he touched up Jack Morris for 300."

Darrell Johnson's days with Seattle were numbered despite the fine job he'd done. In that same year, 1979, the M's established a new position in the front office and filled it by hiring Dan O'Brien Sr. from the Texas Rangers' front office to be the team's president. In two years' time, he officially succeeded Lou Gorman as general manager.

Gorman deserved a better fate. Lou was revered by those who knew him. His reputation as a baseball executive is without question. After minor-league general manager jobs in the San Francisco Giants and Pittsburgh Pirates organizations, Lou began his major-league career with the Baltimore Orioles where he was director of player personnel for the team that won the World Series in 1966. From there it was on to the expansion Kansas City Royals in 1968 and then he became GM for the Mariners when they opened shop in 1977.

It was Gorman who brought the team's first marquee player, Ruppert Jones, to Seattle with the first pick of the 1977 expansion draft. Gorman had seen Jones in the Royals organization. His first draft pick was Dave Henderson, who would delight Mariner fans with his joyous and infectious enthusiasm for playing the game and, later in his career, become a folk hero in New England for his post-season heroics in 1986.

Ken Wilson attests to Gorman's authenticity.

"Lou knew his baseball and I think Lou did a good job in the expansion draft. The organization never seemed to have a lot of money, nor did it ever spend lavishly by any stretch of the imagination. But I think Lou did a very good job. He had a lot of experience...he was an interesting character because he cared about people. Whenever you talked to him, he would go 'good-good, good, good, good-good,' so people behind his back would call him 'Good-good.' When you said something about 'Good-good' people knew you were talking about Lou Gorman. A very nice guy, he knew his baseball, not a real politician by any means; just a real, true-to-life baseball guy."

J Michael Kenyon and Gorman remained close until Gorman died April 1, 2011. Upon hearing the news, Kenyon said it all in two words, "Bad, bad."

As Kenyon reported in the May 25, 1979 edition of the *Seattle Post-Intelligencer* that year, "Manager Darrell Johnson, hired by Lou Gorman, himself now consigned to a sort of twilight zone in the wake of O'Brien's arrival—O'Brien has kept up a running commentary on his Thursday night radio talk show, constantly pointing out (and at the same time insinuating that he's had a hand in) certain changes ongoing in the way Johnson manages a team. Nothing is farther from the truth. Johnson has managed exactly the same way from game one. O'Brien has never spoken to Johnson about the art of managing a baseball team and probably never will."

An all-too-similar scenario was shaping up in the broadcast booth. Dave Niehaus' original pact with Dick Vertlieb expired with the end of the 1979 season. As astonishing as it now seems, Dave came perilously close to leaving.

As Kenyon reported in that same article, baseball fans weren't in the Kingdome watching, but they were certainly at home listening: "It is sometimes forgotten in the whirl of Mariner events that the radio broadcasts—even while game attendance was plummeting a year ago—were steadily growing in popularity. The trend continues in 1979: attendance down, ratings up."

Still, new club president O'Brien was on the fence about the boys in the booth, despite Kenyon's accurate observations.

"Somewhere, then, there are people who care about the Seattle Mariners," Kenyon wrote. "O'Brien has confirmed, for interrogators, his feeling about the broadcast duo. Both Niehaus (whose three-year contract is up this year) and Wilson have stated they would prefer to remain, indefinitely, as the Mariner broadcast team.

"He and Niehaus are both family men, both enjoy the outdoors and both have a lot of fun doing Mariner baseball broadcasts. Tonight's first game from here will be their 391st Seattle game in three seasons and they, alone, have created a sense of continuity to Mariner history."

O'Brien had usurped the authority of Dave's champion, GM Lou Gorman. Vertlieb's penchant for stirring up bad press had led to Kenneth Phillip "Kip" Horsburgh, whom Vertlieb originally hired, taking over his spot. Horsburgh ended up among the worst of choices for the front office. As Dave later remarked, the long-term decline of the franchise could be traced to that decision.

At the 1979 All-Star Game, Marilyn Niehaus had been swept up in the post-game stampede. Blocked by security from joining her husband in the pressroom facilities, she saw Horsburgh and begged his intercession. Horsburgh glanced at the security guard and said, "He's just doing his job," as he turned and walked away. Horsburgh's people skills were a perfect match for his baseball acumen.

Horsburgh had forced a loyalty oath upon all his subordinates in September of 1978. Among those dismissed for refusing to sign was the capable and competent Mel Didier, director of player development and a Dave Niehaus fan. O'Brien had not intervened and by the middle of the 1979 season, it had become every man for himself on the Good Ship Mariner.

Ken Wilson's third consecutive one-year deal required the club to renew him by the first day of August. Wilson aggressively pursued O'Brien for an extension and got it in mid-season. Whether out of pride or simple faith in the job he'd done dictating a renewal, Dave waited for O'Brien to call him. He didn't. Niehaus' contract required a renewal two weeks after the season finale.

The club's decision to renew Wilson and leave Niehaus in the wind was bewildering to any and all who were privy to the information. When the story finally broke and the details became public, there were few, if any, baseball fans in Seattle who weren't steaming mad at the thought of Niehaus' departure. The season came to an end, the deadline arrived and the impasse remained.

On October 25, Mariner fans were treated to the sickening saga when Fred Brack updated the story in the *Seattle Weekly*: "The difficulty—in Niehaus' mind—has been to sit and just talk plain business with his Mariner boss, team President Dan O'Brien. O'Brien has been slow in letting Niehaus in on what's liable to happen. The two, in the company of Niehaus' agent (Tony Attanasio)...have chatted just once, face to face, regarding a new contract—and that only at the outright insistence of Attanasio.

"Yet, O'Brien has indicated to Attanasio, if not to Niehaus, that he believes the broadcaster may not be quite the 'team' man he wants in the booth. Not that Niehaus is unloyal to the Mariners, but that his front-office loyalty and respect may be to the shadow authority of general manager Lou Gorman. Attanasio...interprets O'Brien's displeasure as centering about whether Niehaus' personal likes and dislikes are 'divisive' to front-office policy. Niehaus scoffs at such a suggestion. But he is a proud man. Unwilling to compromise his bargaining power with O'Brien, Niehaus—ever since the logjam began forming in mid-season—has resisted making the first step toward creating a new contract."

Dave had a pretty simple view of how it should work. He felt it was the Mariners' responsibility to make the first move. He'd done not just the work of calling the games, but above and beyond that effort, he'd given the franchise more than a voice. He'd managed to give it a face—while on the radio.

As Dave put it, "If they want me, they should come and tell me. That only makes sense."

Mid-October passed and with it the Mariners' contractual obligation to settle the issue. Incredibly, O'Brien asked for more time to make up his mind. He was due to attend the World Series, spend some time viewing prospects in the Arizona Instructional League, then travel to Ohio for his son's wedding. After that, he was to co-chair the winter confab of baseball's general managers in Scottsdale.

That same week, Dave told a reporter he was headed for eastern Washington to hunt pheasant, a pursuit he'd been introduced to by Mariner ace Glenn Abbott. Abbott was Dave's best friend among the ballplayers and his decision to go hunting with him had been spurred on by two events.

The two occasionally played golf together at Bellevue's Tam O'Shanter golf course. During one of their rounds, Dave had expressed a desire to someday bag a Canadian goose for Christmas dinner. Abbott decided on his next visit to Tam O'Shanter to make that wish come true, sort of. Abbott later recounted the events of that afternoon.

"I used a piece of bread to lure the goose," Glenn said. "I didn't know what the doggone thing would do—might peck the daylights out of me."

Abbott ended up tackling the fowl and, once he had it in his arms, realized that he had managed to snag a very large animal. Knowing that one bad move on his part and the goose would break free, and knowing that could likely be soon, he and his buddy raced for his truck. Glenn, of course, couldn't drive holding that goose, so he jumped in the passenger seat—at which point the goose became alarmed in the way that geese do and began "fowling" the truck so Glenn had to wedge him down where the front right seat met the door.

Abbott planned to ring the doorbell and toss the goose in, but luckily for all concerned, he realized this big goose would take everything off every table and every wall by the time it was corralled. So he rang the doorbell and Dave, ever a man who could tell a joke and take one as well, collapsed in laughter when he opened the door and number 17 presented the goose.

Somehow or other, Abbott got Niehaus to take the goose in his arms, at which point Dave realized the inevitable chain of events that would take that goose from his arms to his dinner table.

"What do I do now?" he asked.

Ever the practical joker himself, Abbott replied, "I just told you I'd get you the goose, the rest is up to you."

There was no way Dave Niehaus was going to ring the bird's neck and feather it and dress it and they both knew it. The two friends howled and laughed their way out onto the Niehaus' second-story back deck and Dave threw the bird up and into the breeze where it righted itself and swooped away.

Through his laughter Abbott chortled, "Mr. Niehaus, this is the last time I'm ever bringing you a goose." To the good fortune of geese everywhere—and the interior of the Niehaus home—that proved true.

Abbott was so delighted by the prank he was determined to play another hunting joke on his good friend. On an excursion to eastern Washington, Abbott shot some meadowlarks, cleaned them and presented them to Dave.

Of course, when he delivered them, he merely told his buddy they were game birds from eastern Washington. The next evening, Abbott's phone rang. It was Dave inquiring what kind of birds he had been given.

"I was on my game that night," Abbott later recalled, "and simply replied, 'game birds' at which point he asked 'what kind of game birds?' 'Well...quail,' I told him.

"Quail?" Niehaus replied, "Hey man, I'm from Indiana, I've had quail. I know what quail is. Those weren't quail."

Abbott held his ground. "Sure they were, Dave. You know, there's white-tailed quail and prairie quail and bob-tail quail. All kinds of quail." Abbott searched for a believable species. "Dave, that's what you call valley quail, yeah, valley quail...got a lot of 'em over in eastern Washington. Why'd you wanna know, Dave?"

"Well the meat was pretty dark and I gotta tell you—it was mighty tough."

The "Tall Arkansan" was rightly thrilled by the outcome of such a solid joke and, as a sign of how much they loved Dave, the players who were on the hunt never told him the "secret of the valley quail." Still, Dave decided from that day forward he wasn't going to eat anything from Abbott unless he knew what it was and was there to see it bagged.

So, that late October day in 1979 with his future uncertain and his family wondering whether another move was on the horizon, Dave decided he'd go hunting with his good friend. If O'Brien wanted to speak to him, he'd have to wait until next week.

The next week came and went and a few more weeks after that. Pittsburgh was calling. The Pirates wanted to make a change in their broadcast lineup and Dave Niehaus was their first choice. As word spread, more clubs expressed an interest. The phone was ringing and doors were opening. Dave knew those doors would not remain open for long. If he wasn't wanted, he'd have to go.

October passed, November passed. December arrived and the stalemate remained. It was a Christmas of genuine uncertainty at the Niehaus home. Marilyn had paid her dues along with Dave in the long climb to his being the lead man in a major-league booth. She had left her family and her adopted home behind in California. She had moved her children north and found them new schools and new friends. The Niehauses were happy in Seattle. The prospect of yet another, possibly short-term move to another baseball metropolis was not something she wished to consider and, truthfully, neither did Dave.

The two sides began talking, but the New Year came without a resolution. Attanasio, who also represented Mariner players Julio Cruz, Shane Rawley, Joe Simpson, and Jim Anderson, brought both sides to the table. It wasn't until Friday, January 18, 1980, that both sides announced an agreement had been reached on a new three-year contract. It was a deal that rightfully included annual salary increases, making Dave one of the highest-paid announcers in the game. His friend Glenn Abbott would not be there to see it through. His friend Darrell Johnson wouldn't either.

If you loved baseball, Dave Niehaus loved you, simple as that. As a self-confessed slave to his regard for the game and as a broadcaster, he had a special place in his horsehide heart for the writers. Especially, for the beat writers who, like he, covered the team day in, day out. They were among his truest pals.

If you've ever been drinking with a sportswriter, you know you'd better have some game. When it's time to belly up, the veteran scribes could pound a cocktail with the same fervor as a typewriter. I recall being informed that one of my buddies was about to be cut off because he'd already had three doubles.

"He's a sportswriter," I told the young bar manager, "it just means he's getting ready to do some drinking."

It was just part of the life, all the more so on the road. The press lounge at the ballpark or the local watering hole were nightly stops for those who plied their trade in the baseball business—especially in the days before sports bars in which the din of a dozen different televisions makes conversation so difficult. On a barstool next to a veteran reporter you could study toward a degree in big-league lore.

The nightly lectures and discourses told tales of Ty Cobb and Tris Speaker and stories about Dizzy Dean and Pepper Martin in the '30s, DiMaggio and Williams in the 1940s and '50s, Mays and Mantle in the 1960s. These barstool chronicles were not confined only to the bright lights of the game. Bit-players and bench jockeys, obscure relievers who specialized in the hot foot, short-fused umpires, and long-forgotten journeymen all were remembered here, served up with a grand helping of stats and stories.

For those who viewed the ballparks as cathedrals, this was a place of communion. Dave Niehaus loved these places like no other and treasured only the company of his family over the company of these men. The oral history of the game was passed on here. Had Homer covered the beat, *The Odyssey* would have been recited here and might have starred a strapping young outfielder from Ithaca, New York or a scrappy third-sacker from Athens, Georgia.

The writers saw the game the way Dave did, lived it, wrestled it into print and prose and found the pursuit worthy of a lifetime's effort.

J Michael Kenyon was the first, but far from the last Seattle-based scribe to befriend the voice of the M's. At the All-Star break in 1980, Tracy Ringolsby left Southern California and his job as a baseball writer for the *Long Beach Independent Press-Telegram* to work at the *Seattle Post-Intelligencer.* He had moved to California from Kansas City where he had covered the Royals and was first introduced to Dave Niehaus during the 1976–77 off-season while covering the Los Angeles Angels. Their friendship grew during Ringolsby's subsequent visits to Seattle for Angel-Mariner series and blossomed fully when Tracy replaced J Michael Kenyon as the Mariner beat writer for the *Post-Intelligencer.*

Ringolsby rented a hotel room while his wife and daughter stayed behind to sell their home. Informed of Tracy's nomad status, Niehaus immediately insisted the writer stay with him and Marilyn.

"Well, you're not going to rent a place to stay until they get here— you're just going to stay with us," Ringolsby recalls Dave telling him. "He was open to everybody. He was everybody's friend. That was his way— his door was open to everybody. I think that's why he became such a key part of the organization, such a key part of Seattle, because nobody was a stranger, nobody was an enemy. You were his friend before you met him— you just didn't realize it."

Hall of Fame baseball writer Tracy Ringolsby with Dave Niehaus.

Marilyn had grown used to her husband's penchant for bringing home baseball strays.

"Seems like he would always call from the airport. 'Honey, I'll be home in an hour and I've got someone with me,'" Marilyn reminisced to me. "That was my cue to get one of the boys up and into his brother's room and get the vacant room ready for company."

Ringolsby graciously declined to displace either of the boys and opted for the downstairs couch. Dave left out the detail that the sofa previously had been the domain of the family beagle, Stephanie. As Ringolsby told me later, "Dave didn't tell me, but the fleas did."

On road trips, the two men would get adjoining rooms so they could talk baseball well into the night, although many a times those conversations ended with Ringolsby closing the connecting door and placing a towel across the bottom. Dave smoked pretty much all the time and sooner or later the smoke would get to Ringolsby. But the door never stayed closed for long.

When I asked Ringolsby what made Dave so memorable, his answer echoed the sentiments of most who knew him:

"He just had fun with whatever he did and he made it fun for everybody else," Ringolsby told me. "For as many years of bad baseball that he announced, he still enjoyed every minute at the ballpark. And so, when you were listening, you wound up enjoying it, too, because you were all having a good time together.

"What stood out was just the excitement that he'd have toward the game, the fact that you're listening to the game and you're having fun—because he's having fun. He wasn't all caught up with everything being technically perfect as much as he was talking with you about the game. He wasn't lecturing you, he wasn't bombasting you, he was just kind of chatting with his friends at the other end of the line and telling them what he was seeing, and what was going on.

"When you see things like how long Kevin Cremin has been there, the fact that Rick Rizzs came back there...if Dave was a jerk that doesn't happen. Rick could have found a job somewhere else. He wouldn't have come back to Seattle. Kevin Cremin as an engineer, it's not like you're going to be set for life when you take that job. You better enjoy it...and he's been there forever. That tells you something."

Ringolsby's stint at the *P-I* included witnessing the ballclub's first change of ownership. The Mariners may have set an expansion-team attendance record in 1977, but the combination of losing baseball and the Kingdome's desultory atmosphere soon slowed the turnstiles. The continued decline in attendance left the original ownership group strapped for cash. They were, in fact, bankrupt.

The cash-poor regime made one crucial mistake after another, chief among them the 1981 dismissal of GM Lou Gorman, whom they essentially replaced with Kip Horsburgh.

Gorman, Niehaus, and Kenyon were baseball birds of a feather with a genuine feel for the game and an extensive knowledge of its history. Dave was clear on this.

"The biggest mistake this organization ever made, to my way of thinking, was when they fired Lou Gorman," he said. "Or maybe the worst thing that ever happened to this franchise was when they hired Kip Horsburgh. They kind of go hand in glove."

The sinking Mariner ship was sailing in a sea of red ink and the original owners saw no option but to sell the team.

Canadian investor Nelson Skalbania looked to be the next in line with a $12.8 million offer. At the eleventh hour, another buyer appeared and Skalbania's effort was foiled. The Mariners were sold to Detroit-born, southern California-raised real-estate developer George Argyros. His principal business entity, Arnel Development Company, was based in Santa Ana, employing some 150 people.

Argyros, a private man, kept a low profile. His chief financial officer, Chuck Packard once remarked, "We don't send out press releases." When asked why not, he replied, "We have no ego."

Well, Argyros had just joined a club consisting of twenty-seven considerable egos, so that circumstance wasn't going to last long. In addition, Arnel Development had garnered quite a bit of ink a couple years prior when it purchased La Casa Pacifica, the San Clemente seaside estate of disgraced former President Richard M. Nixon. George's days as a private man, were, for the foreseeable future, behind him.

The sale agreement was signed on January 14, 1981, and approved by the league later that month. In the end, it would prove a good deal for Argyros. It would also prove a great deal less for the fans and the franchise.

Argyros' Greek heritage was a source of hope to some Northwest scribes. J Michael Kenyon noted that the largely mountainous Greek island of Lemnos was, in both ancient and medieval times, famed for its "Lemnian earth"—said to cure the snake-bitten. If ever a franchise was in need of some of that Aegean topsoil, it was this one. The Argyros ancestry also meant the new owner was never fond of the Mariners' logo, an inverted trident. To Greeks it symbolized bad luck. It came to symbolize bad baseball and bad ownership.

That's not to malign Argyros. He was a man who, in 1962, decided he was "tired of being poor" and left behind his job as a grocery store manager and eventually amassed a considerable fortune. He was a savvy businessman who just didn't know anything much about baseball. It was an investment for George, not a passion. Not that he didn't care, he just cared about the business more than the baseball. Then again, after the opening season, the baseball fans in the Northwest hadn't done much caring, either. Help was needed—and needed right away. So, initially, when Argyros stepped up, the fans stepped in behind him.

I came to know George Argyros from my work with the Seattle Mariner RBI Club, comprised of regional businessmen and civic leaders who made it their mission to help baseball survive in Seattle. The group was formed under the leadership of Jay Porter, president of Unigard Insurance, *Seattle Post-Intelligencer* publisher Virgil Fassio and Andy Smith, president of Pacific Northwest Bell—all tremendous fans and men who understood both the tangible and intangible benefits of big-league baseball.

The RBI Club spread the gospel and twisted arms across the Northwest in support of Mariner baseball. Its members set an example for businesses by buying Mariner season tickets and tirelessly working to persuade their colleagues to do so as well. By keeping the flame burning during some dark times, they made a real difference.

George Argyros wasn't considered a fun guy. It appeared those around him seemed to discourage any sort of levity in his presence. Truth is, I found him quite fun. Upon being introduced, we were, for some unknown reason, left standing together by a buffet. He asked what I did and seemed genuinely surprised that I was a professional singer. I told him a joke and he laughed—a real laugh, not a polite one. So, I told him another and he laughed again. He was motioned to the podium and said "Nice to meet you."

When he walked away, Marianne Wieland, who coordinated special events for the Mariners, came over and asked what I had said to George. She said it was the first time she had ever seen him laugh. I told her I told him a couple of jokes. With complete delight she said, "You're kidding. Nobody tells jokes to Mr. Argyros!"

I never again spoke to George Argyros without telling him a joke. I figured nobody else told him any jokes. He couldn't fire me, so I had nothing to fear, and he seemed to really appreciate it.

What wasn't funny was talking to him about baseball. I knew it was a business to him, but I never could have imagined that anyone who owned a major league team would not be a passionate fan as well. I was wrong, wrong, wrong. George hadn't the slightest feel for, or understanding of the game—incredibly so. I liked him and always enjoyed making him laugh. Not knowing baseball didn't make him a bad guy, but it sure didn't make him a good owner.

Argyros was used to calling the shots. That worked out really well for him in real estate. He knew a lot about real estate. When it came to his baseball team, he also insisted on calling the shots. Again, he did not know a lot about baseball. A great many capable people around him were not given the leeway to make decisions they would have made better than their boss. There are two sayings about baseball owners. When things go right it's: "quality filters down from the top." When things go wrong it's: "a fish rots from the head." In fairness, it's pretty rare not to hear both during one's years as an owner.

Unfairly or not, both George Argyros' and Dan O'Brien's tenures with the Mariners would be forever linked to the hiring of Maury Wills. Argyros simply inherited Wills, but was still a victim of guilt by association. Wills' 6-18 start in 1981, which prompted his firing, simply got the Argyros years off to the worst of starts. Gorman, however, had been instrumental in the whole mess.

Darrell Johnson's stoic run as the M's first skipper came to an end August 3, 1980, after a 4–3 loss to the Detroit Tigers. The previous owners decided to replace him with Wills. It came at the recommendation of Dan O'Brien and was presumably influenced by O'Brien's dealings with Maury's son, Bump, while both were with O'Brien's previous employer, the Texas Rangers.

An extremely bright person, O'Brien was a seasoned baseball man who capably served a number of organizations, especially the Rangers. His term in Seattle showcased a remarkable knack for administration, but perhaps not quite the same skill set when it came to evaluating talent. He was a smooth-as-silk administrator and a superb face for the ball club. He also had vast knowledge of baseball's inner workings from all the years he'd spent in the minor-league office of Phil Piton at Columbus, Ohio. His position in Seattle placed him above GM Lou Gorman in the pecking order and made for a difficult relationship between the two. Gorman's input was largely ignored.

As Kenyon wrote, "(O'Brien) has so far resisted publicly praising any of the myriad deals Gorman made in the two-and-a-half years pre-O'Brien. Under contract through 1981, Gorman is marking time and waiting for a better career opportunity elsewhere."

Gorman opposed the Wills hiring. The M's would have done well to listen to Lou on this one.

I had seen Wills play with the old Seattle Rainiers in the Pacific Coast League and later with the Dodgers. He was a heady player who got the most out of his ability, a terrific base runner and a solid infielder. But baseball history is replete with great stars whose brilliance on the field did not translate to the dugout.

In a 1994 interview, Dave reflected, "The Wills regime was just a nightmare, an absolute nightmare, from start to finish. Some of the things he did. I expected more of a baseball man like that, and I felt sorry for Maury Wills."

Still, Wills did not provide the only foolishness in Marinerville during his first campaign in 1981. By the last day of September, the Mariners were in the middle of an eight-game skid to end the season with 103 losses. With two outs in the bottom of the third of a game at Kansas City, starting pitcher Rick Honeycutt went to his stretch. Willie Wilson danced off second base and suddenly began pointing at Honeycutt and screaming to the umpires. He had noticed something unusual about Rick's glove. The umpires searched Honeycutt and found a tack inside his glove that he was using to cut the baseballs. His ejection and ten-game suspension seemed the fitting, final insult to a dismal year.

Wills' personal demons had him distant and distracted, aloof from his players and inattentive to even the games themselves.

Glenn Abbott, the early stalwart of the Mariner pitching staff, once told me, "Maury Wills would just do the dumbest things, like he wasn't paying any attention to the game."

Take the night of April 12, 1981. In a 6–6 tie with the Angels, Rod Carew stood at third base while Dick Drago, freshly summoned from the pen by Wills, threw his warm-up tosses. Two things should be noted here: if you were a baseball fan and Rod Carew was on third base, you were alive. Carew was the modern-day Ty Cobb when it came to stealing home. Secondly, Drago was warming up from a full windup and his motion to the plate was anything but compact.

I happened to be sitting behind the third-base dugout that night and my buddies and I noticed Carew carefully measuring Drago's throws. From the third or fourth one, he began moving back toward third base and starting down the line with each toss. We weren't the only ones to notice. On the Mariner bench, Abbott and fellow hurler Jim Beattie saw what we saw and thought the same thing. They pointed at Carew and tried to alert their manager:

As Abbott recalled to me, he shoutied, "Look at Carew! He's gonna steal home!"

Wills responded with complete indifference. "What are you guys talking about? He's not gonna do anything."

Many years later, I learned that the mixture of anticipation, disgust, admiration and dismay we felt while watching Carew break the 6–6 tie by

Baby Dave, circa 1936.

Gil Hodges Field in Lafayette Park in Princeton, Indiana.

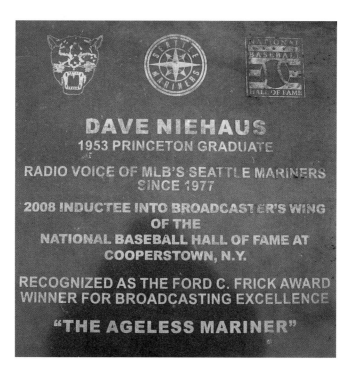

Dave Niehaus' plaque at Gil Hodges Field.

Dave's cousin, Ron Greenfield, with the author
at Evansville VFW Post 1114.

Dave's mother Delania took his picture on the first day of school every year from first grade in 1941 through his freshman year of at Indiana University in 1953. These precious photographs are from the album she left for her son in the last year of her life. Jack Niehaus continued his wife's tradition and took the first day of school photos from 1954–1957.

Clockwise from top left:

First grade—Dave's very first day at school.

Dave begins second grade.

Fifth-grader Dave Niehaus.

Clockwise from top left:

Dave starts the sixth grade.

The first day of sophomore year at Princeton High School.

Opening day for Dave's junior year.

Indiana University freshman, Dave Niehaus.

Sophomore year at IU.

Left: Dave graduated from Princeton High School, 1953.

Dave is now a junior and majoring in radio and television.

Dave begins his final year of studies at IU.

Dave graces the cover of an early 80's Mariner Magazine. Note the inscription to J Michael Kenyon: "JMK, without you & 'Fly Away' it wouldn't have happened."

Dave and one of his heroes, astronaut Neil Armstrong, the first human to set foot on the moon.

Mariner skipper Dick Williams with the author at spring training, 1988.

Dave with Hall of Fame manager Tommy Lasorda and all-time hits leader, Pete Rose.

Dave with Hank Aaron and Ron Fairly.

Dave's fellow 2008 Hall of Fame inductee and lifetime friend, Dick Williams.

Dick Williams and Dave pull a comic stunt at a 1988 spring training dinner.

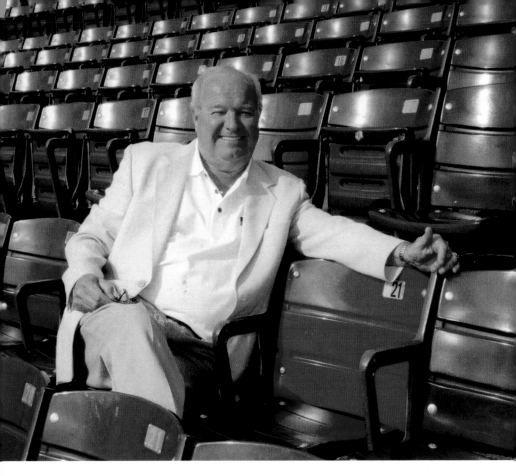

Dave sitting next to the famous red seat in Fenway Park that commemorates Ted Williams' June 9, 1946, 502-foot home run. That home run was hit off of Seattle's native son Fred Hutchinson, for whom the world-renowned cancer treatment center is named.

Dave in his infamous Fourth of July jacket, given to him by Bill Mazeroski, a fellow member of the Hall of Fame.

Right: The author with Manager Jim Lefebvre, the first M's skipper to have a winning season.

Below: The author with Dave Valle in the Mariner dugout prior to a 1990 game at the Kingdome.

Mariner manager Lou Piniella is interviewed by Dave on the Mariners' salute to the Seattle Rainiers night.

Rick Rizzs, Ken Brett and Dave in the broadcast booth.

Marilyn Niehaus with the Drysdale family.

The "Three Amigos"—Dave Niehaus, Rick Rizzs and Kevin Cremin, circa 1990.

George Argyros, Gaylord Perry and Dave in the Mariner dugout at the Kingdome.

Alvin Davis, Dave Niehaus, Edgar Martinez and Jay Buhner celebrate Edgar's induction into the M's Hall of Fame in 2008. Edgar was a lifetime .312 hitter for the Mariners from 1987 to 2004 and the American League's annual Outstanding Designated Hitter Award is named for him.

Marilyn Niehaus (center) joins Mariner Hall of Famers Randy Johnson, Edgar Martinez, Jay Buhner, Ken Griffey Jr., Dan Wilson and Alvin Davis.

sliding under Drago's first delivery to catcher Bud Bulling, was shared by two of our favorite Mariner pitchers who had the only view better than ours.

Manager Wills drove the pitchers nuts. Like the time he took Abbott out of a game in the tenth inning with no one on base and a string of nine consecutive batters retired.

"It was just stuff that didn't make any sense," Abbott told me. "He sent (pitching coach) Wes Stock in an 8–2 game to tell me to be careful with George Brett. Like anybody who ever pitched in the big leagues didn't know to be careful with George Brett. It pissed me off so bad I overthrew a slider and he put it on the lawn on the other side of the centerfield fence."

It was tough on the writers, too. Wills was distant and often unapproachable with the press. His relationships with the guys whose job it was to interview him daily became strained almost immediately during the late 1980 season when he took over. This meant the majority of the inexplicable moves he made during the games remained unexplained. Ringolsby shared that fate with his fellow scribes.

"It was more difficult to cover him than to watch him," Tracy said to me. "I only talked to him about seven or eight times because it was such a waste of time. It came out later that he was hooked on cocaine. You kept trying to say 'this can't be Maury Wills, he was a guy who knew the game, who had a work ethic. He was a guy who made it at thirty.'"

Still, Ringolsby decided he needed to get along better with Wills. In January of 1981 at one of those winter events designed to raise interest in the team, he decided to make a renewed effort to improve the communication between them. After all, Wills wasn't going to be fired. (Wrong.)

Ringolsby remembered starting a conversation with "Hey, Maury, what are you thinking about center field?"

"Well," Wills replied, "We got a guy that isn't the prettiest guy on earth, but when you watch him play, he gets good breaks on the ball and I think he's going to surprise some people. Leon Roberts."

The reporter's next question probably revealed his incredulousness. "Have you talked to Eddie Robinson?"

"Why do I need to talk to Eddie Robinson?" Wills asked.

"Well he's the general manager in Texas," replied Ringolsby.

"So?" asked Wills.

"Well, you traded Leon to Texas six weeks ago."

Ringolsby echoed his mates in the press corps, describing covering Wills as "six months of agony."

Dave Niehaus was equally familiar with the trials of working with Wills. When asked if he remembered him, he'd give a sly smile and say "I remember him altering the batters' box." (A reference to the night Maury had the grounds crew move the batter's box lines, which prompted a protest from Yankee skipper Billy Martin. Wills drew a fine and suspension. There was plenty more to remember.)

"The first full year that he took over," Dave said, "we were down in spring training playing the San Francisco Giants and he went through his entire bench. I remember sitting there in Scottsdale and he motioned for a pitcher and he didn't have anybody up in the bullpen and he didn't realize it! Maury Wills was a guy who would tell you 'look, I can't talk about this' when we were doing the pre-game show with him every day and you'd say to him 'but that's what people want to know' and he's going 'I can't talk about it.'

"I'll be darned. You'd lead him into the interview and he'd just spill his guts and talk about it, anyway. I'll never forget that. Little did we know, but it came out later that he had had a substance abuse problem when he was managing this ballclub. So maybe there were some other reasons. Kind of, as it turns out, kind of a pathetic figure; certainly the worst manager I've ever been associated with."

Despite his trials in Seattle, it should not be forgotten that Wills was a tremendous player. The switch-hitting shortstop was a two-time Gold Glove winner, and played in seven All-Star games. In 1962, he was Most Valuable Player of the All-Star game and National League MVP. Many credit Maury with reviving the art of base stealing. It should be noted as well that, to his ultimate credit, Maury eventuallly confronted and conquered his demons.

The Maury Wills era came to a suitably quick end on May 6, 1981. It ushered out one of the least popular managerial tenures in franchise history and ushered in one of most cherished.

Rene "Lach" Lachemann, skipper of the M's Triple A club in Spokane, was tapped as Wills' successor. At thirty-six, Lach wasn't that much older than the players he managed and brought both a youthful approach and a sense of humor that was welcomed by Mariner fans everywhere. Foremost among them was Dave Niehaus.

The son of a hotel chef, Lachemann was the youngest of three brothers to enjoy long careers in organized baseball, both the majors and the minors. Older brother Marcel had pitched for Oakland from 1969–71 and went on to coach and manage in the big leagues, most notably with the 1995 California Angels, who would play the foil for the Mariners that summer. Oldest brother Bill was the bullpen coach for Marcel's Halos. Bill had managed Class A farm teams for the California Angels and knew Dave when he worked the Angels' booth. Baseball was a family affair to Lach and he quickly made both the team and the fans share the feeling that was quite literally in his blood.

Lach was a favorite of Lou Gorman and had been hired by him as a potential manager-in-waiting. Rene had managed for five years in the Oakland A's farm system when Lou and Mel Didier hired him to helm the M's Triple A farm team, then at San Jose, for the 1978 season. The dream was that Lach would "grow up" right along with all the Mariner draft choices and, eventually, migrate to the big show to manage them. Lou knew as well as anyone that Darrell Johnson's long suit was not developing youngsters; it was handling veterans.

Lachemann's record on the field did not reflect his abilities. The clubs he managed were short on talent and long on key injuries. Just thirty-two games into his 1981 rookie season at the helm, the players' strike silenced the game for two months. The bumpy ride was just beginning.

As you might imagine, the agony of the strike was felt in broadcast booths throughout baseball as well. While guys like Dave Niehaus certainly appreciated some unexpected time with their families, they were all too cognizant of the damage being done to the game. Among the casualties was one of Dave's great delights—baseball's annual All-Star Game. The mid-summer classic was scheduled to be played on Tuesday, July 14, at old Municipal Stadium in Cleveland. Due to the work stoppage, the game had been postponed until August. This particular summer, the exploits of the game's best in the yearly clash between the senior and junior circuits would not fill the airwaves.

Except in Seattle.

A very peculiar set of circumstances gave Niehaus and Wilson a 163rd game to call that season and provided the opportunity for Dave's penultimate call of a game re-creation. Mr. Niehaus was about to meet Mr. Neuhaus.

Barry Neuhaus was a thirty-four-year-old scientific computer programmer for the University of Washington Bio-Electromagnetic Radiation Effects Research Group of the Rehabilitation Medicine Department. Neuhaus was a self-described baseball fanatic who, years earlier, had tried out for the Husky baseball team.

The July 10, 1981 edition of *The Seattle Times* reported:

"Neuhaus, who ruefully recalls he failed to make the UW baseball team in years gone by, hates to see fellow fanatics go without. So he's hunched over the keyboard of a computer terminal in a small back office at Seattle radio station KVI, feeding vital statistics on All-Star players to the plug-in brain. What he'll come up with in time for next week's big game is a substitute, electronic pinch-hitter for the washed-up All-Star game.

"The show will air at 7:30 p.m. Tuesday, with now idle Seattle Mariners' play-by-play announcers Dave Niehaus and Ken Wilson doing the breathless play-by-play. Canned crowd cheers and the occasional cry of a vendor will add realism.

"Station sports gurus Grayle Howlett and J Michael Kenyon chose the lineups on the basis of All-Star balloting to date and season performance.

"The only change is that Cincinnati catcher Johnny Bench was scratched as a starter because he's on the disabled list and replaced by Montreal's Gary Carter.

"Howlett and Kenyon will manage the teams. Based on their decisions and lineups, the computer will spit out quick, pitch-by-pitch accounts of what would be most likely to happen in a real game."

Seattle's well-deserved reputation for being at the forefront of the tech revolution dates back to the early 1980s. Long before PlayStations and X-Boxes, Barry Neuhaus was commissioner of the Northwest Computer Baseball Association, an eight-team league that played exclusively in cyberspace. His love of the game was oddly inspired by the Philadelphia Phillies of the early 1960s, whose penchant for losing baseball included the big-league record of twenty-three straight defeats in 1961. Neuhaus "liked the way they hung on."

So, for Mr. Niehaus, the loss of the real All-Star game was being soothed somewhat by the efforts of Mr. Neuhaus. There was, for Mr. Niehaus, one other small issue: the game was being "played" and taped under strict secrecy. The participants were not to divulge the results to anyone. But Marilyn Niehaus was not about to let her husband keep the secret from her. She prodded him and nudged him and those big brown eyes and that certain smile won out. "I'm sworn to secrecy," Niehaus, forty-six, said with a smile. "But this was fun. It was not the genuine thing but it was still fun. I told my wife who won…but only did that because she kept asking me. I made her promise that she wouldn't tell anyone else, though."

Barry Neuhaus was so committed to the secrecy that he even refused to divulge the outcome during an appearance on the *Today* show with Bryant Gumbel on Tuesday morning.

As scheduled, the broadcast was aired Tuesday, July 14 on 570 KVI AM in Seattle at 7:30 p.m. The results were dutifully reported in the next day's edition of *The Seattle Times*

"A computerized recreation of the All-Star baseball game has finally ended like most of the midsummer classics over the past 18 years—another victory for the National League, 9–4.

"The National League never trailed and scored three runs in both the seventh and ninth innings.

"Neuhaus' computer allotted four home runs, including a two-run homer in the seventh for local favorite Tom Paciorek of the AL Seattle Mariners.

"Milwaukee's Ben Ogilvie homered in the second and Minnesota's Roy Smalley homered in the sixth for the American League. Montreal's Andre Dawson homered to lead off the fifth inning for the National League.

"The winning pitcher was the Dodgers' Fernando Valenzuela."

Some thirteen years later, there would be one final re-created game to which Dave Niehaus would lend his considerable skills.

Back in the real baseball world the tumultuous saga of the Mariners feuding factions and rudderless ownership continued without any All-Star break.

As Kenyon recalled to me: "Of course, mixed up in all this, and, I always thought, lost in the shuffle, was Rene Lachemann, who ought to be, by now—as far as I will eternally be concerned—into his thirty-third season as Mariner manager. If there is anything wrong with baseball, it's that honest guys like Rene Lachemann and Lou Gorman get chewed up by the politics.

"Lachemann was the real peach, though, and someone who's always been tabbed for jobs by the smarter guys in baseball. But, in Seattle, he was caught in the pincer of being a "Gorman man" with Mel Didier's fingerprints all over him, serving between O'Brien's two bad managerial choices.

All this hubbub, never forget, came from the fact the original ownership didn't have the proverbial two quarters to rub together and always was running scared on account of their weak financial positions."

The fans loved Lachemann and still remember him bringing a sense of joy to the Kingdome that only a couple skippers have matched since. His players loved him, too. The 1982 season provided ample evidence of that fact with a nearly season-long saga that involved players, writers, managers, coaches, clubhouse attendants and the Mariners' man behind the microphone.

Nineteen eighty-two was the year of "Mr. Jello."

The chastisement that was the genesis of this saga is of hazy origin, but it involved a play by Mariner D.H./outfielder Richie Zisk. Zisk had come over from the Rangers and was a gritty player who was all business on the field. Lachemann got on him in the dugout during a game and Zisk was not happy—seriously not happy. He decided his manager needed a little payback.

The payback first involved teammate (and future Mariner and Brave broadcaster) Joe Simpson, whose wicked sense of humor is known to all who've had the pleasure of knowing him. Simpson then enlisted Tracy Ringolsby.

The saga of "Mr. Jello," as told to me by Ringolsby:

"Lach took a verbal jab at Richie Zisk and Zisk took it a little harder than he should. So, we go to Chicago and Zisk says, 'Get Lach to stay out a little late tonight' and I go, 'Well, that's the easiest thing on earth. So, all of a sudden we're on Rush Street and it's midnight and Lach wants to go back to his room and I say, 'Lach, we gotta have one more.'

"Finally we wobble back to the hotel, Lach goes up to his room, opens the door, turns on the lights and none of the lights go on. He looks around and there's no furniture in the room. He goes into the bathroom and they've filled the toilet up with Jello. He goes to flush the toilet and all of the Jello splashes up on him. He shut the bathroom door behind him, so now the door's shut, and he goes to get back out the door and can't get the door to the bathroom back open, because they'd covered the handle with Vaseline and taken all the towels.

"He finally gets out and calls down to the operator. They had taken the mouthpiece out of the phone. The operator can't hear a word he's saying. And then he figures, well, maybe Zisk is involved, so he calls Zisk's room, but, remember, there's no mouthpiece. Zisk, knowing this call was coming, says, 'I don't know who this is, but say something or quit calling my room. I'm a professional athlete, I have to get up in the morning.' Meanwhile, Lach is screaming into his phone, thinking he can't be heard. All of Lachemann's furniture is stuffed into his closet and in the tub behind the shower curtain."

"Lachemann couldn't figure out who did it. He had been housesitting when the team was in Seattle and then moved in with me, because we were pretty close. Naturally, Lach looked to me for help, never suspecting my involvement.

"He'd start to figure some things out, and when he did, I'd go tell Zisk and Simpson, so we would go totally throw him off base, so he couldn't figure it out. This became famous as the hunt to find 'Mr. Jello.'

"Lach and Dave Duncan go into a bar in Cleveland and order a beer and they get a bowl of Jello at the table. He checks into the Cross Keys in Baltimore where they always have a gift for the manager, this time it's a silver chalice and this time it's filled with Jello. They come home from a road trip and at the coaches meeting, Dave Duncan takes a sip of a beer only to get a big mouthful of Jello. The equipment truck driver had heard about Mr. Jello and gotten in on the act by punching pin holes in the bottom of the beer cans, draining and refilling them with Jello. Every restaurant they go to, they order dinner and the waiter brings a plate of Jello."

Niehaus was aware of the slippery saga and was determined to do one of two things: find out for his pal, Rene Lachemann, who "Mr. Jello" was, or, get in on the joke himself. It ought to come as no surprise that he chose the latter course.

Back to Ringolsby's account:

"So, the team's in Baltimore and Joe Simpson recruits Dave Niehaus for 'Team Jello.' He goes to Niehaus and asks him to record an interview in which Simpson will claim to know who Mr. Jello is and play that interview for Lach. Simpson knows Lach will confront him and then get Niehaus to provide the tape as evidence. He instructs Niehaus to offer to play the tape for Lach and then erase it, making sure the tape was blank.

"So Niehaus records Simpson saying, 'Yeah, I know who Mr. Jello is— it's gonna be funnier than hell. Lach isn't going to believe it when he finds out. It's hilarious. Lach is never going to figure it out.'

"So, Simpson goes out to centerfield to shag fly balls and Lach is at the batting cage when Dave comes over to him and says, 'Hey, Lach, come here and listen to this' and plays the tape for the Mariner skipper. Lach grins and says, 'Oh really.'

"Niehaus returns to the booth and Lach goes directly out to centerfield to find Simpson. 'Got any idea who Mr. Jello is?'

" 'Lach, I haven't got the slightest idea.'

" 'I think you know.'

" 'Skip, I got no clue who it is.'

" 'I'll bet you a hundred dollars that you know.'

" 'How you gonna prove that?'

" 'I got you on tape.'

" 'You got a bet.'

"The two men proceeded to walk back to the area behind home plate. In old Memorial Stadium in Baltimore, you could scream up to the radio booth, so Lach hollers, 'Niehaus, come down here and bring your tape recorder.'

" 'Yeah, yeah fine.'

"Niehaus comes down from the booth and Lach asks him to play the tape for Simpson. He plays the tape for Joe—the tape is blank. He stammers an apology to Lach for having accidentally recorded over it.

"The next day the team went to New York and 'Team Jello' headed directly to one of those novelty stands that printed fake newspaper front pages. When the team entered the visiting clubhouse that day, there were newspapers plastered all over the walls with the headline:

JELLOGATE TAPES BLANK—LACH BAFFLED

"Dave just couldn't stay out of something like that, he just had to be part of that."

It was emblematic of Dave's relationship with the players that they recruited him and that he remained a willing fellow conspirator throughout the rest of the season. It also reflected his relationship with Lachemann. Dave delighted in being part of such a great practical joke on a good friend whom he knew would take it all in the spirit it was intended.

At the team party in Chicago on the last road trip, the culprits were revealed. Mr. Jello was introduced and a curtain opened to reveal Zisk and Simpson. Ringolsby had left in August for a return stint with the Star in Kansas City, so Lach would have to catch up with him later.

The M's needed the good cheer in 1982. Not only did they endure a losing season on the field, their off-field routine was a genuine grind. Because Seattle is, as NFL coach and broadcaster Jon Gruden likes to say, "right up there next to Alaska," the team annually travels more miles than any other franchise.

Their owner didn't make it any easier on them. George Argyros was notoriously cheap. For the entire 1982 season, the Mariners were the only team in baseball without a charter plane. They flew commercial everywhere they went. As if that wasn't enough, since a non-stop was more expensive than a "milk-run," every Mariner team flight made at least one stop, almost always in Chicago. Except, of course, when they played in Chicago. Those flights stopped in Denver.

The owner's penury had affected his relationship with Lachemann as well. Lachemann was managing the M's farm club in AAA when he was hired to run the big club. When Lachemann came to George and said, "We need to discuss my contract now that I'm with the Mariners," Argyros pointed out that Lach had signed a contract the previous winter to manage "anywhere in the organization." So, Rene Lachemann ended up managing the Seattle Mariners American League team for less than $22,000 per year. It became increasingly difficult for Lachemann to return that kind of disrespect with good humor.

It might have helped if George had any kind of feel for the game. It made Lach crazy to have to explain so much to his boss and it was no different for the people in the front office. O'Brien knew it firsthand.

Argyros was so clueless about baseball that one day GM Dan O'Brien called him to say that the M's had won one of the two games of a double-header. "We won the first game and split," said O'Brien.

The owner testily asked, "Well, why didn't we play the second game?"

"No, George, we did play the second game. We lost it."

"But you said you split."

"We did. We split the doubleheader."

"Oh. I thought you said you left."

In the broadcast booth, meanwhile, big changes were in the wind. Dave's professional life was about to open not one but two chapters that would be ongoing until his death in 2010. Two of his most enduring professional relationships that were also two of his most endearing personal relationships were about to begin. One would be his partner, the other his producer. Both would be his lifelong friends.

George Argyros had his way in the boardroom and wanted his way in the broadcast booth, too. He didn't like Ken Wilson's work. His lack of a gut-level connection to the game made Argyros incapable of understanding how good Ken was at calling a game. Smooth, professional, competent, with a sensitivity to the rhythms of the game, Wilson made a terrific pairing with the excitable Hoosier. Ken brought his own level of excitement, for sure, but his "game" was different.

Wilson recalled the endgame to me.

"I went down to Newport Beach to meet with him," Wilson said, "*on my dime*, and he looked at me and he said, 'Have you ever thought about going into the front office?' Which was his political way of saying he thought I was a terrible broadcaster. That was in July and nothing happened in August. They offered me a contract in the middle of September, because I had talked to Argyros and I wanted to get renewed or at least know that he didn't care about me. They said, 'We'd like to give you a one-year contract with no raise.' I said, "Thanks very much for the contract offer but I decline.'"

George Argyros may not have recognized Wilson's talents but plenty of others did. Wilson would land on his feet.

"About four or five days later WLWT in Cincinnati called and asked me if there was any way I would leave the Mariners to come to Cincinnati and be the television voice of the Cincinnati Reds. So, I took the Cincinnati job and about the same time I got an offer from Chicago to do Chicago Blackhawks hockey on television, which was going to be one hundred games in the NHL and fifty or so in Major League Baseball."

George's failure to renew Ken Wilson's contract was just another in a long series of bad baseball decisions. Like so many of the talented players Argyros sent packing, Wilson proved that the Mariners' owner could be a poor judge of baseball talent both on—and off—the field. "Captain Ken" would not only go on to a multitude of sports broadcasting jobs, but also lived to see the judgment of history smile favorably on the Niehaus-Lassen debate.

"Back then, if you didn't sound like Leo and do things like Leo, you were no good," Wilson said. "Now, of course, if you don't sound and do it like Dave Niehaus, you're no good, or a second-class citizen, anyway."

Surprisingly, Argyros' next decision about broadcasters was far more fortuitous. Scarcely did Argyros guess that the next man he hired would remain in the Mariner broadcast booth even after Dave was gone. It was a solid decision, but one that almost was short-circuited by some Chi-town Girl Scouts and their cookies.

Argyros was down to two candidates, one of them a young man from the suburbs south of Chicago and the son of a local sportswriter. He had been a baseball player for the Salukis of Southern Illinois University where he began doing play-by-play. His impressive minor-league resume began in 1975, when he joined one of his buddies who had gotten a job working for the Alexandria (Louisiana) Aces of the Double-A Texas League. Rick Rizzs showed early on that he was willing to do whatever it took to achieve his dream, even double-duty as the club's launderer.

"I washed the jerseys of Bruce Sutter, Dennis Lamp, Garry Templeton, Donnie Moore, Jack Clark, and lots of players from that league who are stars now," Rick recalled. "I made $200 a month, including tips. So to pay the rent, I also did the graveyard shift at a local radio station as a Top Forty disc jockey. I had to start somewhere and part of the deal in Alexandria was that I could do three innings of play-by-play every home game on another station."

Thanks to the Alexandria manager's wife, who cooked dinner for him five nights a week, the two jobs got him through.

Not long after, Rick became the radio voice of the Amarillo Gold Sox, also of the Texas League. He also had two jobs there: full-time duty as the Gold Sox' man in the booth during the season, and part-time work selling ads for the outfield wall during the off-season.

Rick had grown up listening to Jack Brickhouse, a Hall of Famer, calling the Cubs games in the Windy City. He'd nurtured this dream since his early teens, and if it took doing a few loads of laundry or selling a few billboards, that wasn't about to deter him. From Amarillo, it was on to the Memphis Chicks of the Double-A Southern Association and then a move up to the Triple-A Columbus (Ohio) Clippers of the International League. He also spent two seasons broadcasting Ohio State University football for WBNS Radio where he served as sports director. It was there in the Buckeye State his big opportunity came knocking.

"I still remember the date," he said, "January 7, 1983. I was taking a nap. I'd heard that Ken Wilson, Dave's partner, was leaving Seattle, so I'd sent in a tape of my work. But I'd sent tapes to lots of major-league teams before. This time, though, the Mariners called and said I was one of two finalists."

Argyros liked Rick Rizzs' audition tape and summoned him to Orange County for a final interview. The day before leaving for California, Rick was one of a number of celebrities pledged to a Girl Scout cookie-eating contest for a local charity. Perhaps the only thing Rick works harder at than broadcasting is raising money for charities. (His "Toys for Kids" charity, which he co-founded with former Mariners' center fielder Dave Henderson, has raised in excess of $2.5 million for Northwest children.)

Typically, Rick gave the Girl Scouts fundraiser his all. He ate thirty-three cookies.

Rick Rizzs and Dave Niehaus at Diablo Stadium in Tempe, Arizona, spring training, 1987.

The next day he was hospitalized for chest pains and eventually diagnosed with a bruised sternum, causing him to miss his flight.

"There I was," he said, 'flat on my back, hooked to an EKG, seeing eight years of broadcasting in the minor leagues and my big break going up in smoke. I was still strapped to a table when they let me call the Mariners and beg for an extra day to fly out and see Mr. Argyros."

Argyros was leaving for an extended vacation and Rick now had twenty-four hours to get to Los Angeles. Rizzs checked out of the hospital, headed straight for the airport and made the next day's meeting. It all seemed to go well until the end. George expressed grave reservations about Rick having missed their originally scheduled meeting and made it clear that his decision hinged on the explanation.

Rick gave him the straight story. Argyros was painfully silent and withdrawn. Finally, he stood up and extended his hand. He said, "Anybody that will go that far to help out the Girl Scouts is somebody I want working for me!"

Over the next thirty years, only Dave Niehaus broadcast more Mariner games than Rick. With a brief interruption from 1992–94, Dave and Rick became the all-time tandem in the Mariner radio booth.

During that same 1982–83 off-season, events were set in motion that led to Dave Niehaus' other most enduring professional partnership.

Only a few months earlier, prior to the end of the 1982 season, the Mariners were headed to Kansas City to play the Royals. Grayle Howlett, a producer at M's flagship station KVI, needed a runner. The runner's job was to make sure the post-game guest had headphones and to secure one or more players to appear on Ken Wilson's post-game show. Grayle was the son of Grayle W. Howlett Jr., a member of the Texas League Hall of Fame who served as a front-office executive for the Tulsa Oilers in the 1940s and '50s.

Howlett called up his old buddy, Kevin Cremin.

Kevin was a die-hard Tulsa Golden Hurricane fan. Earlier that year, he had been unable to resist the temptation to take an evening off work to see Nolan Richardson's charges play in the NCAA Regionals against the fabled Phi Jamma Slamma squad from the University of Houston. Richardson had brought Tulsa to heights not seen since Clarence Iba, brother of Henry Iba, coached there in the '50s. Cremin wasn't going to miss his chance to see them defend their 1981 NIT crown. His stellar, eight and a-half years of service to the printing company he worked for made his unusual car synonymous with his presence. As such, Kevin's orange Volkswagen Scirocco was easily spotted by a co-worker as it sat in the parking lot of the Tulsa Convention Center. That co-worker wanted Kevin's job and quickly figured out this information could help him get it.

Although Tulsa lost that night 79–74, Kevin enjoys the memory of that game more every year. He couldn't be happier that his nemesis got his old job. His new job would be the best job he could ever imagine. His departure from the printing business meant Kevin was available to be Howlett's runner. Twenty bucks a game and a great seat at Royals Stadium sounded just fine.

Cremin had grown up in Tulsa and the barbecue joints of Kansas City were his regular haunts. For Dave Niehaus, barbecue was more than just a meal, it was a sacrament. Had Dave Niehaus not found a way to be a professional broadcaster, there's a fair chance he might have found a way to make money at barbecue. He loved barbecue almost as much as a doubleheader. His old friend, Dick Enberg, told me it was his number one hobby.

Right off the bat, Cremin was Dave's man. Kevin made sure Dave saw the inside of Kansas City's best barbecue joints. With Dave, a friendship formed over a plate of barbecue and beans was one destined to last. Cremin also was a product of the Midwest like Dave. He grew up with Cardinal baseball. He was straightforward and kind, not afraid to speak his mind but always respectful and considerate. And he loved the game of baseball.

In October of 1982, Kevin got another call from Seattle, this time from Dave Niehaus. Dave started the conversation with "How's the weather?" "He always started with that," remembered Cremin. Turned out that was the off-speed pitch, the heat was next.

"How would you like the producer-engineer's job?" Dave asked.

Kevin's reply was, typically, completely honest. "That's great," he said, "but I don't know the first thing about it. But if you can push it through, I'm definitely in."

Whatever it was Dave saw in the young Oklahoman, he got KVI general manager Shannon Sweatte to send an outline of the job and a letter of agreement. Kevin proposed to his sweetheart, Margaret, got married, and packed up everything they owned. Then came a third call from Seattle. It was Jay Green, the production chief at KVI, who was not happy with what was going down. He wanted to know Kevin's qualifications.

Once more, Kevin's penchant for the straight truth kicked in. "I don't have any qualifications," he said.

"Then you can't have the job," Green told him.

Kevin wasn't going to let this opportunity elude him. "Look," he replied, "I've got a letter from your station manager, I just got married, I got a twenty-four-foot U-Haul packed and I'm leaving tomorrow, so I'll see you when I get there."

"When I got to Seattle," Kevin recalled, "they dumped everything out on the table and said 'Hook it up.' Fortunately, Rick was coming out of the minors where he had done some of his own engineering and he helped me out a lot. We hooked it up and tore it apart and hooked it up and tore it apart again. I was in Seattle for only three or four days, spent hooking up wires and finding a place to live. Then it was off to spring training and the first game, I was scared shitless. But everything worked and here I am, more than thirty years later."

Jay Green and Shannon Sweatte both became his friends, each earning the ultimate Cremin compliment, "What a guy." Cremin became one of the most respected men in his field and does extensive work on the national stage. The Mariners have never been in the World Series, but their producer-engineer has been, working for ESPN in addition to his off-season work with college football.

The Cremin-Niehaus union was not just the perfect match of two guys who got along and loved barbecue. These two saw the game the same way, came to it from a reverent Midwest perspective and could eat, drink and sleep baseball for seven months a year and still miss it during the off-season. More important for their audience, they heard the game the same way.

Listen to a Mariner broadcast and you'll hear the artistry of Kevin Cremin's touch, a touch that blended perfectly with Dave's approach to calling the game. Dave wanted his listeners to feel as if they were at the park and was keenly aware that Kevin produced the game with the same result in mind. He set the standard for mixing the call of the game from the booth with the sounds of the game from the stadium below.

Where other broadcasts were dry and often sterile, Cremin's mix always had the crowd piped in, often from more than one location creating a genuine ballpark ambience. The occasional heckler could be heard along with the umpire's booming call (especially when it was Durwood Merrill's), Rick "The Peanut Man" Kaminski and, of course, the crack of the bat. When Nolan Ryan pitched, the "pop" of his fastball hitting the catcher's glove was alive in the listener's ear.

It began with Cremin's choice for Dave's microphone and the sound he got on his voice. It extended to the subtle balance of that sound and those in the park. Perhaps it was a result of Kevin's time playing banjo in a bluegrass band, but he mixed the sounds of the game like an orchestra, with each section playing its part.

Cremin's memories of Dave are, understandably, heartfelt and remained undiminished by time. One of his favorites: Dave's penchant for white shoes. The Niehaus fondness for incredibly loud blazers is well-chronicled by writer-broadcaster Ken Levine, most notably Dave's Fourth of July, red-white-and-blue model. It's the white shoes that Kevin remembers. Dave loved 'em. They came into fashion for Dave's generation in the early- to mid-1970s and he could have been the poster boy.

As it happened, Kevin's stamping grounds of Kansas City became Dave's chosen spot to replenish his supply of alabaster footwear. Specifically, Bob Jones Shoes was the place Dave had to visit every time the Royals were on the away schedule. Right up there with barbecue, the white shoes were a staple of each of those trips. His constant adornment in those shoes was only part of the reason for the repeated restocking he required. He had an equal penchant for losing them before he got home. Ask anyone who ever drove him home from the airport after a team flight back to Seattle.

Dave never checked those shoes with his luggage, preferring to carry the precious cargo onboard where they were safely stowed in an overhead bin. There they would all-too-often remain until an Alaska Airlines crew member would discover them, probably right about the moment Dave would be in the passenger seat of the car, headed across one of the floating bridges over Lake Washington, and suddenly blurting out, "%Y**%!, I left my shoes on the plane."

To this day, Kevin supposes there are still a few airline pilots sporting a pair of those size 10 white shoes and never suspecting they have, quite literally, followed in the footsteps of a Hall of Famer.

The lineup had been penciled in for some terrific years of broadcasting baseball in Seattle to come: Dave Niehaus, Rick Rizzs and Kevin Cremin. Mr. Niehaus had his partner and his producer and was genuinely in his prime. Their inaugural campaign together began the following February.

When the spring of 1983 arrived and Rick Rizzs began his first Cactus League season with the Seattle Mariners, one of the first games found him and Dave in Mesa, Arizona at old Hohokam Park to broadcast the game between the Mariners and the Cubs. There they encountered legendary Chicago baseball broadcaster Jack Brickhouse.

When Rick was a mere twelve years old, he had written to Brickhouse and told him of his admiration for his work. He also told him someday he'd like to follow in his footsteps and become a big-league broadcaster, too. Being the kind of man he was, Brickhouse answered that letter with his thanks, plus his advice to go to school, get an education and see where his dreams led him—as Rick described it to me, "all the things you'd tell a twelve-year-old."

Brickhouse could not have known the twelve-year-old had kept that letter, earned his education and never abandoned his dream. The young Chicago Southsider, in fact, became a big-league baseball announcer.

Spotting Brickhouse that day in Mesa, Rick turned to Dave and said, "My goodness, that's Jack Brickhouse, my hero, the guy I grew up listening to."

Dave's simple reply was "Go tell him hello." He paused and continued, "He's your guy, you gotta say hello."

Dave knew from his own experience what that moment was like, what it meant to introduce yourself to your childhood idol no longer as a fan, but as a peer. He knew what that moment means to every broadcaster who ever had the privilege, and he wanted his young protégé to experience the very same thrill of a lifetime. When Rick returned from his rite of passage, Dave simply smiled and, in but a few words, spoke volumes. "Pretty, cool, huh?"

Dave had been there. He'd felt the rush of emotions that comes with an introduction to your hero. For Dave Niehaus, that day had come in February of 1970 in Arizona. His man, Harry Caray, was about to begin a one-year stint with the Oakland Athletics of the American League when the two men met before a spring training game.

J Michael recalls, "I can still remember Dave, every time he saw Harry—the Noose would light up like a Christmas tree, ear-to-ear grin, the full whiskey chuckle, exuberant greetings to Caray . . . He was a life-sized caricature of himself, a horse's ass, even, at times, but he was an American original and pretty much always fun to be around."

Very few of us get to live out the childhood dreams our heroes inspired in us, much less get to meet them. Even fewer get to meet them on equal footing in the very arena in which those dreams took place. We dreamed of meeting those larger-than-life figures we revered knowing full well it was possible only in those dreams. But it's also possible for those dreams to come true. There are few professions in which it is as possible as it is in baseball broadcasting, still a relatively confined community. Stay with it long enough, survive the vagaries of the business and get a break—and there will come that moment when you'll encounter the very guy whose voice inspired you to find your own.

Things had settled into place in the Mariner broadcast booth, but the instability in the organization continued unabated.

The tumult that characterized the early years of the Mariner franchise would sting Dave once again early in the 1983 season. On June 25, Dave and the fans who had come to revere Rene Lachemann and who were so willing to ride out the growing pains with him, woke to the news that he had been fired. Del Crandall, his successor, lasted only until September of 1984, when Chuck Cottier became the team's third pilot in a sixteen-month span.

There were many shameful things about the dismissal of Rene Lachemann. Among the most painful was his being deprived of the chance to manage what Dave Niehaus christened "The Class of '84." The "hope that sprang eternal" among Mariner fans was, at that time, the prospect of a bumper crop of young talent rising to the big-league level.

Left-handed pitcher Mark Langston joined right-hander Mike Moore. Jack Perconte at second, Spike Owen at short and Jim Presley at third solidified a new and exciting young infield. Harold Reynolds, the heir-apparent at second, merited late-season call-ups in '83 and '84, but after cracking the lineup became the only player other than Rickey Henderson to lead the American League in stolen bases during the 1980s.

Nowhere was the impact felt more both on the field and off than at first base. Arizona State University produced a host of major league ballplayers over the years. Among the brightest lights of all was Alvin Davis. A smooth swinging left-hand hitter, Davis burst onto the scene like no Mariner before him. (Nor, after, until the arrival of Ken Griffey Jr.) He led the team offensively, anchored the right side of the infield with solid, steady defense and was named 1984 American League Rookie of the Year.

His impact on the team and the fans was immediate and dramatic. Alvin became the unquestioned leader in the clubhouse and in the community. Davis won the hearts of the Mariner faithful with his engaging and ever-present smile serving to constantly remind us how much he loved to play. He was a consummate gentleman who carried himself with grace and dignity without the slightest hint of swagger. Alvin didn't need swagger; he was the real deal. Ultimately, he became known by the sobriquet bestowed on him by none other than Dave Niehaus. Alvin Davis was "Mr. Mariner."

For the next eight years, Davis was the M's champion and in 1997 became the first player inducted into the Mariner Hall of Fame. He was followed in 2000 by Dave Niehaus, who was elected in advance of Jay Buhner (2004), Edgar Martinez (2007), Randy Johnson and Dan Wilson (2012) and Ken Griffey Jr. (2013)

When asked in 1997 to name his favorite Mariner ever, Dave Niehaus responded, "Alvin Davis by far. He was such a gentleman. But let's not kid ourselves; when Junior arrived on the scene in '89, he was the man who turned the franchise around...He was the guy with his charisma, with that smile, with that hat. He was the first big star that we had here. It was Alvin Davis' records he was breaking...Alvin Davis was so nice and he was the first great player we had here."

Still, all the promise and potential did not keep manager Del Crandall in Seattle through the 1984 season. The job fell to coach Chuck Cottier, who guided the club to a 15–12 finish and was given the reins again the following year. "Chuckles" was a fiery skipper who, like all the Mariner managers, quickly recognized Dave as a solid baseball man, a guy who loved and respected the game, an interviewer who could also be their confidant. Dave loved the managers right back. They were men who had given a lifetime to the game and considered their job the best one in the world. In short, they were just like Dave.

Chuck had indeed spent a lifetime in the game. A delightful man with a trove of tales about his baseball experiences, he was signed by the Baltimore Orioles in 1954 as an amateur free agent. He began his minor-league career with a year with Americus-Cordele in the Georgia-Florida League and a year in the Evangeline League at New Iberia, Lousiana, home of McIlhenny Tabasco and a regional delight called Pickapeppa Sauce.

Cottier went on to play all or part of ten seasons in the big leagues and had a brief stint with the Seattle Rainiers in their final PCL season. He played, coached, managed, and scouted for more than a dozen major-league clubs and was a scout for the Washington Nationals. He is one of the dwindling number who remember baseball as it was once played. He respects the game and understands the respect that is earned in kind by playing it the right way.

Dave Niehaus always loved recounting the story of Cottier's explosion at Yankee Stadium one Sunday afternoon. Chuck's tirade ended with him uprooting first base and flinging it a considerable distance into right field. His record for greatest eruption by a Mariner manager stood for more than a decade. Only the even more explosive Lou Piniella could mount a more memorable on-field tantrum.

As with so many Mariner skippers, a special bond was forged between Cottier and Niehaus, a friendship that truly endured. They sat together on the team plane—front row with the middle seat open.

"He was always great with me," Cottier said of Niehaus. "He loved the game and his friendship meant so much to me. So often we'd have lunch together hours before the game and talk about baseball and family." Chuck admired his work just as the fans did. "He could paint such a beautiful picture of a baseball game. Even if we were losing, you still wanted to listen to the game."

For Dave, Cottier's firing—a mere 217 games later—once again meant parting ways with someone he'd grown to call a friend. His one consolation: this latest turn of the managerial carousel led to a reunion with one of his dearest pals and one of the best managers he'd ever seen. When Dave's pregame interview welcomed new skipper Dick Williams to Seattle, twenty-one games into the 1986 season, they could not have imagined twenty-two summers later they'd be standing together on the stage at Cooperstown.

Dave described Williams as, "one of my best friends. I was with Dick in two places. I was with him when he was with the California Angels and

I was with him here with the Mariners. I may have had a little bit to do with his hiring. George Argyros called me and wanted to know my opinion of Dick Williams and I told him. Dick was out there, a tough no-nonsense type of guy. And let's not forget, until (Jim) Lefebvre got here, Dick had the best record we'd ever had."

Prophetically enough, in that same interview, Dave continued, "I think he should be in the Baseball Hall of Fame…probably will be in the Baseball Hall of Fame as a manager. But, probably, in today's world, he couldn't handle these kids."

Coach Ozzie Virgil, Dave Niehaus and manager Dick Williams "all dressed up" for a 1988 spring training gag.

He could handle them—but he could barely tolerate them.

Williams was "old-school," genuinely no-fooling-around old school. Off the field he was charming and fun to be around. He was one hell of a guy to drink with and tell baseball stories. He was also an old-fashioned gentleman. Marilyn Niehaus recalls being in the back seat of a car with her husband when Dick got in the front. Unaware of her presence, he began to vent his frustrations about his ball club in some seriously salty language. When he turned and saw Marilyn, he was visibly embarrassed. He not only apologized on the spot, but Marilyn will tell you, as she told me, that he apologized repeatedly over the next twenty years. No matter how many times she forgave him, he always regretted his transgression.

The game was changing in the 1980s, and Williams' style didn't resonate with the young players in his charge. Despite an uptick in their performance, the Mariners played less than .400 baseball under him. In less than two seasons, the two old friends worked their final game together. Dave Niehaus had seen some bad baseball and some bad times during his Mariner tenure, but the firing of Dick Williams was one of the more bitter episodes. Niehaus knew how good Williams was, and knew this man who had managed Oakland to successive World Series titles deserved better.

It seemed as though Dave was forever condemned to broadcast losing baseball. A full decade into its existence, the team had yet to even reach .500. Yet he never brought anything to the park but a love for the game and a passion for bringing it to the fans. His long wait was nearing its end. Just as Williams was leaving, some new blood was arriving.

Mariner faithful may recall July 21, 1988, as a landmark day for the franchise. A hometown boy, Ingraham High School's Ken Phelps, had put up some solid numbers. They were solid enough to attract the attention of the New York Yankees, in desperate need of a left-handed power hitter. In perhaps their best trade of the entire decade, the M's shipped Phelps to Gotham for a trio of players. One of them was a Louisville-born, Texas-raised outfielder named Jay Buhner.

Buhner proved to be one of the most rock-solid players ever to wear the Seattle uniform. He became a symbol of baseball in the community and eventually one of Dave's partners on the television side of the broadcast booth. Most importantly, from day one, he brought a new attitude to both the field and the clubhouse.

Fred Brack, long-time baseball writer, recalls Jay Buhner's first game with the Mariners. "After the game, I'm in the clubhouse for interviews and here's this pale white body, bony but obviously fit and strong, clad only in white briefs...walking around the clubhouse, saying to all his teammates, 'We gotta be tougher out there, we gotta be tougher.'"

Brack remembers the guts it took for a rookie, on day one, not only to exhort his teammates, but to challenge them, holding them to a personal standard and one he apparently felt was lacking. There was no arrogance about it. It was sheer earnestness.

"You simply can't give Jay Buhner too much credit for what he brought to the ball club," Brack said. "All the guys who came after Buhner, who came later, they had to be like Buhner. They had to be tough—Buhner tough."

Jay Buhner embodied the spirit that would later be enshrined in the slogan, "Refuse to lose." He simply would not tolerate anything less than the best effort from every man in that clubhouse. He would not tolerate losing and that spirit proved infectious. As important as Griffey's talent was to turning around Mariner fortunes, Buhner's grit was as key an ingredient as any in the Mariner recipe for success. It was no surprise Buhner became one of Dave's favorites.

"The way he played that carom off the right-field wall in the King-dome—he would nail guys going to second base and he'd nail guys going from first to third," Dave said. "He played that like a Stradivarius, those bounces that would come off the wall out there whether they were high, or in the middle, or low. I've never seen anybody play the outfield like that, except maybe Joe Rudi in Oakland. Jay was a master. It was like going to a fronton to watch jai alai. He was unbelievable out there."

Jay Buhner's arrival in 1988, the call-up of Edgar Martinez in 1990, and Randy Johnson's trade to the Pacific Northwest each provided the Mariners with a cornerstone on which to finally build a winning ball club. Their heart and soul arrived in 1989.

Dave's recollections said it all: "Through all that time, the arrival of Ken Griffey Jr. in 1989 was probably the biggest moment in Mariner history. That's really when things began to turn around. Some people say it was 1995, but I don't agree. It was 1989, with the arrival of Junior. That was when Seattle really became, I think, a focal point of baseball. Even though we didn't start to win until 1991, we had one of the great stars in baseball. I've done a lot of games—over five-thousand games—and Junior is still the greatest athlete that I've ever had the opportunity to describe."

Like the thread that stitches a baseball together, there are threads that stitch together a baseball life. In the summer of 1956, Dave Niehaus spent a few days in Evansville with his cousin Ron. They renewed their old summer ritual and spent an evening at Bosse Field watching the Three-I League pennant-winning Braves play ball. There was no earthly way Dave could have known the pivotal role the Braves' nineteen-year-old catcher that evening, Roger Jongewaard, would play in his life.

Fast-forward to 1988, when the Seattle Mariners had the first pick in the draft. Owner George Argyros wanted pitcher Mike Harkey, believing his college experience would place him on the big club's roster sooner than later. Orange County-based Argyros knew about Cal State-Fullerton's Harkey, who played just eighteen miles from George's Arnel Development offices in Costa Mesa. Roger Jongewaard was now a scout for Seattle, and he thought his man was the right choice. He held firm against all objections and ended up getting his way. His man was Ken Griffey Jr.

It was Jongewaard who was at Junior's home in Cincinnati the night he was drafted. His tenacity changed the fate of baseball in Seattle and the face of the game.

As fans in Seattle may recall, Griffey's debut was a special one. On the road at Oakland-Alameda County Coliseum, the rookie's first at-bat yielded a ringing double off Dave Stewart. His maiden Mariner voyage at home was even better—first at-bat, first pitch. Dave was ready for him.

Here he is, Ken Griffey Jr. at the age of nineteen and listen to the ovation. Ken Griffey Jr. trying to give his father a birthday present today because Senior is thirty-nine years of age. So, here comes the wind-up and the pitch on the way to Junior…
AND IT'S SWUNG ON AND BELTED DEEP TO LEFT FIELD…KITTLE TO THE TRACK, THE WALL—FLY AWAY! WELCOME TO SEATTLE KEN GRIFFEY JR.! MY OH MY!

On the first pitch thrown to him from Eric King, we are tied at one. Wow, electricity here at the Kingdome and a standing ovation, and they want The Kid to come out! It was a fastball on the outside corner and Griffey hit a rocket—a line drive over the wall.

This same year brought yet another skipper to the helm of the good ship Mariner. Jim Lefebvre's youthful enthusiasm seemed a good fit for the young and talented team. He would, during his tenure, finally bring a winning record to the franchise.

The door was revolving again in the owner's box as well. Argyros wearied of the public nature of being a baseball owner and the struggle to build a winner within the confines of his business model. Ever-escalating salaries and ever-present public relations battles took their toll.

Argyros never fielded a winning team nor did he ever win the hearts of Seattle fans. He was, however, responsible for a number of accomplishments that showed his heart was often in the right place.

It was his suggestion that the Mariners' Kingdome lease include a special codicil that came to be known as the 120-day clause. This clause stipulated that any owner of the Seattle Mariners who put the team up for sale would be required to allow 120 days for a local buyer to be found. Just a few years later, the clause kept big-league baseball from leaving Seattle a second time.

It would be patently unfair to George Argyros to hold him accountable for the shortcomings of his ownership without crediting him for some of his noteworthy accomplishments as well.

Argyros was the chief advocate for expanding baseball's pension plan to non-players, including clubhouse and front-office employees. He led the way in establishing a college scholarship fund for players who were drafted out of high school and chose to forego further studies to pursue a major league career. In 1987, he oversaw the first-ever drug test administered to a major-leaguer, one in his own organization.

One of his greatest accomplishments was the Boeing Junior Mariner baseball field project.

In 1985, George Argyros assigned Mariner executive Bill Knudsen to oversee a new project. Knudsen set up meetings with T.A. Wilson and Stan Little of the then Seattle-based Boeing Company at which he pledged to convert AirCal's entire fleet to Boeing jet airliners in exchange for Boeing's promise to spend $1 million each year to build Little League fields in and around Seattle. The first Boeing Junior Mariner field was built in Carnation, Washington. Thousands of area children have since been afforded the opportunity to play at first-rate facilities.

Still, the contentious relationship between Argyros and the fans continued to deteriorate. For more than two years, the specter of the franchise

Mariner broadcasters Joe Simpson, Rick Rizzs, Kevin Cremin and Dave Niehaus, 1988.

moving had played out in the press on an almost daily basis. Prior to the 1987 season, three different groups began maneuvering for the opportunity to buy the franchise. Potential owners had surfaced in Miami, Tampa Bay, and New Jersey and they were serious.

Among their guarantees: a team attendance of two million fans a season for ten years at baseball's average ticket price, $10 million to pay legal fees should litigation result, $10 million for new ballplayers should no litigation result, and a stadium lease "as good or better than any in baseball." It was becoming increasingly clear that somebody was going to pay George Argyros a lot more than the $13.1 million he had originally shelled out to own the Mariners.

Through it all, Dave remained confident that Seattle was a baseball town, but the very real possibility of uprooting his family again weighed on him. Marilyn was happy in Seattle and had raised their children there. Those children had been in the Northwest for over a decade, gone to school there, made friends and a life there. Yet, the entire Niehaus family knew the simple truth: if the team moved, Dave would have no choice but to move with them or to another market.

Fortunately for Dave, and for all Seattle baseball fans, somebody at the top was looking out for them. On September 8, 1988, A. Bartlett Giamatti, president of the National League, was unanimously elected to succeed Peter Ueberroth as baseball's commissioner.

The former Yale president was an eloquent and thoughtful man, deeply committed to the game. Included in that perspective was the need for social justice, specifically as it applied to the long-ignored problem of the lack of minority hiring. Be it managers, coaches, scouts or front-office executives, Giamatti was determined to see that baseball not only reflected society at large, but also recognized that a sport so long enriched by players of color should be more inclusive of people of color.

He was also a champion of the fan and, as such, committed to the notion that franchises were immensely valuable to the communities they served. In a view similar to the one embraced by the Seattle Mariners RBI Club, he believed that value to be both tangible and intangible. He believed that baseball had an obligation to its fans and every effort should be taken to maintain the stability of those franchises.

When Giamatti took office on April 1, 1989, his commitment to that stability was of consequence as serious negotiations to sell the Mariners began. A group headed by Jeff Smulyan, head of Emmis Broadcasting Corporation, and Michael Browning, president of Browning investments, a real-estate company, reached an agreement in principle with George Argyros. The agreement stipulated that, for now, the Mariners were staying in Seattle. It, of course, meant the Niehaus family was staying as well.

Mariner fans were aware that until the agreement was finalized they had reason for concern. On September 1, Bart Giamatti died of a heart attack, the only commissioner to die in office other than Kenesaw Mountain Landis. Dave was especially saddened by this loss. Giamatti was his kind of guy, literate and well-spoken and a man whose writings Dave found genuinely moving.

The ascension of his deputy, Fay Vincent, to the post of commissioner made certain the commitment to Giamatti's ideas would endure. On September 14, the owners met in Milwaukee and approved the sale.

The tandem of Jeff Smulyan and new team president, Gary Kaseff, was an early hit in the Northwest and the two seemed to grasp the show-business side of the game. Their promotional team, led by executives Stuart Layne and Bill Knudsen, came up with some creative ways to get fans back in the Kingdome. Among those ideas was baseball's only "Guaranteed No-Hitter Night."

Nolan Ryan had thrown his record sixth no-hitter Monday night, June 11, 1990, in Oakland. His subsequent start was on Saturday, June 16, in the Kingdome against the Mariners' Matt Young. Niehaus had broadcast Ryan's first no-hitter for the Angels in 1973.

When informed of the upcoming promotion, Dave Niehaus said, "I didn't know what they were talking about. But it's show business, you know. We're in show business. I wouldn't go out on a limb to predict a no-hitter, but I know every time Nolan Ryan goes out to the mound, there's that possibility."

Neither Ryan nor Young pitched a no-hitter (Young did throw a three-hit, 5–0 shutout), but fans attending the game were able to use their ticket stubs for a $4.50 general admission seat for a game with the California Angels on July 11.

In truth, Ryan's recent feat was not the only catalyst for the unusual promotion. The event came on the heels of the first no-hitter in Mariner history only two weeks earlier. Randy Johnson tossed the gem against the Detroit Tigers on June 2, and the night proved to be one of the most electric in Kingdome history. The game made every Top Ten list Dave ever compiled. Those lucky enough to be listening remember hearing this:

Randy Johnson…a man all alone with himself, but not all alone here as twenty-four thousand incredibly rabid Mariner fans are looking for that final strike that will set Mariner history. Here comes the lefthander's wind, the 0–2 pitch on the way…STRIKE! IT'S OVER! HE HAS DONE IT…HIGH FASTBALL, RANDY JOHNSON BEING MOBBED BY SCOTT BRADLEY, DOWN TO GREET HIM AND THE ENTIRE MARINER TEAM!

Here on the second of June, it ends at 9:51 Pacific Daylight Time. Randy Johnson with the first Mariner no-hitter in history AND THEY ARE GOING CRAZY…everybody saluting the tallest man to ever put on a uniform in the history of baseball. Randy Johnson has done it, he has no-hit the Detroit Tigers tonight, 2–0. MY OH MY!

Fans might have noticed Dave's small homage to Vin Scully's call of the September 9, 1965, Sandy Koufax perfecto by inserting the precise time of the final pitch. It was much like Coltrane inserting a Johnny Hodges riff into a solo.

Dave was now in his fourteenth year in the booth in Seattle and had truly become a fixture—beloved by both those to whom he broadcast and those about whom he broadcast. His special relationship with the Mariner players and players throughout the league was never more in evidence than on June 22, 1990. The night before, on the team flight to Arlington, Dave had uncharacteristically walked to the back of the plane. There sat Griffey, Buhner, Martinez and Mariner catcher Dave Valle. Valle looked up and wondered what could bring Niehaus to the back of the plane. It was Valle's attention the Veteran Spieler wanted.

He said, "Hey, Val, you know Nolan Ryan's pitching tomorrow night?"

"Yeah," Valle answered. "Why?"

With an impish grin, Niehaus said, "Because he's never struck you out."

Valle, knowing the world's biggest jinx had just been laid on him, told Niehaus to get back to the front of the plane and get there now. But Niehaus knew what he was doing.

The next night at the old ballpark in Arlington, Valle came to the plate against Ryan and rifled a sharp single to left. It's worth remembering that the previous season Ryan had hit Valle twice in one game. (That would have put a lot of guys on the disabled list.) So, you can bet Ryan was steamed— Valle was a tough customer and not a man who would give in.

The next at-bat against Ryan came in the fifth inning and "The Express" quickly ran the count to 0–2, at which point Valle suddenly remembered the Broadcaster's visit on the plane the night before. Sure enough, Nolan whistled a third strike past the M's backstop. Valle paused on the way to the dugout and looked up at the booth, arms outstretched, saying, "Are you happy now?"

Niehaus was doubled over with laughter. He would never delight in the misfortune of a Mariner, especially such a good man as Dave Valle. But in the long, wearying parade of the baseball season, these practical jokes are rare and, frankly, to be treasured among comrades.

The next day, Valle came into the clubhouse to find a plain paper sack on the chair in front of his locker. He opened the bag and found a baseball inside. It was inscribed with the words "To Dave, 'Gotcha.' Welcome to the club—#5,167 and #5,169—Nolan Ryan." A beaming Niehaus stood on the other side of the locker room. Dave Niehaus was so respected that he got Nolan Ryan to autograph that ball and bring the caper to an ending all three would cherish. Valle could only look across the locker room and grin back.

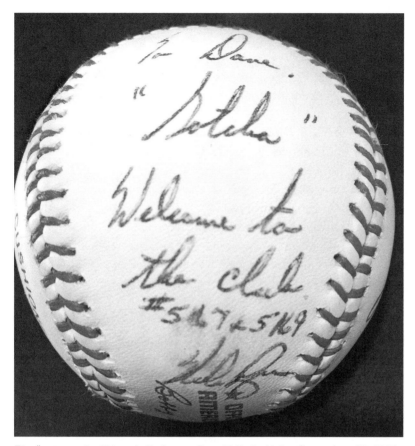

The "autographed" baseball given to Dave Valle by Nolan Ryan, June 23, 1990.

A scant three years later at the Kingdome on September 22, 1993, Dave Niehaus called the final pitch of Ryan's career. The incredibly game Ryan, after tearing a muscle in his arm while facing Dave Magadan, bravely threw one more toss. It was clocked at ninety-eight miles per hour

Dave had a great relationship with most of the players, but his relationship with Ken Griffey Jr. was special. Junior's admiration for Dave was no secret, and his respect for him always evident. One of Dave's favorite stories involved a night in Detroit.

"We're in Tiger Stadium; the deepest centerfield in baseball," Dave recalled, "Junior is in right-center and a left-handed batter slices the ball into left-center field and, man, Griffey is flying over there and he gets his glove on the ball and the ball goes off his glove. Just a tremendous effort, and I said, 'Junior usually makes that catch.' So we go to New York and the next afternoon he yells at me, 'Hey, Niehaus! My people tell me you said I should have made that catch last night in Detroit.' I said, 'Your people tell you wrong.' He said, 'What did you say?' I said, 'I said you *usually* make that catch.' He got a grin on his face and said, 'Yeah, I usually do, don't I?'"

It was Junior who affectionately labeled Dave's white loafers his "prom shoes."

Still, 1990 was the fourteenth consecutive losing season for the Mariners. There would not be a fifteenth.

In 1991, Jim Lefebvre accomplished something no other Mariner manager had accomplished: he finished a season with a winning record—83 wins, 79 losses. The euphoria was short-lived, thanks to the pall cast by owner Jeff Smulyan's announcement in November that he would be selling the team. He was, in fact, strongly considering moving the team to the Tampa–St. Petersburg area. It was no secret the Florida market was hungry for a team and with local officials offering strong support, Smulyan knew he could make it work.

Curiously enough, despite all of the heat he had taken, both deserved and undeserved, George Argyros had one final chapter to write in his Seattle saga. With the announcement, Smulyan had triggered the 120-day clause. Much to his surprise and most of Seattle's, there was a hero waiting in the wings.

U. S. Senator Slade Gorton of Washington was part of the group seeking to find a local buyer. He found one, sort-of. Nintendo of America was headquartered in Redmond, across Lake Washington from Seattle. Gorton approached Nintendo about the possibility of finding a Japanese investor. Commissioner Fay Vincent and a number of owners got wind of the idea and strongly opposed it, going so far as to refuse to sanction the sale to a foreign-born owner.

Nintendo President Hiroshi Yamauchi, a brilliant businessman who transformed Nintendo into the video game giant we know today, stepped forward. Expressing his gratitude to the United States and to the Pacific Northwest, he generously offered to buy the team and keep it in Seattle. He teamed up with local cell-phone magnates and Microsoft executives to create a new and lasting ownership group. Baseball was in Seattle to stay. The new owners also made another thing clear: Dave Niehaus was in Seattle to stay as well.

The new ownership was not the only cause for celebration in the Niehaus home that winter. Dave's son, Andy, and his wife welcomed the newest member of the clan on January 31, 1992. Dave and Marilyn's first grandchild was a boy, Zachary. Dave's illustrious resume now included one of his proudest appellations: grandfather.

The new ownership's maiden voyage was not without its miscalculations. Despite his achievement and his popularity with the fans, Manager Jim Lefebvre was let go before the 1992 season and replaced with long-time Mariner coach Bill Plummer. The results were not pretty as the team went 64–98. The enormous step backward taken by the club made for some genuine frustration among the fans who had supported the team and Lefebvre, only to see the revolving door in the manager's office spin once again, with all-too-predictable results. Dave was justifiably exasperated, too. Yet his work never suffered for it.

When you visited him in the booth, he could be caustic and devilishly dark-humored between pitches when the mic was off. What went out over the airwaves was nothing but his best, nothing but his love for the game and his undying hopes for the franchise. In fact, late in that frustrating 1992 campaign, he gave us what remains one his most entertaining calls ever. Randy "The Big Unit" Johnson was "mowin' 'em down" that day at the Dome and Dave was loving it. When RJ sealed the shutout with his 288th strikeout of the year, Dave treated us all to this:

He is one strike away from the shutout, his seventh consecutive victory, his 288th strikeout of the year and his eleventh of the night. And everybody is up pulling for the Big Unit to do it, with his brand, with his "K." One-two pitch on the way—SWING AND A MISS, AND IT'S OVER! And he did it, he put it right on the rump of the ol' steer and burned 'er right in there!

In 1992, Mariner radio fans had to endure another bit of heartbreak. Dave's sidekick of nearly a decade, Rick Rizzs, had been offered the job of lead announcer for the Detroit Tigers broadcast team. Rick was a Chicago boy raised on the South Side and his roots were in that region. Leaving Seattle was not in Rick's plans, but the overwhelming consideration was that he had been chosen to replace a legend.

Hall of Famer Ernie Harwell had been inexplicably forced out by the Tigers' front office, and it was quite an honor to be chosen to fill Harwell's considerable shoes. It also was a testament to Rick's courage and belief in his ability that he took on such a task. Harwell's controversial ouster meant that Rick was walking into a hornet's nest, a possible no-win situation.

Niehaus was genuinely proud of his big-league protégé and, of course, thrilled to see Rick get such an opportunity, even if it meant having to part ways.

"I'm very happy for Rick, just elated," he said. "He'll do a heck of a job. He's very good mechanically on plays, but he's probably 180 degrees different than Ernie and Paul (Carey), in that he's a very excitable young man, and they're very low key. So the fans there will get a different perspective as far as, 'There's a deep fly ball up against the wall!' He'll make it really come alive for them. He and I are both quite that way. As I've said before, I know it's going to be a tough situation for whomever got that job, but he'll do a good job. I just hope the fans are fair with him. He'll put some zip in the broadcasts."

Rick wasn't the only one leaving the nest. Former Mariner outfielder Joe Simpson (a.k.a. Mr. Jello) had just wrapped up another year working primarily television with Dave. He was a delightful and entertaining man who brought a great sense of humor to his work. His promise had not gone unnoticed. On January 23, the announcement came that Superstation WTBS tapped him to become the newest member of their Atlanta Braves broadcast team. He found a genuine niche there and became a fixture on Braves TV.

Dave Niehaus was always there to help his colleagues, see them on to greater success. His willingness to create opportunities for deserving talent extended to young broadcasters as well. Northwest sports radio host, Jeff "The Fish" Aaron, had moved to Seattle in 1992 to work for KIRO Radio, the Mariners' flagship station.

"I had the opportunity to interview Johnny Vander Meer," Jeff told me, "the only man to have thrown back-to-back no-hitters. It was on the anniversary of them...it was a good interview and I was quite proud of it. Then suddenly this voice, like the voice of God, comes through the headphones and it's Dave Niehaus and he says, 'You know, son, we'd like to use that interview on the pre-game show.' I had no idea that board was wired to the board at the Kingdome and Dave Niehaus could hear every word I was saying...and his voice scared the bejesus out of me...they played it on the Saturday magazine show and it opened up a lot of doors for me."

Years later, when Jeff left KIRO before moving on to KJR in Seattle, it was Dave Niehaus who called him to wish him well and to remind him that every door closing leads to another one opening.

That egalitarian spirit extended to all of his colleagues. Mike Gastineau recalls his early days in Seattle producing a sports show for rival station KJR.

"The thing I remember about Dave," Mike told me, "was he treated me like I was a big-timer from day one. He didn't have any airs about me being a producer at a rival station. He was gracious. You knew in your heart 'I'm not an equal, I'm kind of a peer, I'm in the same business,' but he treated you like you were. That's part of what made him such a charming guy. I never heard him go after anyone or slash anyone."

Like so many others, Mike, too, thinks these qualities reflect Dave's Indiana roots.

"I think it's the Midwestern upbringing," he continued. "I think Dave was just brought up that way to be a polite and charming individual, a guy who wasn't putting on act, that was just how he was raised, how we was brought up. He tried to see the good in people and he tried to see the truth in people, too—that was a good combination."

Gastineau further reflected on a familiar note sounded by so many that knew Dave and worked with him—how genuine Niehaus was.

"He was the same guy on the air as off the air," Mike recalled. "A lot of guys in broadcasting end up with two personas. Dave was a big influence on me. He showed you can be a pretty big star in this business, and you don't have to be 'broadcaster guy' when you're on the air and somebody completely different off the air."

"If Dave had been a banker, he still would have been a wonderful guy to sit at a ballgame with because of what he was, he was such a great storyteller. He had that ability—and it's tough man, it's just an innate thing and you've either got this or you don't—that ability to tell a story within the pace of a baseball game and knowing when to begin a story and when not to begin a story. If you sense something's about to happen in a game, you don't want to be telling some goofy story that has nothing to do with anything."

"But he had that great sense and that flow of knowing maybe when a game was in a little bit of a dull patch that you could tell a fun story and string it out over ten or twelve or fourteen pitches or even a couple innings."

As is true of so many of Niehaus' listeners, Gastineau had his own favorite memory.

"I remember they're playing St. Louis at St. Louis and the stadium's right there on the river and there's an air show going on out over the river with all these old bi-planes and World War II aircraft. And Dave's talking about the planes as he's calling the action 'Yes, think that's an old B-29," as it flew over and you could hear them. Just effortlessly—talking about what was going on the field and at the same time drawing you into what everybody there was experiencing with the planes flying over.

"And he was really good at that—at just understanding that the way a game unfolds that it's necessary to have some entertainment in there. It was Dave's world and here's what Dave finds interesting—whether it was about a player from some little town or what's going on at the ballpark.

"That's what happens when you have the confidence and the belief that you are entertaining."

Long-time Northwest radio host Dave "The Groz" Grosby, Gastineau's former co-host of the legendary Seattle sports talk show "Groz and Gas" on KJR radio, echoes Mike's sentiments. He recalled to me how Niehaus' special ability to weave the game together with the backdrop against which it was played made Grosby part of the congregation.

"My first season here was in 1991 and the Mariners had no cable package. So, the first year I was here, I went to as many games as I could, so I didn't get to listen to Dave all that much in the first year.

"But I'll never forget, the second year, spring training, I was driving up from Portland and the Mariners were playing their final exhibition game in Las Vegas. It's the first inning and Randy Johnson throws a 1-2-3 inning, I mean nothing happened, nothing at all. I think he had one strikeout out of the three outs, but Niehaus was *singing a song!*

"I mean it was like all of a sudden I heard him for the first time. I thought, Oh my god, listen to this guy—the tenor of his voice, using his voice, going up and down, drawing you in, telling a story about this, an absolute nothing half-inning was like poetry. And all of a sudden I got it! I'm thinking, holy goodness, I understand why this guy's so good all the time. I didn't believe that people really knew how good he was."

Grosby would, shortly thereafter, be introduced to Dave and learn what so many had learned.

"As it turned out, you know Dave, he loved a good joke, and loved to laugh—so it took about thirty seconds to be a friend...he laughed at his own jokes as hard as anything and with the right person that is the single most endearing quality you can possibly have...the right person laughing at their own jokes...it's perfection, it's artistry. How could you not want to be around this guy?"

Like Aaron, Gastineau and Grosby, a host of others would have their opportunity to experience the joy of entering Dave's world.

I can tell you first-hand how gracious Dave Niehaus could be to those

Dave in the Diablo Stadium radio booth, 1990.

who worked with him, and how that spirit infused the people around him. In the mid-1980s, I won a contest sponsored by the Mariners and KIRO Radio. The prize was the opportunity to call an inning of Mariner baseball on the radio alongside Dave Niehaus.

For one glorious inning of completely uneventful baseball, I was Dave's sidekick as Juan Guzman and the Texas Rangers squared off against the M's at the Kingdome. There are few moments in my life I would give more to re-live than that one. It was, quite literally, the thrill of a lifetime.

Prior to the game, Kevin Cremin told me that he and Dave were headed for the press dining room to eat. I told them I would find something to eat and join them later.

"You're not coming with us?" Kevin asked.

"Well, I can't," I replied, "that's for the pros, the big-leaguers."

"Well," Cremin said, "today you are a big-leaguer."

I looked over at Dave. He had the kindest look on his face. With a warm smile, he nodded and said, "He's right, you know."

Rick Rizzs asked me to do the post-game show and we had more than a few laughs as we went through the night's results around the major leagues. I could not have been made to feel more welcome or more worthy.

It was as true in the broadcast business as it was in the music business. The very best treat the people they work with as though those people were the very best as well. The king and his subject are both most elevated when they stand on common ground.

The departures of Rick Rizzs and Joe Simpson meant more changes in the Mariner broadcast booth. Over the next two years, Dave was about to get two new partners, each of whom became dear friends. For those who felt Mariner baseball was in need of some comic relief, the addition of Ken Levine in 1992 was a welcome choice. Levine was an Emmy-winning writer whose work on *Cheers, M*A*S*H, The Jeffersons,* and *The Simpsons* had garnered well-deserved praise from critics, viewers and industry peers. His delightful and youthful sense of humor seemed to make an immediate impression on Dave.

Few knew, however, that Dave had known Levine for many years, and it was that shared sense of humor that began their relationship. Levine was a student at UCLA when he landed a job as a sports intern at KMPC radio. Dave was, at that time, in his "jack of all trades" period with the station, doing sportscasts, football and basketball pre-game and post-game shows. Among those responsibilities was hosting the "Ask the Manager" show on the Angels pre-game broadcast.

Levine joyously reminisced about it with me.

"Listeners would call a voice-mail machine and leave questions for the manager," he said. "Dave would use the questions and if your name was selected you got Angels tickets. I was also on the campus radio station and, back in those days disc jockeys had names like 'Charlie Tuna,' so I was 'Johnny Lizard'—that was my name. So I'm working the Saturday night shift and I decide to call the Angel hotline and I ask some legitimate question as 'Johnny Lizard from Woodland Hills.' The next morning the Angels are back East and Dave is doing the program live and Dave goes 'and our next question is from Johnny Lizard of Woodland Hills' and the engineer goes 'Johnny Lizard—that's Ken at the sports desk.' And it's about 9:30 in the morning, I'm sleeping soundly and my phone rings and I pick it up and (sleepily) go 'Hello?' And he booms, 'If you think you're getting those #$%^**% tickets, you have another think coming' and then laughs that Niehaus laugh. And I said, 'Dave! Good morning, how are you?' We kind of bonded as a result of that."

Years later, Levine's aspiration to broadcast baseball took a deeper hold on him. He began to take a tape-recorder to games and literally practice.

"I would see Dave from time to time when I was practicing play-by-play. I would go to the upper deck of Dodger Stadium or Anaheim Stadium and when the Mariners would come to town, I'd try to get a press pass and see Dave. He was always encouraging."

Dave was encouraging enough (and Levine persistent enough) that Ken eventually got his entree into the business, calling a year of minor-league baseball for Toronto's farm team in Syracuse and following it up with a two-year stint with the Mets' Double-A team in Tidewater. His work caught the attention of the Baltimore Orioles and it was there he ascended to the big-league booth in 1991.

The job with Baltimore meant that, like Niehaus and Caray and like Rizzs and Brickhouse before him, Levine was reunited with his long-time idol as a fellow member of the profession. It is understandable then, his salient memories of that year include an encounter with Dave Niehaus. He recounted the story with a mix of delight and gratitude.

"We were finishing a road trip with a night game in Kansas City," Ken told me, "and the Mariners were coming into Baltimore to begin a home stand with us the following night. But they had a day game and flew in from Milwaukee. So, as they're busing in from the airport, Dave used to have a transistor radio and listened to the other broadcast. So, he's listening to me, he's listening to the Orioles game. The next night when I see him in the press box, he was effusive with his praise and thought I just sounded great.

"To me that was like...God has paid you a compliment."

Little did either of these gentlemen know what fate had in store for them.

"We kept in touch and I'd see him when we'd play the Mariners," Levine remembered. "So, at the end of the year, the Orioles offered me a three-year contract, but they wanted me to move to Baltimore...I was still making ninety percent of my income as a TV writer. Although it killed me, I had to turn it down. So, I'm back home about a month and Rick Rizzs gets the job replacing Ernie Harwell in Detroit and I get a call at home from Dave asking would I be interested in coming to Seattle. I said, 'Heck, yeah!'"

The Mariners made it official on February 19, with the formal announcement of his hiring.

The new Mariner owners, Jeff Smulyan and Gary Kaseff were in the radio business. I had the pleasure of meeting Smulyan and sharing a couple evenings with him in the owners' box at the Kingdome. I learned first-hand that Jeff understood that being in the baseball business meant you were simultaneously in the entertainment business.

It seems a small thing in retrospect, but one of those nights in the box I spotted Rick "The Peanut Man" Kaminski, legendary for his prowess tossing bags of peanuts right into the hands of his customers from considerable distances with remarkable accuracy. I tried repeatedly to get him to throw a bag to the new owner, but he understandably resisted. Finally, I got Jeff Smulyan to stand next to me, and Rick made one of his patented behind-the-back laser tosses—a sure shot into Smulyan's waiting hands. It was the kind of genuinely human moment, the kind of shared experience as a *fan* that you can never envision sharing with an owner. Neither Rick nor I ever forgot it. Despite all the controversies that would later transpire with Smulyan's exit, I will always remember that moment and always remember him fondly.

Ken Levine was aware of the ownership group's entertainment savvy as well.

"One of the reasons why they hired me," he said, "was because at the time the team was terrible. They wanted the broadcasts to be entertaining."

Make no mistake, Levine's comic skills were certainly part of the equation in the decision to bring him onboard, but his obvious love for the game and his genuine talent for broadcasting were both at the heart of that decision. It didn't take long for his sense of humor to show up in his work.

The tumult surrounding the change of ownership left the TV deal for the new season in limbo. There was still at that time a reluctance in certain markets to increase the number of games, particularly home games, broadcast on television for fear of negatively impacting the live attendance. So, it wasn't until the beginning of the 1992 season that the TV deal was announced and, with it, the selection of Ken Griffey Sr. and Billy Sample as analysts.

Niehaus and Levine introduced Sample to the Mariner faithful on a radio pre-game show. Levine had two specific questions in mind for Sample, but Niehaus went first and asked Sample one of Ken's prepared questions. Dave then followed up with the second query Levine had ready. Sample's brief answer meant Dave quickly tossed it to Levine who had to think fast.

His question: "So, Billy, is it okay to pet on the first date?"

Ken Levine was an immediate hit with Mariner fans and with his sidekick from Indiana. It wasn't long before they were best of pals and seen daily together at local eateries. Levine saw up close the reverence with which Mariner fans treated Dave, how meeting him impacted their lives.

One such chance meeting was at the Rice Paddy, a Chinese restaurant in the Seattle suburb of Bellevue. It had long been one of Dave's favorite haunts because he enjoyed the company of the bartender, Marilyn Fleek. Marilyn was a pro who made it a point to know her customers, which meant Dave would walk in and find his vodka and soda ready and waiting for him before he sat down.

In the early morning hours of May 8, 2014, I was in Seattle-Tacoma International Airport awaiting a flight to Los Angeles. Despite working on only a couple hours of sleep, I couldn't help but notice the man in the Seattle Mariners hat and Mariners shirt. His wife was seated next to him and I moved to the empty chair on the other side. I inquired if I might ask a few questions about Mariner baseball.

"Sure," he said.

I asked, "What did Dave Niehaus mean to you?"

As with so many to whom I have spoken, I was not prepared for the depth of his response. He inhaled sharply, held his breath for a moment and whispered, "Everything."

This gentlemen, whose name was Kevin, was nearly sixty, and still played hardball in the Puget Sound Senior Baseball League. He and his wife, Chris, played couples softball for years. Baseball had been his passion for his entire lifetime. He, too, frequented the Rice Paddy for lunch and happened to be there the day Dave brought his new partner, Ken Levine, in to show him the place. When Dave Niehaus sat down at an adjoining table that weekday afternoon, Kevin couldn't believe his eyes or his good fortune. He and Dave exchanged hellos. Kevin mentioned he was a big Mariners fan—that's all it took to open the vault.

"I couldn't believe it," Kevin said, "...he immediately made me feel at ease...like he had known me my whole life. It was just like he did with his broadcast, only in person...it was amazing. In that moment, I realized what he meant to me. I'll never forget that day as long as I live...as long as I live."

It was Dave's way. He really viewed the fans as his family—not just metaphorically but viscerally. No fan went ignored, every fan's story was important to him. Five minutes with Dave Niehaus and it was clear: if you had a place in your heart for baseball, he had a place in his heart for you.

Like so many of his counterparts, Levine remembers the respect and care Dave showed for those who worked with him.

Ken Levine, Kevin Cremin and Dave Niehaus in the booth at Tiger Stadium.

"It was great for me," he recalled. "The thing about Dave that was so great was there was a genuine quality to him on the air and he really didn't have a big ego...there were a lot of lead announcers who would feel threatened by a number two guy who had a personality or would develop a following or just could offer something that they didn't. That was not the case at all with Dave, he was completely supportive, he rolled with my humor—we made each other laugh on the air. It's like the great actors, like Kelsey Grammer, who understand that having a David Hyde-Pierce on your show doesn't detract from you, it makes you better."

Levine particularly recalls the road trips. Any broadcaster will tell you how the travel and the hours spent away from home and in hotels can weary the soul.

"He was a wonderful travel companion...we would go to movies. We would go to art museums. You might not think of Dave as an art connoisseur, but quite often we'd take a day and go to a museum."

But also like most of Dave's counterparts, Levine remembers Dave's choices of restaurants being considerably less highbrow.

"I shudder to think of how we used to eat," Ken recalls, "fried chicken in Kansas City at midnight."

Yet, like all of Dave's partners, Levine remembers the travel, the road, the food, the schedule—none of these ever impacted Niehaus' commitment to his work.

"The thing that always struck me about traveling with Dave, there's usually a team bus that takes you to the stadium—Dave would never take the team bus. We'd always get out to the park early—if the first bus was 4 o'clock we'd leave at three. There is a level of preparation and a level of commitment that rubbed off on me. Remember, we were a terrible team—it was not like these were big games, not like they even meant anything. It's August and we've lost six out of seven, and we've got to go out to Tiger Stadium, and there's going to be nobody around, and it's a thousand degrees, and it's hot and humid and there's a forty percent chance of rain…and David's out there at three o'clock in the afternoon doing his preparation, you know, reading and studying. He's down there talking to players, talking to managers.

"That's the other thing about traveling with Dave—Dave knew everybody. I found myself developing relationships because of Dave. When I was with the Orioles, I would go around and introduce myself, say to the manager of the Texas Rangers, and say 'Hi, I'm the new guy in Baltimore.' But Dave, Dave would take me around and introduce me to people. We'd be up in the press room with all the scouts and Dave knew everybody. He knew the names of the usher's wives and the names of their kids.

"He was like the great mayor of baseball."

Levine once wrote that Dave's broadcast booth led the league in laughter every season and he was probably correct. The two of them had their own special routine. When the Mariners fell behind by ten runs or more, they would sing "The Wabash Cannonball" on the air. It happened all too often, so often, in fact, that Dave carried the lyric sheet in his scorebook, always at the ready.

Levine also found himself, like so many Mariner fans, mesmerized by the language of Dave's broadcasts.

"As good as he was on television, I thought he was always better on radio, because he had that blank canvas. I quickly learned that quite often the best thing I could provide was silence. To interrupt with comments like 'You know, Dave, this guy hits .280 against lefties,' was often just unnecessary. I would chime in, but I knew there was nothing I could add that Dave couldn't articulate better. When Dave was unspooling some story, sit back and listen like everybody else.

"He had marvelous ways of describing things. We were in Baltimore and a guy hit a high pop fly and as the ball was in the air, he described it as a white dot against the black sky. Tremendous, right in the middle of the play!"

Levine's voice at that moment trailed off as the reverie beckoned him to the silence of memory. His regard for the moment and for Dave Niehaus was evident, inaudibly pronounced and heartfelt.

For all the years of their friendship, Ken called Dave every Christmas Day. He still calls Marilyn on that day and on Dave's birthday as well.

Another old southern California comrade would join Niehaus, replacing Levine the following year.

Former Dodger first baseman Ron Fairly had retired after twenty-one seasons in the big leagues. Moving into the broadcast booth, he had followed quite directly in Dave Niehaus' footsteps, joining up with Dave's former team of Dick Enberg and Don Drysdale to do the Angels games for KTLA in Los Angeles.

From there, Fairly moved on to KNBR in San Francisco to work the Giants games. He well understood the challenge Dave Niehaus had faced in Seattle with Leo Lassen fans and the one Rick Rizzs was up against in Detroit. Fairly replaced long-time Giants voice Hank Greenwald. There was also the issue of Fairly being a Dodger. He took some hard knocks from the Bay Area press but showed his mettle by lasting six seasons there. After the 1992 season, wholesale changes by new team owner Bob Lurie prompted Fairly's exit from the KNBR radio booth.

Ron and Dave had first met back in southern California in 1965. The expansion Angels were in the process of building their new stadium, the "Big A," in Anaheim and were sharing Dodger Stadium with the primary tenant. From 1978 on, their friendship was annually renewed at spring training in Arizona as the Angels and Giants were fellow Cactus League members with the Seattle Mariners. Hearing of the opening in Seattle, Ron called his friend and Dave arranged for what turned out to be a successful interview with long-time Mariners Director of Communications Randy Adamack. Fairly was a man who was respected both as a player and as a broadcaster. When the Mariners played in Kansas City, none other than Hall of Famer George Brett, a California kid who grew up admiring the Dodgers' first-sacker, would come up to the press room after games just to visit with Ron.

Fairly and Niehaus shared the same passion for the game that had marked Niehaus' pairing with Rick Rizzs. After all, Fairly's two decades in the game certainly had Dave's respect. Not only did Fairly win three World Series rings and play in two All-Star games, but he was one of only two men to ever play one thousand games in the outfield and one thousand games in the infield. A fellow named Stan Musial happened to be the other.

Spring training is a joy of its own and part of what makes baseball special. Particularly for those from northern climes, the annual trek to the Cactus League in Arizona or the Grapefruit League in Florida offers welcome relief from winter. All who experience it bask in both sunshine and an aura of languid preparation for the season-long grind ahead. It's a time for remembering and for reconnecting. Major-leaguers, minor-leaguers, ex-ballplayers, coaches, and scouts all co-mingle across adjacent diamonds. Baseball friendships often separated by leagues and divisions, schedules and obligations are again renewed.

It's where you see one of the game's smallest of rituals played out again and again, one that has been repeated countless times dating back to the days of sharpened spikes and gloves piled behind second base in-between innings. It still endures. Just about every ballpark has a wire mesh fence behind home plate and, in most, that fence extends partway or all of the way down the left and right field lines. The openings are too small to fit a hand through. As veterans of the game greet each other from opposite sides of that fence, they stick as many fingers as possible through and, unable to shake hands, they "shake" fingers. Look closer and you will see that there is always a smile on either side of that fence, and a kind word, and a precious moment shared.

As few announcers will readily admit, as much as they love spring training as a whole, the spring training games can be a different story, at least from the sixth inning on. They can be a test of patience for even the most ardent broadcaster. The rosters shift daily with prospects and try-outs constantly inserted into the lineup at the last minute with no advance warning to even the managers, much less the guys on the radio. As a result, names are often missing from information sheets and the numbers assigned to those names often incorrect or duplicated. Fairly once saw three players on the field simultaneously wearing number 27 for the Giants in a spring game at Scottsdale.

Tim Hevly, the M's senior director of baseball information and winner of the 2013 Robert O. Fishel Award for excellence in his profession, fondly remembers Dave's reaction when he'd bring names and numbers of late-inning substitutions to the Peoria booth.

"Get out of here!" Dave would yell. "We don't want to know."

During the late innings, as the replacements mount and the identities of the substitutes blur, any announcer will testify that the ball hit by an unknown batter will be hit directly to an equally unknown fielder. So it happened early in spring training in 1993, Ron Fairly's first year in the M's booth, he informed the late-inning audience that, "Sammy Jorgensen has taken over in right field and in center that's a young man from the University of Oklahoma, Kenny Campus, spells it with a 'C.'"

After the game, Dave expressed his appreciation of his new partner's preparation and asked, "How did you find out who that was in the outfield in the eighth inning?"

Fairly replied with complete honesty. "I don't know who the hell those guys were—it's radio."

Turned out that Sammy Jorgensen and Kenny Campus would appear in spring training games for some twenty-eight years, all in games called by Fairly—and nobody had a bigger laugh about it than Niehaus. The two shared their roster secret for the entire span of their fourteen-year association behind the microphone as Messers. Jorgensen and Campus continued to make their Cactus League "debut" an annual rite of spring.

In addition to Ron Fairly, another special member joined the broadcast crew in the spring of 1993. Chip Caray, grandson of Dave's boyhood idol, Harry Caray, was hired by the Mariners. Fairly would spend fourteen years with Seattle and Caray four.

Fairly and Caray were spared the agonies that Dave had endured through fifteen summers in the Kingdome. Their arrival coincided with that of new skipper Lou Piniella, and they witnessed Mariner baseball as it had never been played before.

Among the most memorable nights of Lou's first year came early, on April 22, 1993. The second no-hitter in Mariner history was fashioned by Chris Bosio. Like Johnson's gem three years prior, it took its rightful place on Dave's Mariner highlight reel.

Bosio, his 2–1 pitch on the way—swung on, high-chopper over the mound, charged by Vizquel...BARE-HAND THROW, AND IT'S OVER AND BOSIO HAS DONE IT! MY OH MY! WHAT A PERFORMANCE BY CHRIS BOSIO! The second no-hitter in Mariner history and he is being MOBBED BY HIS TEAMMATES OUT BEHIND THE MOUND!

Great defense. Great pitching. And the fans indeed have had a chair on baseball history here at the Kingdome tonight to see one of the more brilliant performances in history as Bosio faces only one over the minimum and no-hits the Boston Red Sox, beats them by a score of 7–0. You will never see a better-pitched game. Congratulations to Chris Bosio, being embraced by all of his teammates and he did it in only ninety-five pitches. Indeed, MY OH MY!

The 1993 Mariners finished 82–80, but over a lifetime in the game and decades of chasing pennants, the wins and the losses are not what are remembered most. It's the enduring friendships formed in the sea of ever-changing faces and ever-turning calendars. Dave would look back on 1993 as the year he began one of his greatest friendships, the one with skipper Lou Piniella. Tragically, however, one of his most precious friendships came to its conclusion that summer as well.

Dave's closest friend in the game had been one of its fiercest competitors on the field and one of its nicest guys off of it. Don Drysdale joined with first, Brooklyn and, later, Los Angeles Dodger teammate Sandy Koufax to form arguably the premier 1–2 pitching combination of the late 1950s and early-to-mid 1960s.

Drysdale's Hall of Fame resume included a 1962 Cy Young Award for a 25–9 season, six consecutive shutouts, fifty-eight consecutive scoreless innings in 1968, three World Series rings and a lifetime ERA of 2.95. He led the National League in strikeouts three times. He was named to ten All-Star teams. His athletic prowess extended to the batter's box as well. He set the National League single-season record for home runs by a pitcher and, in 1965, was L.A.'s only .300 hitter.

Drysdale was the kind of guy who even made it hurt when you beat him. Umpire Jocko Conlin once warned him he'd be fined $25 if he threw at the next hitter.

"You might as well go back behind the plate, Jocko," Drysdale's replied, "I've got a hundred bucks in my pocket."

Once ordered to intentionally walk a batter, he hit him instead. When asked why, he explained, "Why waste four pitches when one will do?"

After fourteen big-league seasons, Drysdale retired to a career in broadcasting. Over a span of twenty-three years, he called games for the Dodgers, Montreal Expos, California Angels, Texas Rangers, and Chicago White Sox. It was the stint with the Angels that cemented his relationship with Dave Niehaus. For the next twenty years, they shared one of those special friendships a baseball life sometimes bestows upon members of its devoted fraternity.

The two men ate and drank and lived the baseball life together including many an after-game session in the Bards' Room in Chicago's Old Comiskey Park. The Bards' Room was the in-stadium watering hole for the press and players and among its many fabled stories is the night Drysdale and Niehaus and Cremin found themselves alone there after the game and after the bartender had closed up. It was Dave and Kevin who stood guard while Don picked the lock on the liquor cabinet.

On July 3, 1993, Don Drysdale was found dead in his hotel room in Montreal. "The Big D" was a frequent guest in the Niehaus home and his wife, UCLA athletic legend Ann Meyers, remains to this day one of Marilyn's dear friends. Drysdale had, in fact, stayed with Dave and Marilyn that January. The loss was doubly felt in the Mariner broadcast booth as Ron Fairly and Drysdale had been teammates, friends and fellow broadcasters for more than thirty years. The loss remained an empty spot in Dave Niehaus' heart forever. Coincidentally, Dave's friendship with Fairly went a very long way toward helping him heal from the loss of his irreplaceable friend.

The business of professional sports was changing rapidly in the early 1990s. The escalating salaries and the pressure to be profitable were reflected in the need for franchises in every major sport to maximize revenues. Organizations began to focus on not only getting fans into the park but also on maximizing the revenue per capita generated by fans. The emergence of ever more luxurious corporate suites and the focus on amenities to enhance the "experience" of the high-end customer began to price the common man out of the box seats.

Over two decades, the price of season tickets in Seattle went from $1,100 a pair to $7,000. Presenting just the game to the hard-core fans was no longer enough to sustain a professional baseball franchise. The casual fans were not going to feast on the 2–1 pitchers' duel. The ballpark itself became the product.

Big-screen scoreboards, family picnic areas, playgrounds for the kids, and higher-end eateries were all becoming the norm in new stadiums. Bill Veeck's original idea of fireworks when a home run was hit was expanded to include all sorts of video games and crowd-engaging routines, accompanied by cranked-up audio over constantly improving public address systems.

The casual fan found these sideshows every bit as enthralling as the long-time fans found them annoying. Distracting and contrived at best, the marketing departments had a new opiate they found impossible to resist or even control. Two decades later, there is hardly a moment at the ballpark between innings, during a pitching change, or a time out during which the high-decibel strings aren't being yanked by the puppeteers in the multi-media booth.

The ballpark's greatest social impact is based in its sense of connection. Prior to the pricing of the average fan out of the box seats, the baseball stadium was a place of genuine equality. The democracy of the stadium sat the banker next to the baker and the stockbroker next to the steelworker. The community and the sense of the ultimate common bond of being fans was integral to the experience, as were the conversations that took place between so many whose lives would not otherwise intersect in such a way.

Something equally precious has been lost: the sounds of the game. The chatter of the players as they take grounders from the first baseman between innings, the rattle of the bats in the rack, the thump of the warm-up pitches in the glove of a utility man as the catcher dons the tools of ignorance. All are lost in a sea of pumped-up pop hits and the roar of the engines from the car or boat race on the Jumbotron. The game itself stands as testament to the long attention span. It is played without a clock. The experience has now been altered in a way that is disconnected from the soul of the game.

Only at the ballpark could you hear the catcher whistle to the second baseman and shout, "Coming down!" before his toss to him after the last warm-up pitch. Then came the sounds of the players throwing the ball around the infield. Only there could you hear the "chatter" as that ball went from catcher to second to short to first to third, then to be walked to the mound with a "Let's get 'em." An old disco record accompanying a dancing animal on a three-thousand-square-foot television can be heard at any circus.

This drove Dave nuts. He wanted fans to love the game for its intrinsic beauty, its unique lexicon, its singular soundtrack.

"The game itself is enough for me," he said. "If you are a real baseball fan, the film clips and the sonic boom or whatever it is, I think it gets on your nerves. It does on my nerves. But I also understand that this is 1994 and not 1974. But to the real fan, it is a pain in the neck, too much noise." But that horse was out of the barn as a night spent at any modern ballpark will show.

The Mariners did have a new stadium in 1994, at least for spring training, saying good-bye to Diablo Stadium in Tempe and hello to Peoria Stadium. Their expansion status had, for sixteen years, extended to their spring-training facility as well. The first year, 1977, Diablo was genuinely remote and featured an impressive jackrabbit population. Dave recalled them being everywhere, even on the field during games.

Manager Darrell Johnson and bullpen coach Donald "Bear" Bryant regularly had to build the bullpen mound by hand. Diablo Stadium was also remembered as the place a young Mariner pitching recruit named Colin McLaughlin learned he was to be cut. Knowing that the news had to be delivered in person, he lit out in the middle of the night to hide on one of the surrounding buttes. He was found there the next day, meditating—in his long johns. He figured if he couldn't be found, he couldn't be cut. He was summoned back to camp and released. Tempe was also remembered for an amazing 1989 spring that earned young prospect Ken Griffey Jr. a spot on the club.

Fittingly enough, it was a Junior grand slam in the first game at Peoria on March 3 that christened the new yard.

As for Dave, there was little to miss about Diablo Stadium. The broadcast booth was a cinder-block cubicle measuring about twelve feet across and eight feet deep. It had a single, formica-topped counter in front. It was just one step up from the bleachers at Sembower Field back at Indiana University.

Few associated with major league baseball have fond memories of 1994. It remains the most tumultuous, cantankerous year the sport ever endured. For many who went through it, the pain still lingers. For its part, the '94 edition of the Seattle Mariners struggled, to say the least. Lou Piniella had brought a new level of excitement and along with it a new level of expectation. Yet that year's club just couldn't seem to find the combination to achieve consistent results. Fortunately, neither did any other AL West squad as they were all ten or more games below .500 by mid-summer. The promise of Piniella was as yet unfulfilled. Mariner fans looked to the heavens in hope that perhaps something from above could save them. It did.

As the M's and the Baltimore Orioles readied themselves for their July 19 tilt at the Kingdome, the sky fell in on baseball in Seattle. Literally. Dave Niehaus was standing next to the batter's cage preparing to interview Piniella for the pre-game show. He could see third-baseman Mike Blowers stretching in the outfield. As Blowers recalled, "We just heard a big crash and somebody said something about one of the tiles falling. We sat out there for what seemed like a couple of minutes until someone had the bright idea that—you know what? –those things are pretty big and maybe we should get inside."

A combination of factors, involving shoddy materials, cost-cutting and substandard work but mostly an ill-advised decision to pressure wash the Kingdome roof, resulting in the saturation of the materials, led to the descent of more than a dozen ceiling tiles from the roof of the Kingdome to the left-field bleachers below. Section 111, row 17, seats 1–4 gained their place in Seattle baseball history that night as did season ticket-holder Norm Lacher, who was forever glad he didn't come early that night.

The game was postponed. The rest of the series was postponed. The rest of the home season was shipped off to the home parks of Mariner opponents. Suddenly the Seattle Mariners were as homeless as the guy on the corner with a sleeping blanket and a cardboard sign—have stadium, will travel. The Seattle baseball team faced spending the last two months of the 1994 campaign living out of a suitcase as the building was declared unsafe and a costly ten-month renovation was set in motion. The Seahawks were forced to move their exhibition games and two regular-season contests to the University of Washington's Husky Stadium.

The Mariner organization lost in excess of $40 million in revenue giving up the next fifteen home games. The repair bill exceeded $51 million, more than three-quarters of what it cost to build the stadium in the first place. On August 17, 1994, two workers lost their lives in a crane accident during the repairs. In the end, the facility did not reopen until November.

Among the options discussed: minor-league stadiums in Tacoma, Washington and Portland, Oregon and Vancouver, British Columbia. But the Major League Baseball Player's Association didn't want players playing in minor-league facilities. So began the logistical nightmare of rescheduling home games to road games for the Mariners and road games to home games

Dave dressed for a luau-themed event at the Kingdome—with his white shoes.

for their opponents. Traveling secretaries across the American League had some serious work to do.

Over the ensuing twenty-one days, the Mariners would play twenty road games and travel 10,425 miles in the process. According to designated hitter Edgar Martinez, "It was the longest road trip, the biggest laundry bill and the most suitcases."

There were, however, two unexpected developments in the offing. The first was the lockout that would ensue in just a couple of weeks, rendering the seventy-day road trip moot. The other was even more unexpected. A team that could have come apart, that could have consumed itself in the drudgery and weariness the road always dishes out, instead took to a much higher road. The 1994 Mariners chose to have each other's back, to pick each other up, to join together and band together. They took a most unusual advantage of a most unusual disadvantage.

The first four games were shifted to Boston where the M's took two out of the first three. The Red Sox decided to price all seats at $10, a well-intended gesture to the fans that resulted in some of the rowdiest crowds Dave had ever seen at Fenway Park.

As Dave dryly observed, "You had a lot of people sitting in seats they normally couldn't get into."

The novelty of the situation wore off quickly. The team dropped the finale in Boston and then six in a row to Detroit and Chicago. As if the mood wasn't ugly enough, the August 12 "strike date" was announced during the series with the White Sox. A team meeting was called and the result was a commitment to make the best of the situation. Ten years later, Mike Blowers recalled the change in attitude.

"From a team standpoint," he said, "it might have been the best thing that happened to us. We really got to know each other a heck of a lot better. A lot of us ended up becoming really great friends during that time. Usually, on the road, three or four guys might go out together. But it seemed like, on that trip, we had a bunch of times when we would all go out basically as a team. You rarely see that, and it was really cool."

The Mariners then swept the Angels in a three-game set in Anaheim, took two out of three from the Royals in Kansas City and won all three tilts against the Rangers in Texas. Their 8–1 shellacking of the A's in Oakland on August 12 was their ninth win in ten games.

"Everybody wanted to keep playing," Blowers said. "If we had had to stay on the road the rest of the year, guys would have gladly done it…I think it really set up what was to come the following year."

The 1995 Mariners were conceived during those three weeks in the summer of 1994. The group of men who chose to endure as one, win or lose as one, took the step all great teams take when the common goal becomes more important than any individual achievement. They found something in themselves that, in 1995, would coalesce into something memorable, something enduring.

Somewhere in that bitter darkness that enveloped the awful end of the 1994 season, the Seattle Mariners had put flint to steel. That light at the end of the tunnel was no longer the proverbial oncoming train, it was the bright light of a season that would forever shine in the memories of Mariner fans who were there to see it and hear it.

We lost something special that summer. The baseball gods owed us big time.

They were about to pay up.

Lou Piniella, who managed the Mariners from 1993 to 2002, being interviewed by Dave.

The Magical Mystery Tour: The 1995 Mariners

One day the Mariners will win the World Series—they will, and they will hang the bunting and raise the flag out there in centerfield. But it will never be what it was like in '95.
—Dave Niehaus

THE SHADOW OF THE STRIKE fell over baseball in August of 1994 and remained throughout the bitterly contentious offseason. The following spring, a season heretofore the harbinger of hope, proved this year the auger of impassable and intractable acrimony. Recalling that year's spring training, it was the pallor of a divided game that was foremost in the memory of Dave Niehaus as well as the recollection of the day it all ended.

"The strike," he said, "that's what I remember most, because we went to spring training with what they called replacement players. Guys who were trying to make a roster because the other guys were out on strike. And I'll never forget we went through a whole spring training. We went over to Dunedin, Florida, to play the Toronto Blue Jays. Lou Piniella said to me, 'If you see me walk down the right-field line in the sixth or seventh inning you'll know the strike is over. These other guys are going to be coming in a couple days.' I saw Piniella take off down the right field line and said, 'This strike is over.'"

To adequately frame the snapshot 1995 represents in the great photo album of baseball history, one must first travel back to the late summer of 1994.

Everyone knew a strike was possible, but the idea it could come at the expense of the rest of the season was hard to imagine. That it would come at the expense of the World Series was genuinely unthinkable. In 1994, Major League Baseball became the only major sport to sacrifice its postseason to a work dispute.

Randy Johnson's third strike blew past Oakland's Ernie Young at 9:45 p.m. on Thursday night, August 11, 1994. More than just a season ended with that pitch. Tony Gwynn's pursuit of .400, Matt Williams' pursuit of Roger Maris, the Montreal Expos' pennant chase—all abruptly ended. The hopes of long-suffering Seattle Mariner fans were dashed as well.

Their young star, Ken Griffey Jr. echoed their sentiments: "We picked a bad season to have a good year."

Sometimes a "good year" is relative. Despite being fourteen games under .500 at 49–63, the Mariners were only two games behind the 52–62 Texas Rangers when play stopped.

Reminiscing about that awful September, Dave Niehaus said, "(did I) …miss it? God, yes. The last ten days of the season, I couldn't wait to get to the park. The team was playing great. I really believe they'd have won the division.

"The first pennant race in franchise history. People were getting pumped, and I'd have turned this town on in September. Of course, the crime was there would have been no place for the fans here to have come to see the team (referring to the closing of the Kingdome), except on television. They sure weren't going to be able to play here."

The silver lining was that all those September hopes and the opportunity to turn the town on only had to wait one more year.

Typically, Dave felt not only for himself, but for the players. He knew how precious every year became for the veterans. Unlike broadcasters, the career window opens and closes all too quickly for the players. Those whose last game would be played on August 11 were foremost in his mind. Little did he know the ballplayer for whom he felt the most sympathy would stand beside him at Cooperstown fourteen summers later.

"I felt for a guy like Goose Gossage (whose twenty-two-year career ended in a Mariner uniform). It shouldn't end this way for a class man like Goose, and he had tears in his eyes that night. It reminded me of the September this team finally clinched a .500 season, players like Alvin Davis and Dave Valle were crying. Those were tears of happiness. These weren't."

For many months, years actually, the festering tensions between the players' union and the owners had left both sides bitter and uncompromising. The strike lasted 234 days. The owners began spring training with replacement players and only a court order (and Orioles owner, Peter Angelos) saved the 1995 season from beginning with those recruits. Finally, an agreement was reached to begin a truncated 144-game campaign on April 25.

For the fans, the wound was further salted by the resumption of play under the old collective bargaining agreement. Nothing had changed. Their lifelong trust in the integrity of their game had been shattered for nothing and it would, in fact, be years before a new agreement was negotiated.

In 1993, the year before the lockout, National League attendance had risen an astonishing 50%. The average attendance at MLB games in 1994 was 31,612. The turnstile count did not reach that level again until 2000. It took until 2007 for attendance to peak briefly at 32,568, but an immediate decline left the average attendance numbers where they remain today—below the 1994 average.

In 1995, attendance fell over twenty percent and the fans who did show up made their voices heard. The Pirates' home opener was delayed seventeen minutes by a barrage of debris hurled onto the field. Ballparks across the land echoed with catcalls, for players and management alike.

On a more positive note, for Dave Niehaus the onset of the 1995 season meant a reunion with his Mariner mate of nine years, Rick Rizzs. Among its remaining, old-time characteristics, baseball shares a common trait with Kansas: there is no place like home. In 1995, Rick decided that, for him, the greener pastures were back in Seattle with Dave. He said goodbye to Detroit and once again saddled up with his dear friend and colleague in a partnership that lasted for the rest of Dave's career. Ken Levine departed, but Ron Fairly and Chip Caray remained part of the television and radio crew through the 1995 season.

Rick's return was as timely as an extra-inning RBI.

After a year devoid of the World Series, the fans' alienation was unprecedented. It was palpable at the ballpark and wherever enthusiasts gathered to bemoan the damage inflicted upon the grand old game. Against this backdrop—and almost as counterpoint to it—the Seattle Mariners' most magical season unfolded. Amid this dark storm of discontent, baseball's longest-suffering expansion franchise would emerge as the bright ray of sunshine, the proverbial hope that springs eternal and become what *Sports Illustrated* later would dub "the team that saved baseball."

This was no Caesar's march through Gaul, no German blitzkrieg—in fact, anything but. The youthful over-achievement of the 1994 M's had disappeared with that lost season and 1995 began as a gut-wrenching return to mediocrity—the same mediocrity that had for so long marked the fortunes of Seattle's hometown nine. From the onset of the campaign, it seemed the fleeting promise of 1994 had not survived the cruel winds of the long and acrimonious winter of diamond discontent.

Third-baseman Mike Blowers recalls the mindset entering that year. "At the start of the season," he said, "there were no expectations of us winning the pennant. We were talking about improving and playing over .500. There weren't many fans to start the season."

Lack of fan support had serious repercussions, too. Talk of moving the team was once again at center of the local baseball conversation. Tampa Bay-St. Petersburg had the Seattle franchise in their sights and appeared to have the money to make it happen. The players knew the possibility was real.

As Randy Johnson said, "That was the year a lot of people were talking about the franchise going on to Florida. Had that team folded and not risen to the occasion, the franchise might be somewhere else, without a doubt."

Just prior to opening day, the owners abandoned their plan to use substitute players, necessitating a three-week delay before opening day. Dave Niehaus, like most everybody associated with the game, just wanted to get back to normal.

"It was the only way to put the whole mess behind us. We hadn't played a real game in eight months, we couldn't wait to get back to real, major-league baseball."

On April 27, as the M's squared off against the Detroit Tigers, Johnson gave the fans the first glimpse of what was to be an extraordinary summer for him, blanking the men from the Motor City, 3–0. Seattle took three out of four and finished April with a 3–1 record. May saw the M's play one game over .500 for over three weeks, sitting at 15–12 on May 26. But something was sure to go wrong. Something always went wrong. This time what went wrong made every Mariner fan sick to their stomach. I was doing a show that night at a Seattle venue and the news spread quickly through the club.

At the Kingdome that fateful Friday night, May 26, 1995, the Orioles' Kevin Bass lashed a line drive deep into right-centerfield, just to the right of the 407-foot marker. No more than a few who ever played the game could have chased that ball down. But "The Kid," Ken Griffey Jr., as he did so often, did what mere mortals could not. Streaking toward the wall, he hauled in Bass' shot as he crashed into the blue padding on the

Dave with Ken Griffey Sr.

outfield fence. Everyone in the Dome was on their feet, everyone except Ken Griffey Jr. He lay on his side, hunched into a fetal position on the warning track.

As Griffey grimaced, a hush quickly enveloped the crowd of 15,256 anxious on-lookers. There was no worse nightmare for Mariner fans than to be forced to dream of their star player sidelined by injury. More than their best player, Griffey was the literal embodiment of the bright hope that had infused long-suffering Mariner fans since his arrival. Just as Bass' drive had been no routine fly ball, this was no routine bad dream.

Arguably, it had been Griffey's greatest Kingdome catch, topping even the clinging-to-the-wall robbery of Rubin Sierra near the same spot, almost four years to the day before. "My team needed a win," a matter-of-fact Griffey said. "I had to go get that ball. I want my pitchers to be comfortable."

The catch helped protect a 4–3 lead for Randy Johnson (Seattle eventually won, 8–3) whose immediate reaction, seeing Griffey hurt and sprawling, was to fall on his back in disbelief.

Mariner fans awoke the morning of May 27 to the confirmation of their most dreaded nightmare. Griffey's left wrist was broken. He underwent surgery the next day, Saturday, to insert a small plate in the radius, the smaller of the two bones in his lower arm. Dr. Larry Pedegana, an affable man who served as the team's orthopedic surgeon, predicted a full recovery, but not before three months' time.

Team President Chuck Armstrong, shaking his head, remembers, "It just looked really bleak at the start. We had the replacement debacle, the players were on strike…they decided to put the stadium issue up for a vote within King County, and polls showed us losing, two-thirds to one-third. The strike finally ended, and we started off kind of slow. And then when things started to pick up, Junior makes that all-world catch and gets hurt—just a disaster."

The Kingdome was a new baby—and an ugly one. It was as utilitarian a design as ever made it through construction, far more like an enormous fallout shelter than a cozy ballpark. Concrete walls, concrete roof, concrete ramps. It had all the aesthetic charm of a courthouse basement with bleachers. As Dave commented years later, "The Kingdome is not a ballpark. There are no elements, no effect on the baseball. At Fenway, you can see the grass grow on some days. Fenway smells, you can see Ted Williams, Babe Ruth playing there. I darn near genuflect when I walk through the gates at Fenway Park."

You were far more likely to genuflect upon *exiting* the Kingdome.

The Kingdome resembled a giant concrete mushroom, the biggest basement in town. We all remember the kid with the biggest basement in the neighborhood, the kid who had the Ping-Pong table or maybe even a pool table. This basement was so big it could hold a baseball team. The fences were blue and everything else was grey. It always felt like a seventy-two-degree November day.

Everything was about cost-control. Mariner fans quickly learned one of the Kingdome's concession-stand rules: during a day game, never order a hot dog until the fifth inning unless you wanted a re-heat from the night before.

For those of us who spent more than two hundred hours every summer, over nearly two decades, entombed in that concrete-covered, Astroturf-floored bubble watching the Mariners rack up baseball's worst record over that span, there had been precious little to survive on other than love for the game and the thrill of actually being a season-ticket holder. Yes, we were all-too-often terrible, but Alvin Davis, Harold Reynolds, Mark Langston and the Class of '84 had sustained us through most of that decade. Rene Lachemann, Chuck Cottier and Dick Williams had given us hope, but ownership hadn't given them enough talent on the field or time in the dugout to give them a fair chance at delivering.

But the long decade of mostly so-so 1980s Mariner baseball was a decade that ended with the ray of hope and sunshine that was Junior's 1989 arrival in centerfield.

Griffey's steady maturation mirrored that of the franchise, culminating with a league-leading forty home runs in 1994. He brought Seattle multiple one-hundred-plus RBI years, multiple .300-average years, a string of Gold Gloves that ultimately numbered eleven straight. Still, that didn't tell the entire story of what Junior meant to the hearts of Seattle fans. His contagious smile and immense popularity, overwhelmingly with children, had given Mariner fans their first nationally visible superstar.

In a town in which Seahawks and Supersonics fans were constantly able to needle Mariners fans, Griffey gave baseball fans in the Pacific Northwest the player whose presence on the national stage outshone any Seattle professional sports figure before him.

In 1994, Griffey was not just elected to the All-Star Game, he was elected with the highest vote total ever. He had a way of rising to special moments and the All-Star Game that year was no exception. Ken Griffey Jr. stepped into the batter's box, hat turned backwards, and proceeded to win the first of his three titles in the annual Home Run Derby.

The infectious joy with which he played the game reminded us all of why we fell in love with baseball in the first place. On a nightly basis, he made you glad you went to the ballpark. Like Willie Mays, Griffey did *something* every night to delight the paying fan. With his glove (ask Kevin Bass) or his arm (ask Lou Whitaker) or his speed (ask the Yankees) or his bat, Griffey would give you something to tell your baseball friends about the next day.

Yet to fully understand the pall Griffey's injury cast over Seattle baseball fans, you would have to know Griffey's other great achievement of 1994—being named the recipient of the annual Celebrity Recognition Award from the Make-a-Wish Foundation, his favorite charity. He was baseball's "Pied Piper." I saw first-hand how children everywhere connected with him, admired him, flocked to him wherever he went.

Teammate Jay Buhner told *The Seattle Times* for its April 5, 2009 edition, "What people don't hear enough about is the amount of time and money he gives back to charities and people less fortunate...he opens his heart and wallet to various charities, especially the Make-a-Wish Foundation.

"He'd bring the kid into the clubhouse, literally take the jersey off his back, sign it and give it to the kid. Give him a bat, take him around and introduce him to everyone in the clubhouse, make him a sandwich—make the kid feel great. He didn't want people to see that side; he didn't do it for acknowledgment. He knows what it means to kids, and for that hour, he totally made a difference in the kid's life, and the family's life. I saw him do it over and over and over. Sure, that's part of the responsibility of being a professional athlete, but he became a totally different person. He would let his guard down and roll out the red carpet.

"Junior has such a huge heart. Sometimes, we don't talk about that... We forget the little things he does that go way above and beyond "

Joe Chard, M's vice-president of community relations, recalls a similar story.

"I can't remember what year, but there was a boy who had cancer. He was having bone-marrow treatment. Junior was supposed to see him in spring training, but the Make-a-Wish people called and said the bone marrow hadn't taken, and he wasn't doing very well.

"So I called Ken, who was in Atlanta at the time. I explained the situation to him. He said, "I'll fly back early. Where can we meet?" So we met at the hospital. We went up to the room. The kid didn't look well. I was just blown away by the fact he went in and sat on the kid's bed, talked about riding motorcycles, held his bed pan when the kid got sick. I could not have done it myself without showing some sort of discomfort, but Junior just went about it, and made the kid feel just normal. They were laughing and talking about things teenagers do.

"We walked out of there, just kind of in awe. Junior flew back early and had just taken over the whole situation. He made the family feel great, made the kid feel great. It was as heart-wrenching a situation as you could see.

"It was just one of those humbling experiences. Junior had given the boy his jersey. The parents called after the boy passed, asked if it was OK if he was buried with Junior's jersey. Very humbling. A lot of guys are not comfortable in a hospital setting, but he has the ability to make people feel very comfortable.

"His thing has always been, 'I'll do it, but I don't want anyone there. This is for the family and the kid; not for PR. I want to give the person special time.' "

Long-time Seattle advertising executive Jim Copacino, who has worked on countless Mariner commercials, recalls the television shoot at which Griffey was nowhere to be found when lunch was served. Junior was off playing catch with the crew members' sons and daughters who had come to see him. He really did care more about the kids than about whether or not he got fed.

To be sure, there were temperamental moments—would any of us be immune to having virtually every waking moment the subject of public scrutiny? There may have been run-ins with adults, but for kids Junior was the man. And to Seattle baseball fans, most of whom were privy only to the Junior they saw on their screens, he carried the hopes of the franchise.

The night after Griffey was injured, Seattle lost to Baltimore. Still, they spent Sunday making the most out of nine singles to beat Baltimore 5–2 and followed it up with a three-game sweep of the New York Yankees. The combination of the fans' continuing resentment about the previous season and Griffey's absence showed itself at the turnstiles as fewer than forty-three thousand fans filed into the Kingdome for the entire series. The Yankees always drew in Seattle, but not this year. The pallor had settled in with alarming swiftness.

June began with the M's being swept at Boston, shortly followed by a five-game, mid-month skid. Save for Johnson's brilliance, Edgar Martinez' steady bat, and Jay Buhner's rock-solid defense, the M's spent those four weeks on their heels. But unlike so many campaigns before, that five-game losing streak was to be the longest of the year. The Texas Rangers pounded Mariner pitching for ten runs and thirteen hits on June 30, and Seattle finished the month winning only eleven of their twenty-eight games.

With the AL West-leading Angels at 34–26, the Mariners were 30–30, still at .500 and a mere four games back. But all across the Pacific Northwest, fans were not ready to believe the annual swoon was anything but imminent. Hopes were steadily sinking.

Jay Buhner, Edgar Martinez, Mike Blowers, Tino Martinez had all played with grit and determination throughout. Griffey's absence, however, seemed too often to mean that key hit or defensive gem that he contributed nightly was absent at a key juncture of the game. Great baseball teams rely on a combination of timely individual efforts, the winning web woven strand by strand.

Griffey missed seventy-three games in all, just over half of the 145 games the Mariners played that season. The Mariners showed how good they were without him by playing at .500 during that stretch, pretty doggone good. But with him back they would play at a .622 clip. That proved to be just good enough.

July was as kind to the Angels as it was indifferent to the Mariners. Seattle went 13–14 that month, continuing to hang tough without their bulwark in centerfield. The Angels, however, were the only thing in American League parks hotter than the thermometers, going 20–7 for the month. That left the Seattle nine a full eleven games behind and fingernails dug into the side of the cliff. It seemed, once again, time to wait 'till next year.

There was little comparing the two clubs. The Angels' rotation included former Seattle all-star and A.L. strikeout leader Mark Langston, a member of the Mariners' fondly remembered "Class of '84" that included Alvin Davis and Harold Reynolds. Traded to Montreal, Langston had, like so many other Mariner castoffs, returned to haunt them from within their division. California's ace, lefty Chuck Finley, who in 1990 had bested Frank Tanana's team record for southpaws with a 2.40 ERA, was fully worthy of leading the staff.

Seattle's six-game winning streak in early August gave the fans some hope of another season above .500 but there was no reasonable expectation of anything beyond that to salve the annual baseball wound. On August 20, Seattle's four-run rally in the ninth fell short in a 7–6 loss to the Boston Red Sox. That same night Langston improved to a sizzling 13 wins and 2 losses by beating the Yankees, 10–5. The Mariners woke up on August 21 to find themselves a seemingly insurmountable $12^1/_2$ games out of first place.

By comparison, the 1951 New York Giants, who came from so far back to catch the Dodgers and win the playoff, awoke on August 21 of that year only eight games in arrears.

It appeared what was left for Seattle was another stagger to the finish line, reduced to hoping once again just to finish above .500. For yet another year, baseball would draw ten thousand fans only on the nights when the giveaway was enough to lure an additional few thousand souls into the mortar mausoleum down by the end of the Alaskan Way Viaduct.

I did say *seemingly* insurmountable.

Just as it takes two to tango, an astonishing come-from-behind surge requires an equally astonishing collapse from the front-runner. In 1951, the denizens of the Polo Grounds, the New York Giants, do-si-do'ed with the Brooklyn Dodgers. In 1995, another of those classic baseball melodramas played out on the West Coast as Seattle and California locked together in their own two-team two-step.

As the dog days drew to a close, it was California's turn to stagger. Beginning with an 11–2 shellacking from Baltimore on August 25 and ending with an 8–1 loss at Fenway on September 3, the Angels suddenly, almost inexplicably, dropped nine games in a row, scoring only twenty-three runs in the process. They lost twelve of thirteen, fifteen of eighteen. They dropped two of their next three but momentarily steadied themselves by taking four of their next five from Minnesota and Chicago.

Then the truly unforeseeable and unfathomable happened. For the second time in fewer than thirty days, California lost nine in a row. A team that had won sixty-six of its first 107 games, a .617 pace, won only six of its next thirty, an astonishing month of .200 baseball. When Langston bested the Bronx Bombers on August 20, California was twenty-five games over .500. When Chuck Finley lost to the Texas Rangers 5–1 on September 23, they were a mere seven games above even. To their credit, they won six of their final seven to finish the year at 78–66, but, like jockey Jorge Velasquez aboard Alydar, they went to the whip a furlong too late.

As gut-wrenching as those final six weeks in Anaheim proved to be, as cruel as the baseball gods were to the Angels, that last month and a half in Seattle was the most delirious thrill ride ever taken by Pacific Northwest baseball fans—a truly unforgettable, genuinely magical stretch run worthy of Silky Sullivan, one of horse racing's legendary last-to-first closers.

It would prove to be the season that saved baseball in Seattle, the campaign that ended the testy courtship and began the continuing love affair with baseball, the season that would carry Seattle forward to a glistening jewel of a new stadium and a newly successful franchise. It proved to be the season in which the Mariners took their rightful place in the hearts of Northwest sports fans.

It also proved to be the year that David Arnold Niehaus, whose journey from Princeton, Indiana to New York to Los Angeles to the outpost of Seattle, took his rightful place in the hearts of Northwest sports fans as well. This was the season that brought to the attention of fans everywhere his passion for the game, his nuanced and melodic command of the English language, his deep connection with the lexicon of his beloved sport and his unabashedly joyous pursuit of his chosen profession. This special year, this once-in-a-franchise season, made everyone who "refused to lose" fully aware of this man's immense talent and inexhaustible devotion to both his craft and to the game he so loved.

This was the campaign that made fans near and far aware of what those of us who had thrilled to his work for decades had known for so long. Dave Niehaus was the real deal, one of the greats, the legitimate heir to Barber and Brickhouse, Allen and Caray.

For those of us who knew him and cherished him, he never needed anything but a microphone and a ballgame. For the world at large, however, there was another requirement, one beyond even his great ability to manufacture. In 1995, during one extraordinary summer, the baseball gods not only smiled on the Seattle Mariners, they smiled on their devoted champion, their unwavering voice.

All he ever needed was a pennant race.

Rick Rizzs put it this way, "1995 put him on the map—the whole baseball world knew how great he was."

All Mariner legends seem to begin with Ken Griffey Jr., Edgar Martinez, or Jay Buhner. This particular legend is no exception. Buhner and Griffey would go first and Edgar had their backs.

As of Thursday night, August 24 the Mariners were 54–55, 11^1/$_2$ games behind the first-place California Angels. By Yankees-Mariners standards, it was not an impressive crowd. The next day's *New York Times* described the Kingdome as a place "where it was apparent that the 17,592 fans had not embraced the wild-card race." The events of this evening changed all that.

Lost in the ninth-inning heroics of that game is where it all began and how. It began on the mound sixty feet, six inches from home plate and ended some 437 feet from the dish in the left-center field stands. That's where Jay Buhner deposited David Cone's first-inning fastball for a grand-slam home run and a 4–0 Seattle lead.

The fireworks that started it off were eventually overshadowed by the blast that finished it off. The M's surrendered the early lead and trailed, 7–6, heading into the bottom of the ninth. Cone had weathered the early storm and gone on to strike out ten as he gave manager Buck Showalter eight gutty innings. Showalter went to the pen for John Wetteland.

In 1995, Wetteland was as good a closer as there was in the game and he got two quick outs. But John McGraw's famous words were about to be spoken again: "Oh, those bases on balls." Wetteland walked speedy Vince Coleman, who promptly stole second and third. Joey Cora's single off Tony Fernandez' glove scored Coleman with the tying run. That brought Junior to the dish. Despite Griffey's prowess, he'd never homered off Wetteland

and, for that matter, never in his already storied career had he hit a game-winning four-bagger. That was about to change, too.

A pennant race was about to break out in one of baseball's unlikeliest places. It would bring Lou Piniella and his charges to the forefront of the baseball headlines and forever change the visibility of a downtrodden franchise. Countless casual fans that were unaware of this talented group of players would make them their "Cinderella story." Countless more fans would also discover the extraordinary talent behind the voice that carried their exploits out over the wires.

The Seattle Mariners were about to become overnight sensations and so was their sixty-year-old broadcaster.

Griffey stood in the box "waving that black bat" and, this time, Dave's call was *fortissimo* from the get-go:

> *…there goes Joey—the pitch SWUNG ON AND BELTED DEEP TO RIGHT FIELD THE MARINERS HAVE DONE IT! FLY AWAY! JUNIOR WITH A TWO-RUN HOME RUN! THE MARINERS WIN IT 9–7! MY OH MY!*

Griffey hit Wetteland's first pitch on a rising line into the right-field bleachers. Not even the bouncing gaggle of Seattle players gathered at home plate to greet Griffey had any idea what was about to happen. Nobody did.

From the "swung on and belted" in the first to the "fly, fly away" in the ninth, Dave Niehaus crackled in the booth that night. Throughout his often-difficult seasons with some less-than-stellar Mariner ensembles, Dave had witnessed an uncanny amount of Mariner success against the New York Yankees, most notably at the Kingdome. He relished every "W." That night was as sweet as any and so was that entire weekend. The electricity of Thursday's finish carried over into Friday's broadcast.

The guys in the dugout knew it was a seriously special night. Mike Blowers remembers it well.

"Junior missed a ton of time, and when he came back, we were playing real good baseball." Blowers said. "One of his first games back, he ended up hitting a home run off John Wetteland, upper deck, to win a game. We all looked around. If this guy is healthy and ready to go, we had a chance to do something special. His injury had been so serious we didn't know what we'd get. He comes right back and turns a ninety-six-mile-an-hour fastball right around. We all smiled and said, 'Here we go.' "

Jay Buhner knew it as well.

"I think that's when everyone kind of said, 'Hey, something really special is happening,'" he recalled. "We got on a roll, and we had an unbelievable amount of confidence. We had the mentality we could beat anyone. Anyone could be the hero. People were contributing in every way, from top to bottom. The few games we did lose, we thought we just ran out of outs."

On that Friday, August 25, just as the Mariners took flight, the Angels began their descent. The Mariners won their second straight over the Yankees, carried to a 7–4 win by Edgar Martinez' twenty-third and twenty-fourth round-trippers of the season. Starter Chris Bosio's 5 $2/3$ innings were backed solidly by Norm Charlton's two innings of hitless relief. The next night, Mariner ace Randy Johnson equaled Langston's torrid 13–2 won-loss record by going the distance, shutting out New York on three singles. Jay Buhner and Mike Blowers each homered and despite the 5–2 loss in the finale on the 27th, the M's were a game above .500.

Although no one yet imagined it, the race had begun.

Over the ensuing week, the Angels lost their next six contests while Seattle went 4–2, winning two out of three in back-to-back series in Boston and Baltimore.

"We were about ten games back, playing really well." Mike Blowers said. "After one game we had won, another one of those eighth-, ninth-inning deals, I remember sitting at my locker. At one side is Jay, the other side Tino. We're all talking about the game, and Tino looks at me and says, 'You know what? I have a feeling the Angels are going to start losing.' Right after that, the next day, was the first time I started paying attention to what the Angels were doing."

And so it was that the Mariners began the final four weeks of the 1995 chase for the American League West crown a mere three games above .500 at 61–58. Twenty-five games remained and, despite the Angels being on a nine-game slide, the Mariners were still 6 $1/2$ games out of first place. They won two of three games in Baltimore but dropped two of three in New York. The long and draining trip to the East Coast was made all the more taxing by having to stop in Cleveland on their way West. A 4–1 loss left them 3–4 on the road trip and back to a single game over .500.

A bone-weary Dave Niehaus signed off the broadcast that night seeing another promising year slipping away. The truncated 1994 season had left him with renewed hope that somehow, someway, the tide would turn this year and the Mariner ship would at last come in.

Dave's Seattle Mariners 1987 publicity photo.

I remember that night. I was performing at The Edgewater on Seattle's waterfront not too far uptown from the Dome. As had been my custom for almost two decades, I kept the audience apprised of the score of the game and taped it on my portable cassette player. After the show, I returned to my fourth-floor room to change clothes and listen to the recording of the post-game show. I intended to drive home to the small farm I share with my wife east of Lake Washington, but as the loss to Cleveland sank in, I was in need of some comfort.

I happened to have with me a very special cassette tape and decided to sooth my Mariner soul by listening to it that night. I had been lucky enough to receive the recording from Kevin Cremin. Seattle fans weren't the only ones who felt cheated by the abrupt end of the 1994 season. That team was special and nobody knew that better than the team in the broadcast booth. They knew that their chance at calling Seattle baseball's first-ever postseason action had been stolen from them as surely as had the fans' chance of watching it.

Dave and Rick and Kevin had decided the previous fall to give Mariner fans a very precious gift. Recalling his days with the tickertape in both New York and California, Dave, along with his cohorts, took the art of baseball recreation to a higher level. Envisioning a 1994 World Series match-up of their young and beloved M's with the then-National League powerhouse Atlanta Braves, they "broadcast" the seventh and deciding game of that World Series.

Cremin took to his basement with a yellow notepad and a pencil. Pitch by pitch, inning by inning, he crafted the game Mariner fans all dreamed of for so long. From the fertile imagination of the veteran producer sprang a baseball fantasy worthy of the Strat-O-Matic games he played as a kid. His script would be their tickertape and the numbers would reveal themselves just as magically as they had on the chalkboard at Dave's Palace Pool Room in Princeton.

This broadcast remains special for many reasons. It was born out of deep and abiding passion for the game and represents both a snapshot of an otherwise lost postseason and the dearest of gifts to the fans and to the game. It was a gift from two guys who loved the game to everyone else who cherished it.

It's also special because it is, as far as I can discover, the last "re-created" game broadcast by a major-league announcing team. Dave Niehaus had done recreations in New York in the 1950s and in Los Angeles in the 1960s and here he was again, some thirty-plus years later, doing it one last time. Dick Shively, Red Barber, Leo Lassen—all the "veteran spielers" who had ever worked the tickertape—were alive in the booth that night, all represented in that broadcast. The great art of extemporaneous hardball theater had maybe its last great revival and perhaps the last great practitioner of the art was at the microphone.

The game was recorded over several nights at the studios of KIRO radio in Seattle with the able engineering assistance of the late Brad Perkins.

To listen to it is to marvel at the nuance and subtlety of Niehaus' use of language, his story-telling ability and appreciation for detail. Cremin's script is every bit as delightful as the screenplay for *It Happens Every Spring* or the book for *Damn Yankees*. It's baseball as only radio can deliver it. It is extraordinary. I have boxes of tapes of Dave Niehaus broadcasts. If I were allowed to keep only one, this would be it.

Until almost sunrise, I lay on my bed in the hotel, listening to the greatest game in Mariner history, a game that never happened. I fell asleep about the same time the road-weary Mariners were hitting their pillows after crossing three time zones, landing at Boeing Field and driving home. That simulated game was, of course not the greatest game in Mariner history, it was just a dream. But baseball dreams can and do come true. I didn't know it and neither did Dave, Rick, Kevin or any of the slumbering Mariners—but the game that would make countless baseball dreams come true was mere weeks away.

The Mariners had been six games above .500 only once that year, at 19–13 on May 31. On September 8, a week after returning home, they got back to that high-water mark—and kept going. Over the ensuing two weeks, they were torrid. They won fourteen and lost only two. Meanwhile, the trap door again sprung open beneath the California Angels. For the second time in less than a month, the Halos, incomprehensibly, were losing nine straight.

The Mariners had caught them.

The town was beside itself and Dave Niehaus was at the epicenter of the dizzying hurricane. Everywhere he went, he saw it and heard it. His calls of the game were on local sports radio, news radio, on television and, in the tech-savvy city of Seattle, all over the internet.

He heard it from the dry cleaner and the grocery clerk and the guy in line at the bank. Suddenly they all knew him. Dave was certainly proud of the recognition and the appreciation, but a deeper feeling brought him a more enduring joy. His town had come to know what a pennant race felt like. Indeed, he looked around to see all of Seattle decked out in Mariner blue. "Refuse to Lose" signs were seemingly in every window. The town finally seemed to be in lockstep with his passion for the sport.

The city, at long last, was becoming aware of what baseball meant to Dave Niehaus. It also, finally, was becoming aware of what Dave Niehaus meant to the city.

ESPN was not only showing Mariner highlights on a nightly basis, they were also replaying the radio calls of the action. The thirty-five-year veteran "pronouncer" was an overnight sensation. Millions who had never heard his work now marveled at his cadence, his modulation, his ability to describe the action in detail, in sequence and, most of all, the unbridled enthusiasm for the game he brought to the audience. Fans across the country wondered how they could have spent their baseball lives not knowing who this man was. With each new highlight, they understood how lucky his listeners were.

Dave at Tiger Stadium, Detroit.

Mariner baseball had gone from New Haven to Broadway and their voice was more than ready for the Great White Way. It was a pennant race all right, one for the books, one to be remembered, the one Dave deserved.

His supporting cast was right there with him and he delighted them along with the rest of his fans.

His early years with the California Angels had given birth to his signature expression, "My Oh My." An evening's drive through the spring training desert with sportswriter and friend J Michael Kenyon had spawned his classic home run call, "Fly, fly away!" These two iconic phrases were to be joined by a third. Niehaus was a broadcaster who never stopped getting better, who never ceased searching for yet another lyrical expression to add to his repertoire. The birth certificate for this delight reads Detroit, Michigan, the Motor City.

"It was 1995," Dave said, "when Tino Martinez seemed like he was hitting a grand slam home run every other at-bat, but he wasn't. But I've always called a grand slam home run a salami. And I went back to the hotel one time and said, 'Well, what goes well with salami?' And I came up with rye bread and mustard, and then I thought when I was a little kid, and never got my way, I went to my grandmother's house—I wanted that extra piece of candy, and I'd go over there, and Grandma would say, 'You mean they won't give you another piece of candy?' and she'd say 'here.' And I've never forgotten that, so it was sort of a salute to her.

While it appears the idea for this occurred to Dave during a three-game, Fourth of July weekend series with the Tigers, it would be a few more days before its actual debut. On Sunday afternoon, July 9, the Mariners faced off against the Cleveland Indians at Jacobs Field. With one out in the seventh, ex-Mariner lefty Bud Black intentionally walked Edgar Martinez to load the bases. The next batter was Tino Martinez, who drove Black's 2–2 offering beyond the wall in right field for the inaugural Grand Salami.

Dave recalled, "…Ron Fairly was with me on television, and it was Tino Martinez who hit another grand slam. And I said, 'Get out the rye bread and the mustard, Grandma, it's grand salami time!' He looked at me like I had taken a step on the other side, and I looked at him, and I knew I *had* taken a step on the other side."

Working the radio side of the broadcast, Kevin Cremin didn't hear the phrase but was asked about it a few days later by Mariner press secretary Pete Vanderwarker. It would make its first appearance on radio the following week.

It happened against Detroit at the Kingdome on July 17. This Grand Salami off the bat of Tino Martinez propelled a 3–2 fastball (the eighth pitch of the at-bat) from Wedsel Gary "Buddy" Groom Jr. deep into the right-field bleachers. The shot also sent Groom to Florida as he was waivered into a Marlin uniform, after which he remarkably lasted another ten seasons, becoming one of baseball history's most-used relief specialists.

Rick Rizzs recalls the mix of delight and surprise in the booth when Niehaus let it rip. "I'm already excited," he said, "because I'm watching the ball leave the park and here's Dave just exploding with this incredible call, I mean, coming out of his chair. It was just tremendous. I mean, the guy was so good. Here he was, all those years behind the microphone and still coming up with great material."

Dave Grosby was doing pre- and post-game work for Mariner broadcasts in 1994 and 1995. He first heard the "Grand Salami" call on the radio driving back from Pullman, Washington.

"I pulled over and called Kevin Cremin in the booth," Grosby recalled. "I said, 'What is going on?' and Cremin just said, 'The old man's on a roll, the old man's on a roll.'"

The phrase was so popular it spawned a new and different outpouring of affection for Niehaus' work.

Niehaus told *The Seattle Times*, "I got back here and the town went bananas about that phrase. The 'Oh Boy! Oberto' people had salamis sent up to the booth. At the Kingdome above me, there was the upper deck and people used to drop jars of mustard tied on ropes and twine down into the booth for me so I could make my own sandwiches...they would send sandwiches down."

The call later became the name of Jon Wells' new independent magazine, *The Grand Salami*, sold outside the Kingdome and, later, Safeco Field.

The baseball events of the previous four weeks had been incredible. Night after night, improbable victory followed improbable victory. Unlikely heroes rose to the fore and expected heroes performed as advertised. Through it all, Niehaus was at his very best.

Randy Johnson fondly recalled, "I just remember the electricity of that year, and the things that continued to domino, where we'd be behind in the game, and something magical would happen. And the roles that certain people played off the bench. They always seemed to come through—Doug Strange, Joey Cora, Luis Sojo, Alex Diaz—just a lot of the people that weren't the Edgars and the Juniors. You need to have quite a few of them to exceed everyone's expectations in order for things to fall in place the way they did that year."

It started benignly enough on September 8 with The Big Unit's four-teenth win in sixteen decisions, a 4–1 besting of the Kansas City Royals. Mid-season acquisition Andy Benes, former Evansville University Purple Ace, upped his mark to 4–1 with a three-hitter in a 6–2 victory the following night. Going for the sweep, it was Joey Cora's turn for heroics as he doubled home Vince Coleman in the bottom of the eighth to make it three straight. Norm Charlton picked up his eighth save of the year and his second in three nights.

Minnesota came to town next and pounded out twelve runs in the opener, enough to overcome the home team tallying four in the seventh and five in the eighth. The following night, the young Mariners came back with a vengeance. Jay Buhner was torrid, slugging his thirty-second and thirty-third of the summer to go along with Mike Blowers' twentieth in a 14–3 drubbing of the Twins. That same night in Chicago, former Mariner ace, Mark Langston, won his fifteenth. As good as Seattle was going, the Angels were now sixteen games on the plus side of .500. The Halos were six games up with only sixteen more to play. They would not win again for another twelve days.

The series with Minnesota hung in the balance on Wednesday night, September 13, and once again the "Refuse to Lose" motto proved apt. Trailing 4–0, the Mariners struck for a trio of runs in the home half of the seventh, capped by Blowers' twenty-first. Still not out of rabbits to pull from their hat, the M's once again called on their star right-fielder. Jay Buhner's thirty-fourth round-tripper with two aboard in the eighth carried the surging squad to five games over .500. Charlton, nicknamed "The Sheriff" by Dave, got save number nine. The improbable was taking shape. The 67–62 M's now trailed the California Angels by only five games.

Mariner employee Tony Pereira had been charged with posting the wild-card standings at the Kingdome each night. Jay Buhner had taken notice and wasn't impressed. In early August, a reporter had asked Buhner about the Mariner chances of securing the American League wild-card playoff spot. Buhner told the reporter that he wasn't interested in the wild card—he was out to win the division. While the remark had been typically long on guts and toughness, Jay might have been the only one to believe it. He was no longer alone. It was beginning to sink in—this could actually happen.

Reliever Norm Charlton remembered what a jolt Buhner sent through the clubhouse, "We started creeping and creeping, and there was some talk

about the wild card. I think Jay stepped up and said, 'You know what'—
and I don't know how you're going to print this—but basically, 'bleep the
wild card.' For me, that probably was the turning point, where everyone
looked around and said, 'You know what? The way we're playing, he's
right. Not only is it a possibility, it's probably going to happen.'"

Charlton further recalled how pivotal that moment was. "The apocry-
phal story is true. We had flags at the Kingdome denoting the standings.
One day we said, 'We're kind of out of it. Let's put up the wild-card flags.'
Buhner said, 'What's going on?'"

As for Jay, he told the story this way. "I said it very politely, I thought.
I was shagging in right field that night, and a kid was putting the banners
up right above me. I yelled at the kid, and he came down to the field. I said,
'What are you doing? Take that bleeping banner down.' He said the front
office told him to do it. I said, if they had a problem, to come down and talk
to me. When they did, I told them, 'Look, we're playing great right now. I
don't think we should be setting our sights on the wild card. Let's not settle
for second best.'"

Buhner's play typically matched his words. His teammates, one after
the other, one night after the next stepped into the spotlight. The Mariners
headed for the Windy City, taking their magic show on the road. In the
first game, the new guy, Benes, improved to 5–1, scattering eight hits and
allowing only two runs. That night's hero was Vince Coleman, whose
seventh-inning RBI-double to right plated Luis Sojo with what proved to
be the winning tally.

The following night, September 16, Buhner belted his thirty-fifth
circuit clout. Still, the hero's laurels fell to catcher Dan Wilson, whose
ninth-inning solo shot made Tim Belcher a ten-game winner and set the
stage for Charlton's tenth save. Meanwhile, the Angels fell in Oakland and
their lead shrank to three games.

The entire city was, as Dave would say, "going bonkers."

When the M's lost a 2–1 heartbreaker in the series finale, the wound
was salved by California's fourth straight defeat, a 10–8 loss in Kansas City.

Returning home to face Texas, Seattle sent Randy Johnson out to toe
the slab in an effort to match Langston's fifteen-win total. The Big Unit did
not disappoint, handcuffing the Rangers on three hits as Blowers had three
RBI and once again went yard with his twenty-second. Edgar Martinez, on
his way to his second AL batting crown, hit his twenty-eighth. California
lost again.

The M's were only two back.

There were few non-believers left in the city by the Sound. Game after improbable game, both likely and unlikely heroes had come to the fore.

Yet, in addition to the blossoming pennant race, there was another baseball drama unfolding in Seattle. On September 19, Seattle voters went to the polls to vote in a special election. That election was to decide the fate of a $111 million property-tax levy that included funding for a new baseball-only stadium for the Mariners. The widely held view was that the ability of the franchise to remain in Seattle hinged upon approval of the measure.

Early returns began filtering in by the third inning and they were not good. The measure was failing and the fans at home and in the stadium had every reason to believe their cause was lost. There was now every possibility the 1995 Mariners would not return in 1996. The measure trailed all night and was eventually defeated by a 53–47 percent margin.

But for those of us who are fans, part of the mystique and the magic is that baseball transports us from the realm of our daily lives into a universe in which seeming miracles really happen. Not only is the sometimes mundane and tedious and worrisome world held at bay for nine innings at a time, we willingly surrender to the equally real realm of hope and possibility and an occasional gift from the baseball gods.

Incredibly enough, the election results would not be foremost in the minds of Seattle baseball fans the next morning. The ballot box would end up taking a back seat to the box score.

Instead it turned out that the September 19 contest against Texas filled whatever seats were still left on the bandwagon. Despite Junior's thirteenth blast of the year, Texas had a 4–2 lead going into the bottom of the ninth. With Mike Blowers on base and one out, manager Lou Piniella knew the gritty Blowers had been playing for some time on a bad knee. He sent Alex Diaz into pinch-run.

The Texas closer was Jeff Russell, a formidable pitcher who brought serious heat. Piniella needed a left-handed stick and nodded toward utility infielder-outfielder Doug Strange. As memorable as any calls he made during that stretch run, Dave Niehaus' description of what happened next was absolutely seismic. Throughout the Northwest, kitchen tables were pounded, headsets were inadvertently yanked out, and car horns were blasted when Strange sent Russell's 0–2 fastball into the right-field bleachers. Pandemonium ensued wherever the faithful were that night.

*Jeff Russell is set to go to work on Strange. Here comes delivery
on the way to Doug and it's SWUNG ON AND BELTED—
DEEP TO RIGHT FIELD AND IT WILL FLY AWAY AND
WE ARE TIED AT 4–4! I DON'T BELIEVE IT! MY OH MY!
First pitch to Doug Strange, a bullet that just screamed over the
National League sign of the scoreboard, AND THEY ARE
GOING ABSOLUTELY CRAZY IN SEATTLE!*

And it wasn't even over. Strange was not done for the night. He singled with one out and nobody aboard in the eleventh inning and scored the winning run when Junior whistled a two-out, line drive between short and third.

*The 2–2 pitch to Ken Griffey Jr. now from Dennis Cook here
it comes and it's swung on and LINED OFF THE GLOVE OF
THE THIRD BASEMAN ORTIZ—HERE COMES STRANGE—
THE MARINERS WIN IT 5–4, MY OH MY! THE MARINERS
ARE ONE GAME BACK OF THE CALIFORNIA ANGELS,
AS JUNIOR HITS A LINE DRIVE RIGHT OFF THE
GLOVE OF LUIZ ORTIZ AT THIRD BASE AND NOW
THEY ARE THREE GAMES AHEAD OF THE TEXAS
RANGERS AND BABY IS THIS LOOKING SWEET!*

It had happened again. The M's were finding ways to win, ways both great and small.

Farther south, Troy Percival had given up a run in the bottom of the tenth at Oakland, sending the Angels to their sixth straight defeat, Seattle was within one game of the division lead.

The baseball season is intrinsically about the long haul. Over a stretch of 180 days, 162 games are played. With the doubleheader now a rarity, twenty-seven games a month are played over six consecutive months. Many of those eighteen days off are spent in transit.

The very best teams in history lost ten times a month. So, to watch a pennant winner is to learn the remarkable manner in which good teams win consistently. The outcome may seem to be the result of the big hit in the late innings, but the second-baseman's smooth pivot on a rally-killing double play in the second inning made it possible. The base runner who went from first-to-third on a base hit and scored on a sacrifice fly back in the fourth inning was instrumental as well.

Each succeeding night, the same cast performs a different play. Some nights there is a single hero, other nights many. It's why baseball fans cherish the names of role players and superstars alike. The memories of a great season are replete with stories of games won by platoon players and pinch-hitters.

The role players who rise up with a key hit or a spectacular catch at the most opportune moment are every bit as key to a team's success over the long haul as the superstar who tears it up on a nightly basis. To those fortunate enough to watch a winning team over a season, those "lesser lights" shine as brightly in the memory as do the household names. Years later, simply remembering their names brings a smile to the fan who followed them that year, that memorable season.

Strange knew, as did most of the players, that they were winning hearts as well as ballgames, recalling, "We were so far out, it seemed no one was interested in baseball staying in Seattle. Next thing you know, we get on a roll, and we're right there. Whether it was Diaz hitting a pinch-hit homer to win a game, me doing the same, Sojo breaking his bat, Randy being unbelievable, Junior being the fantastic player he was, (Rich) Amaral contributing every time he went on the field—everyone found a way."

The wrap-up game of the three-game set followed the next night. Seattle got a little home cooking at both the Kingdome and at the Oakland-Alameda Coliseum. Ken Griffey Jr.'s first-inning rocket started the 11–3 romp at home. In the East Bay, Todd Stottlemyre, son of former Yankee great, Mariner broadcaster and long-time Dave Niehaus pal Mel Stottlemyre, took care of the reeling Angels, striking out twelve over 8 ⅓ innings.

At the Kingdome, Mariner reliever Jeff Nelson came on in the ninth facing a bases-loaded, nobody-out jam and proceeded to strike out the side on ten pitches. When Mark McLemore swung and missed a 0–2 slider, Dave Niehaus could barely contain himself.

Jay Buhner, a man who every day gave every ounce, sat before his locker. There weren't many places he wasn't sore. In his eighth year of sacrificing his body on a daily basis, his medical chart led the team in every category. Still, this night, he never felt better in his life. His August dream had become a September reality and he'd had plenty to do with it. He knew it wasn't over, that he needed to coax his body through another ten days and hopefully more. But the M's had caught the Angels. Thursday would be an off day. He needed the rest. Other than that, he couldn't wait to get to the park on Friday.

Years later Buhner reflected on how it felt to be part of that clubhouse. "Ask anyone, it was crazy," he said. "If you got to the park at two, you were the last to get there. We were there at twelve, one, the whole month of September. We got superstitious—we had to have a pepperoni pizza from Pizza Hut. The guy would show up with the pizza, we'd play cards and shoot the cud. That's the way baseball is supposed to be played—playing baseball and having a blast. We'd pull up a cooler after the game, sit around talking about the game until late at night, and then hurry home so we could come back."

Had it been a movie script, it would have been rejected as implausible, too feel-good to be true. Sometimes baseball serves to remind us that the plausible and the possible are two very different things. Ask any fan of the 1969 Mets. Ask any fan of the 1995 Mariners. Those fans were a part of

Dave in the Kingdome booth with Kevin Cremin.

the magic. John McLaren was the bench coach in 1995, and he was the one who took what the fans were feeling and literally made it a part of the team's credo.

"The fans would not let us quit," McLaren said. "They absolutely supported us, pushed us to the hilt. We were on the bench one day, I'll never forget it. We're waiting for the umpires to come out, and I'm looking out toward left-center, and there's this sign: 'Refuse to Lose.' I said, 'That's a neat thing, Lou.' And Lou started talking about it. He said, 'You know, that's got a little rhyme to it.' As we kept going, there were ten, twenty signs, and they were all over the place. After a while, we rode it. Refuse To Lose. That was our thing."

The Oakland A's rolled into Seattle fresh off their sweep of California and ready to continue in their role as spoilers in the AL West race. With six runs in the first three innings, they made it clear they took that role seriously. Then Junior led off the fourth inning with a drive deep into the right-centerfield seats. It was as if a charge had gone off in the third-base dugout and by inning's end, the game was knotted at six apiece. Still, the A's were unrelenting and a single tally in the seventh gave them a 7–6 lead going into the home half of the eighth inning.

Edgar Martinez stepped into the batter's box to face reliever Jim Corsi. With his familiar, toed-in stance and bat cocked high above his head, he called the meeting to order. When Corsi's 1–0 pitch soared over the left-field wall, Rick Rizzs was at the ready:

> *The pitch on the way...swing and a drive...deep to*
> *left field, this game is tied! GOODBYE BASEBALL!*
> *Edgar Martinez with a lead-off home run—it's even at seven.*
> *This shot lands above the aisle-way in left-centerfield.*

Three nights earlier, it had been role-player Doug Strange who had carried the mail. This night, one of his mates on the bench brought a very special delivery to the 57,555 gathered under the concrete roof next to Royal Brougham Way. Alex Diaz put his stamp on the saga of Mariner role-players who came up big during the final month of the 1995 campaign.

Amid all the heroics performed by Mariner players, a salient strength evidenced itself throughout the incredible September: Lou Piniella was a hell of a manager. Lou was both a great motivator and a great tactician.

Mike Blowers remembers Lou the motivator.

"Another thing I remember," Blowers said, speaking of 1995, "is just how relentless Lou was. It's a 162-game season, and I don't think guys ever take a day off, but it's a grind. And, I think at times, you can lose a ballgame and just think, well, that's just one loss out of 162 games we're going to play. But, the thing that I got from playing for Lou for four years was that every loss means something. I mean, this guy would lose a game in May, and it would drive him crazy. And, that's infectious on everybody and you get to a point where you don't accept losing at all, even though you know you're going to lose games. I remember Lou, early in the season when we weren't playing particularly well, saying that to us.

"And it took a while for us to really get it, but I think that's one of the reasons that we had the success that we did. And as it turned out, we did need every win that year."

Ask anybody who ever played for Lou Piniella, coached for him, worked with him in any capacity what they remember most about him. They will tell you the same thing. The man hated to lose.

Lou Piniella the tactician was equally imposing.

Time and again, he pulled the right string, used his personnel wisely and called on his National League experience to execute the double-switch. He had adapted the strategy to the American League with considerable acumen. In the Senior Circuit, the ploy is used most often when a pitching change occurs and a substitute bats in the pitcher's spot in the order, usually moving the pitcher's turn to hit back as far as possible.

With the designated hitter in effect in the American League, Piniella regularly applied the concept when he used a pinch hitter. He was a shrewd observer of the game and the opportunities available to him both at the moment and a few innings down the road. Most of all, he was a manager who knew his players and how to use his bench. He'd assembled a team of guys who were versatile as well as capable when called upon.

As the bottom of the eighth opened, first-baseman Tino Martinez singled. Piniella's wheels began to turn. He needed speed and sent Rich Amaral in to run for Tino Martinez, knowing that third-baseman Blowers could move across the diamond to play first base the next inning. He had Doug Strange on his bench to take over at third.

Ever true to his commitment to do whatever it took to win, Jay Buhner deftly sacrificed Amaral to second. Thinking ahead, Piniella sent Alex Diaz into the on-deck circle ostensibly to hit for shortstop Luis Sojo. Felix

Fermin was on the bench and available to play shortstop. If it all worked out, Diaz could play left field and Fermin could take left-fielder Vince Coleman's spot in the order. Diaz was a switch-hitter and, if Blowers got on, A's skipper Tony La Russa probably would bring in the left-hander warming in the bullpen. Blowers ran the count full, then drew a base on balls.

Sure enough, La Russa made a change. He went to the pen for a ghost of the Mariner past, summoning southpaw Rick Honeycutt to the mound. Piniella had played his card and now had the edge. In 1995, Diaz hit .237 from the left side and .307 from the right. Piniella pressed the advantage. With both the element of surprise and the tall Honeycutt's lanky delivery on his side, he gave Amaral the steal sign. One pitch later, Amaral stood at third, the potential tying run, and Diaz was ahead in the count 1–0.

Most managers will confess that they look brilliant only when their hunches pan out. Lou's did. But great managers make those choices based on a careful reading of the situation. When Honeycutt threw the next pitch out of the strike zone, he was in no position to miss with the next one. He came across the middle of the plate and Alex was sitting on it. Diaz lifted Honeycutt's 2–0 offering high into the Kingdome ether. Left-fielder Rickey Henderson ran out of room. In the booth, apoplexy reigned. Once again, Rick Rizzs had the call:

He's got a huge gap on the right side of the infield, everybody up close, pitch on the way. Swing and a fly ball deep to left field—GOING, GOING, GOODBYE BASEBALL Alex Diaz jumping up and down as he passes first base. A three-run home run—the Mariners lead Oakland 10–7! WHAT A MAGICAL NIGHT HERE IN THE KINGDOME!

The Seattle Mariners were all alone at the top of the American League West.

Randy Johnson's 1995 season was about as dramatic as one could imagine. Time and again he stood every bit as tall as his 6–11 frame. Once again, he brought the Saturday Night Fever to the ballpark. Fifteen of the twenty-two outs he recorded were strikeouts. Oakland managed four singles and Jay Buhner's thirty-sixth homer of 1995, with two aboard in the first, gave Seattle's ace all the support he needed. Still, Buhner added number thirty-seven in the fourth. Yet another night the ballpark in Seattle was rocking as more than fifty-four thousand fans jammed the Kingdome.

It was now the California Angels who were two games back.

When the Mariner faithful kneeled to pray on Sunday morning, September 24, they surely offered up an orison of thanks for what may have seemed like divine intervention to many. One can only imagine that the heavens were just as intently petitioned for the manna to continue, for the baseball seas to remain parted long enough to reach the post-season Promised Land. To complete the Exodus, the Mariners would have to leave their past behind.

Some 1,200 miles to the south, Angel fans, too, were casting a glance heavenward, beseeching the baseball gods to bring an end to their second nine-game losing streak in five weeks. As it happened, on this particular Sunday, all prayers were answered. The Angels got their tourniquet in the form of Jim Abbott's sparkling three-hit, 5–0 shutout of Texas. As for the Mariner fans, they got a serious dose of answered prayer as well

That Sunday afternoon, Chris Bosio struggled through four innings and combined with Bob Wells to give up six runs. Luckily, this was a night for the offense to shoulder the load. The Mariners pecked away—one in the third, two in the fourth, one in the sixth and two more to tie in the seventh. Baseball is a game in which the most successful hitters in the game fail 65% of the time and the pretty good ones more than 70%. Yet, hitting and confidence are both considered contagious for a reason. The Mariner mindset was bending spoons.

In the bottom of the eighth, LaRussa inserted Craig Paquette at third base. Paquette promptly threw wild to first on Jay Buhner's inning-opening ground ball. Buhner wound up at second. Buhner never wanted to come out of a game in his life. Even a manager as tough as Piniella couldn't have relished the prospect of having to face Buhner after replacing him. Still, both men knew what Jay had sacrificed that year, the limits to which he had pushed his body. Yet, part of what made both these men great was their commitment to winning, to the team. Piniella needed speed at second and even Jay understood when the skipper sent Alex Diaz out to run for him.

Third baseman Mike Blowers was cut from the same cloth and gave himself up, sending Diaz to third with a perfect sacrifice bunt down the first-base line. Dan Wilson added to Jim Corsi's rough weekend with a sharp ground ball through the hole on the left side. The good ship Mariner seemed unsinkable.

Then the unsinkable gave way to the unthinkable.

Ex-Mariner Danny Tartabull had burst onto the Seattle scene in 1986 with twenty-five homers, ninety-six RBI and sky's-the-limit potential only

Ron Fairly, Dave Niehaus and Kevin Cremin, 1995.

to be traded away to Kansas City the following year. He represented so many of the Mariner nightmares of the past: a young superstar traded away for a group of players, none of whom matched the five one-hundred-RBI seasons he'd produce with the Royals, Yankees and White Sox. He was back with yet another bad dream.

The Mariners had made two terrific mid-season moves to bolster the pitching staff. One was the acquisition of starter Andy Benes from St. Louis, the other dealing with the Phillies for reliever Norm Charlton. Charlton became the closer of choice for Piniella and chalked up twelve saves in a few short weeks. This Sunday afternoon, he quelled the A's uprising in the eighth, but in the ninth he followed a walk to Mark McGwire with the only hit he gave up that day. It was a towering blast off the bat of Tartabull that put the white-shoed Athletics up, 8–7.

Rick Honeycutt got Junior to line out to Stan Javier in left to start the ninth. LaRussa again went to the pen for his man Dennis Eckersley, one of the game's all-time great relievers. Recall, however, this was to be a day of answered prayer and, whoever whispered the one about Eckersley not getting anybody out today, got through on the heavenly request line. Edgar Martinez, who had clubbed his team-record, fifty-first double in the sixth inning, lined a single into center. As the left-handed-hitting Tino

Martinez stepped into the box, LaRussa made the decision to stick with his man. Tino made him pay with a rope into the right-field stands—Seattle 9, Oakland 8.

Like the Leviathan, the unsinkable rose from the deep and put the unthinkable to rest.

It was all too much. In the space of seventeen days in September, this .500 club had played at an .824 clip, winning fourteen of seventeen. At the same time, the Angels had lost ten of fifteen. Can anyone blame Dave Niehaus for blowing a gasket over this latest installment of the 1995 Magical Mariner Tour? Those who had their headphones on must have nearly passed out.

Here's the pitch to Tino, swung on and belted, deep to right field and that will be FLYING AWAY! And the Mariners win it, 9–8, in perhaps the most incredible game in their history! Back and forth, back and forth and Tino Martinez, his second home run of the game! UNBELIEVABLE! OFF DENNIS ECKERSLEY! And forty-six thousand fans are losing their minds here in Seattle! TONIGHT I'LL GUARANTEE YOU IT WILL BE SLEEPLESS IN SEATTLE FOR EVERYBODY WHO WAS HERE TODAY, INCLUDING ME!

It was pure unadulterated bedlam in Marinerland. The "Refuse to Lose" signs were now as ubiquitous as the raindrops. Mariner t-shirts seemingly adorned half the town. The city, which had endured so many baseball ills, over two long-suffering decades, had itself a brand new disease. Seattle had its first case of pennant fever.

And California was coming to town.

It was certainly a gift from the schedule makers that Monday, September 25, was an off day. It seemed like the whole city needed to catch its collective breath. The broadcast crew was no exception. Niehaus, Rizzs, Fairly and Cremin had been pedal to the metal ever since returning home from Cleveland on September 7. A day's rest before the two-game set with the Angels was a welcome relief.

The Angels came in with their rotation at the back end, so game one pitted Shawn Boskie against Andy Benes. The Mariner right-hander gave up eight hits, only two for extra bases, and Seattle's Griffey (his sixteenth) and Buhner (his thirty-eighth) went deep. Seattle's 10–2 shellacking put the Angels in a three-game hole.

The ace of the California staff was southpaw Chuck Finley, a six-foot-six product of West Monroe (Louisiana) High School and Northeast Louisiana University. Chuck was in the middle of a twelve-year run in which he racked up double-digit wins in eleven seasons. He was among the toughest pitchers the M's faced and, in the second game of this crucial series, Finley was again as intimidating as ever. Despite giving up five walks, he allowed only three singles—two to Edgar Martinez and one to Blowers—combining with Troy Percival and Lee Smith on a 2–0 shutout.

Had Finley faltered that night, his ball club would have been four games out with four to play and the race all but finished. His big effort that night contributed mightily to the dramatic finish of the 1995 campaign. The Angels won their last five.

The Mariners finished up in Texas and the first game of four with the Rangers brought another special Niehaus moment—a deli treat, now oh-so-familiar to Seattle fans. Mickey Tettleton, a man who could hit a one-iron about as far as you could see, golfed a low fastball from Randy Johnson into the stands for a 2–0 lead in the second inning. Jay Buhner answered in the fifth by touching them all for the thirty-ninth time, this time with Edgar Martinez aboard. Deadlocked at two apiece in the top of the eighth, it was time for Grandma to get busy in the kitchen. With Rich Amaral on third, Dan Wilson on second and Vince Coleman on first, Griffey came to the plate.

Junior right down on the knob of the bat, wavin' that black
beauty right out toward Pavlik, has it cocked and Pavlik is set.
The pitch on the way to Ken Griffey Jr. and it's SWUNG ON AND
BELTED DEEP TO RIGHT FIELD! GET OUT THE RYE BREAD,
GRANDMA, IT IS GRAND SALAMI TIME! I DON'T BELIEVE
IT! ONE SWING OF THE BAT—THE FIRST PITCH—AND KEN
GRIFFEY JR. HAS GIVEN THE MARINERS A 6–2 LEAD OVER
THE TEXAS RANGERS! MY OH MY, WHAT A SHOT BY
JUNIOR...AND HE HAS NEVER HIT A BIGGER ONE!

You'll forgive Dave if this one time he left off the mustard. There was plenty of it on the call. Junior's "one swing of the bat" gave Randy Johnson his seventeenth win against only two losses, eliminated the Rangers from playoff contention and reduced the Mariners' magic number to two.

Two up with three to play, there was one last regular-season escape trick to be performed on Friday night. The Rangers' Mike Witt took a 3–2 lead into the eighth, but back-to-back sacrifice flies by the Martinez boys plated Coleman and Amaral. Charlton's fourteenth save put the Mariners two up with two to play.

Norm Charlton, in his final 15 games of 1995, was 2-0 with twelve saves in twelve chances. With the first postseason in team history on the line, it's hardly surprising that Dave's call crackled with anticipation.

> *A ball and two strikes and the 1–2 pitch on the to Maldonado—*
> *HE WENT AROUND THERE'S NO DOUBT ABOUT THAT!*
> *SO MALDONADO WENT AROUND…and the Mariners are*
> *coming out of the dugout to congratulate Norm Charlton on another*
> *phenomenal performance but there's no jumping up and down—*
> *that will all come three hours later if the California Angels*
> *lose to the Oakland Athletics because the Seattle Mariners have*
> *just clinched a tie for the American League West championship*
> *with a 4–3 victory over the Texas Rangers tonight…*
> *and the chant right now is ONE, ONE, ONE!*

I've always been intrigued by this call, by the subtle changes Dave's voice went through. It's one thing to simply modulate up, but to set the scene, rise to the action, then temper that excitement with the reason born of experience, the knowledge that the job was yet unfinished, and then to rise again to the full import of the pennant-clinching number now being "ONE, ONE, ONE!"—it truly was like song. That night in the Lone Star state, Louie Armstrong had nothing on Mr. Niehaus.

Charlton's fourteenth save put the Mariners two up with two to play. The magic number was indeed at one.

Saturday night proved to simply be Texas' night. Benes had his only bad start of the season and the Rangers prevailed, 9–2. Later that night the news came in that California had bested the A's, 9–3. One game left and one game separated the two division rivals.

Sunday, October 1, would be the final day of the 1995 season and the AL West crown was on the line. The new month brought some old results as nemesis Mickey Tettleton bedeviled the Mariners and Chuck Finley carried the Angels. Tettleton's three-run bolt in the first catapulted Texas to a 9–3 win over Seattle. Finley held Oakland to four hits on the way to his fifteenth victory of the campaign and his second big-time win in his last two starts, an 8–2 triumph.

Six months and 144 games had come down to a dead heat. The fate of the two combatants would be decided in a one-game playoff on Monday.

A decade later Dave reminisced: "The Mariners can win the World Series one of these days, and they will, I might not be here, you might not be here, but let me tell you something, it will not be as exciting as 1995. It'll be much talked about, it'll be nice to hang that pennant out there that says 'World Championship,' but nothing ever will take the place of 1995."

Dave Niehaus finally had his pennant race and some lagniappe to boot. Regular seasons have ended in a tie only a handful of times in baseball history. One game for all the marbles creates a sense of drama and history and excitement exceeded perhaps only by a seventh game in the World Series. The sense of drama and urgency was all the more compounded by the fact the playoffs were scheduled to begin on Tuesday. That meant no day off, no rest, no chance for either squad to regroup and prepare.

Monday afternoon, October 1, two teams would dig deep into the hidden reservoir of will for a showdown at High Noon. One of these two teams would get Tuesday off and the rest of the winter as well.

As it happened, someone in the offices of Major League Baseball had considered the possibility of a tie. Accordingly, the Mariners and the Angels participated in a coin-toss to determine who would host a one-game playoff should such a result occur. The Mariners won that flip and with it the right to host the game. It was just one more thing that went their way that incredible year.

Despite sweeping Oakland to salvage a regular-season tie, the Angels knew what they were up against. Infielder Rex Hudler recalled, "On the bus, after sweeping four from the A's and knowing there would be a playoff, we were thinking, if they throw (Tim) Belcher, we're going to the playoffs. If it's Randy . . . we don't know."

California GM Bill Bavasi would later say, "It just came down to Lou having saved Randy. If he didn't save Randy, I really believe we would have beaten them."

Nobody could quite foresee what that afternoon in the Kingdome would be like. I had seen The Beatles, the Super Bowl, the seventh game of an NBA Finals, stood on the side of the stage with James Brown and Tina Turner before seventy thousand people—but I had never seen anything like this.

The fire marshal had to be sweating bullets, knowing how many fans were packed into the Kingdome that Monday afternoon. It wasn't just loud; it was astonishingly loud. Sixty thousand pennant-crazed, bleary-eyed fans sandwiched their way into the ballpark with, seemingly, a single purpose: this was not only going to be the most exciting game in Mariner history, it was also going to be the loudest. They didn't disappoint.

It was classic baseball drama, almost Shakespearean. On May 25, 1989, Randy Johnson had been traded by the Montreal Expos to Seattle, along with right-handed pitchers Brian Holman and Gene Harris, as part of a deal for fellow southpaw Mark Langston. Despite being the ace of the staff, Langston was set to be a free agent at the end of the 1989 season. Rather than allowing him to walk away, the Mariners chose to make the swap. Langston had three times led the AL in strikeouts and, at the time, the trade was considered another in a long list of deals benefitting the Mariners less than their trading partner. This was epic.

"It was just kind of interesting," Johnson said, "I was now pitching against Mark Langston, whom I got traded for. I don't think, up to that point, I had ever pitched against him, and now I was, obviously, in a very big game. It was everything you thought it was going to be."

Neither team gave an inch, as Johnson and Langston traded goose eggs through the first four frames. Vince Coleman's RBI single in the fifth gave the home team a tenuous, one-run lead. Johnson pitched with a level of intensity that was wilting and was damn near unhittable.

"Randy was throwing pellets." Hudler remembered. "You could barely see the ball."

Through 106 pitches, Langston kept the deafening crowd from blowing the roof off the Kingdome. Pitch number 107 opened the floodgates, and yet another unlikely hero pulled the lever. With ducks on every pond, second-sacker Luis Sojo cued Langston's first pitch off the end of the bat just inside the bag to the left of diving first-baseman J.T. Snow–"that ugly bleeder," as Hudler later described it. The ball more crawled than rolled, seemingly forever, all the way down the right-field line, clearing the bases. Langston's errant throw home allowed Sojo to score as well.

It was Rick Rizzs' turn to call the action and his final two words became part of Mariner history:

Here's the pitch. Swing, and it's a ground ball, and it gets on by Snow. Down the right-field line into the bullpen. Here comes Blowers. Here comes Tino. Here comes Joey. The throw to the plate is cut off. The relay by Langston gets by Allanson. Cora scores! Here comes Sojo! EVERYBODY SCORES!

Sojo still speaks of the moment with genuine excitement: "Bases loaded...the first thing I said, 'you have to put the ball in play.' Langston had pitched an unbelievable game, him and Randy Johnson going at it. I said to myself, 'this is your moment. Concentrate on what you're doing.' It was kind of a lucky shot, but it worked. I've never heard a place as loud as the Kingdome after that play. We weren't able to talk for the next twenty minutes."

Jay Buhner echoed his sentiments: "Every pitch, every out was very intense, nerve-packed. And as the game drew closer and closer to the last inning, it was more and more nerve-racking. That whole Sojo play, the way that whole thing transpired, it was almost in slow motion....the way it all ended, with him sliding in, made it that much more special."

Two innings later, the Big Unit shook off Tony Phillips' lead-off round-tripper to start the ninth. Two outs later, he whistled a 1–2 fastball past Tim Salmon putting a final exclamation point on the 9–1 win. Dave Niehaus was behind the microphone with the call and made us remember his "rump of the steer" call the previous year.

Now the left-hander ready, branding-iron hot, the 1–2 pitch...
K INSERTED! IT'S OVER! RIGHT OVER THE HEART
OF THE PLATE! RANDY LOOKS TO THE SKY THAT
IS COVERED BY THE DOME, AND BEDLAM
AS THE MARINERS NOW ERUPT! NINETEEN
LONG YEARS OF FRUSTRATION IS OVER!

Not one single person knew the meaning of those words better than Dave Niehaus. Nor did anyone feel them as deeply, as viscerally. No one could. Surely his mind called forth a tableau of images from Diego Segui to Mike Moore, from Enrique Romo to Bill Caudill, from Bob Stinson to Dave Valle—the cadre of men he'd known and watched, described and befriended as each took his turn in a Mariner uniform. He had to have pondered all it took, all he endured—but, knowing Dave, he unquestionably thought every road trip, every inning, every pitch was worth this moment.

In the locker room, Jeff Nelson took it all in. "After the game, people were just all over the field," he recalled. "People were taking dirt off the mound. They were trying to cut out the plate. We were just going crazy in the locker room. This was something a lot of us had never experienced before."

Nobody wanted this moment to end—not the fans, the players and certainly not Coach John McLaren.

"We needed to get on a plane to New York, but no one cared," McLaren said, "We'll worry about that later, let's enjoy this. I mean, there were guys in Jacuzzis, guys smoking cigars. When we finally left the stadium, it was something you might not experience again. We had probably a twenty-five-police-car escort, and the whole street was lined up, wishing us well, air horns. It was absolutely fabulous."

An exultant band of Mariner broadcasters could all be seen standing in the booth overlooking the bedlam. Dave Niehaus, Rick Rizzs, Kevin Cremin and Ron Fairly were taking it all in as well. There were suitcases to be packed and scorebooks and notes to gather and a plane to catch to New York. This moment had been far too long in the making not to savor it. High above the rollicking mayhem below, a smiling Dave Niehaus breathed deeply. He'd seen other teams clinch the pennant against the Mariners, like the White Sox in 1985. He'd paid more than his share of dues, sung more than his share of the blues. This was the sweetest moment of his career.

It was by far the most memorable, most exciting moment in the history of the franchise. It would remain so for only a few days.

The 1995 American League division series between the Mariners and the Yankees is now the stuff of baseball lore. Yet, the beginning of the series was far from the headline story of the day in Gotham. The bleary-eyed AL West champions awoke that day to the news that the verdict in the O.J. Simpson trial had been announced with Simpson acquitted of all charges. The Mariners were about to make a few headlines of their own.

Chris Donnelly's book, *Baseball's Greatest Series: Yankees, Mariners, and the 1995 Matchup That Changed History,* tells in great and exciting detail how the Yanks took both games in New York to open the five-game series. The second game, a 7–5 New York victory, ended on a late-night, early-morning fifteenth-inning home run by Yankee backstop Jim Leyritz. It was the kind of defeat that breaks most teams.

The post-game assault by the press on Seattle hurler Tim Belcher, a genuine gamer who every start gave every ounce, was equally brutal. Not only did a crush of reporters surround Belcher, they did so mere moments after he'd surrendered the gamer-winner. It led to the adoption of what some call the "Tim Belcher Rule" allowing players a little time before enduring the onslaught of the Fourth Estate after a game, and requiring reporters to give their subject a few feet of breathing room.

A weary Dave Niehaus had lost a lot of sleep but little hope. He recalled, "I'll never forget seeing Jimmy Leyritz hit that home run about 1:15 in the morning with the rain coming down at Yankee Stadium. And we had a three-thousand-mile flight home, and you had to win three games. That wasn't going to happen. Ah…but it did. Yes it did. That was the magic that captured the imagination here in Seattle."

Nobody in the visitor's clubhouse in Yankee Stadium that night had to worry about the resolve of the men around them. Certainly their skipper wasn't about to let his feelings be unknown. He told his team to pack their bags and get ready to go back to Seattle and win three games.

When he walked to the team bus, Lou Piniella stopped before the throng of thousands of Yankees fans standing in the rain, deliriously celebrating their 2–0 lead in the series. He looked at them and said, "It's good to see you all out here in the rain. Over ninety percent of people have jobs in the morning. Apparently, you guys don't. I'm glad you're supporting your team, because you've just seen the last home game of 1995." It was vintage Lou, no brag—just fact.

Edgar Martinez was equally convinced: "I knew we were in trouble, and this would be tough, down two games. But I also felt that if we could just win that first game at home, we had a great chance to win the series, because the fans were such a big part of '95. All we needed was one game, one big game."

The M's won the first game back at home, 7–4, with Johnson pitching into the eighth. It was once again the long arm of the law that shut the door on this one.

Pat Kelly trying to hang on for New York and
Charlton back with the 2–2 pitch and it's SWUNG ON
AND MISSED AND THERE WILL BE A TOMORROW
AS THE MARINERS KNOCK OFF THE NEW YORK
YANKEES 7–4 BEHIND OUTSTANDING PITCHING
BY RANDY JOHNSON—WHO ELSE—AND THE
SHERIFF COMES IN AND SHOOTS THEM DEAD!

The Mariners headed into game four, down 2–1.

While game five is etched in memory, the penultimate contest was just as big for the man who would deliver the decisive blow in the finale a day later.

For six-plus years beginning in 1983, Edgar Martinez toiled as a Mariner farmhand. From 1987 through 1989 he averaged .344 at Triple A Calgary. Finally, given his full-time shot, he proceeded to hit .302 in 1990, .307 in '91 and a league-leading .343 in '93. In 1995, he had his greatest season ever. He won a second batting title, blistering AL hurlers at a .356 clip and, as in 1993, led the junior circuit in doubles, this time with fifty-two. He was the premier designated hitter of his era. As good as his 1995 season was, Edgar's playoff series against the Yankees was simply heroic.

Edgar hit .571 over that five-game span with a slugging percentage of 1.000. He had five extra-base hits and ten RBI. He also had the biggest hit in Mariner history. In game four, the Yankees scored three in the first and two in the third. The Mariner miracle seemed destined to end that afternoon. Martinez had his own miracles to deliver that day. Cora and Griffey opened the third with consecutive singles, Martinez followed by lining Scott Kamienicki's 0–1 pitch into the left-field bleachers. New York led 5–3.

Edgar wasn't through.

Despite scratching out single runs in the fifth and sixth to take a 6–5 lead, the Mariners gave up the tying run and came to the plate in the home half of the eighth knotted at 6-apiece. Buck Showalter sent John Wetteland to the hill for the Yankees. He walked Coleman and couldn't quite field Cora's drag-bunt single.

Memories of late August were alive in the stadium as Griffey stood in. There was to be no repeat of the drama that began this run as Wetteland's third pitch hit Junior, loading the bases. This was Edgar Martinez's night. Bat held high above his right shoulder, right foot turned slightly in, Edgar hammered Wetteleand's 2–2 fastball off the blue tarp behind the center-field wall, the deepest part of the yard. High above the Kingdome turf, Dave Niehaus served up Edgar's blast with a side order of cold cuts and condiments:

But with two strikes you've gotta protect the plate. 2–2 on Edgar. And John Wetteland one more time set, and here comes the 2–2 pitch

*to Edgar Martinez now and the fastball swung on and hit to deep
center field, Bernie Williams goes back and it is…GET OUT OF THE
RYE BREAD AND THE MUSTARD THIS TIME GRANDMA,
IT IS A GRAND SALAMI! AND THE MARINERS LEAD
IT 10–6! I DON'T BELIEVE IT! MY OH MY!*

The Mariners prevailed 11–8. Two dingers and seven RBI from their DH saw to it the M's would play another day. Still, Edgar wasn't through. Neither was Niehaus. Game five was the next day, Sunday afternoon in the Kingdome.

His affinity for his very first Mariner broadcast notwithstanding, Dave Niehaus knew full well he would not be remembered for that April night in 1977. Instead, it would be an October evening in 1995 that was to be replayed again and again in highlight reels and in the hearts of the Mariner faithful. There is not a single Mariner fan who does not remember where they were at that moment. It is the kind of moment that remains forever crystallized in the memory, the kind of moment every fan dreams of witnessing. It also was the kind of moment every baseball announcer dreams of calling. It was the moment for which Dave Niehaus had endured, the single moment that washed away a thousand disappointments and decades of agonizing defeats.

It was arguably among the most dramatic games ever played—a fifth game of a five-game series played by two spent and bone-weary teams trying to find enough reserve to carry them through to victory. It was a game in which the stalwarts on both teams rose to the occasion.

Andy Benes lasted a gritty 6 ²/₃ innings, giving up only four runs. His counterpart, David Cone, gave New York 7 ²/₃ innings, surrendering four runs as well. Joey Cora's unlikely round-tripper in the third was answered by Paul O'Neill's two-run blast in the fourth. Jay Buhner's RBI single in the bottom half squared the contest. Mattingly's two-run double in the sixth was answered by Griffey's one-out solo blast in the eighth. Five batters later, with two out and Seattle trailing 4–3, Doug Strange's bases-loaded walk knotted the game. Four-plus games, thirty-one innings, and six thousand miles in a week's time and it was all even.

It was the kind of game everyone who suited up will remember a lifetime, replaying every pitch, every at-bat. I remember few more anguished looks on the diamond than that of an exhausted David Cone's skyward glance as Strange trotted toward first. Dave Niehaus had great respect for the gritty, veteran hurler and there was even a touch of empathy, even poignancy to his call:

This is the action pitch, it all happens here. The stretch, the Mariners runners go, the 3–2 pitch to Strange, IN THE DIRT, AND WE ARE TIED! HE WALKS DOUG STRANGE, MY OH MY!"

Six years later, in 2001, Cone would collaborate with the great Roger Angell on the book, *A Pitcher's Story*. In that work, Cone reflected on that ball-four, split-finger fastball to Strange that allowed the tying run to score.

"It took me forever to get over that," he said. "I couldn't sleep. I almost didn't go out of my house for a couple of weeks after. I'd thrown 146 pitches in the game up to that point, and I had nothing left, but I was still sure that was the right call. I just didn't execute. Maybe I'm stubborn, but I have this conviction that I should be able to deliver any pitch in any situation.

"I'll never forget that flight home. My catcher, Mike Stanley, kept telling me it was his fault for calling the pitch, but I wouldn't let him get away with it. Buck Showalter, the manager, must have known that he was finished with the Yankees after the loss, and Donnie Mattingly is somewhere else in the plane, going home for good and knowing that he's never going to play in a World Series. I'd let them all down."

Truth is, David Cone never let a teammate down during his entire, stellar career.

It was a crucial moment and the noise level in the Kingdome was ear splitting. Strange, too, remembers the import of that at-bat and the tidal wave of noise that accompanied it.

"I still can't believe I didn't swing at the pitch," Strange reminisced. "First, I can't believe he threw a forkball. If it had been one inch higher, I would have swung for sure...As a player, we were used to tons of people watching us. It's part of the gig. You're in the spotlight. But during that at-bat, I remember stepping out of the batter's box and saying, 'I can't believe how loud it is.'"

As the eighth inning drew to a close, the apparently inexhaustible crowd exploded anew. Randy Johnson emerged from the dugout and headed for the bullpen. It simply wasn't possible that he could take the mound that night. Johnson remembers letting his manager know he'd be ready.

"I went to Lou and told him I'd be available," Johnson said. "At that time, he told me, 'Go get your spikes on.'"

Then, with two on and nobody out in the ninth, a most extraordinary event occurred. Lou Piniella took the baseball from closer Norm Charlton and the man he summoned from the bullpen was indeed Seattle's ace, Randy Johnson. The playoff game against California meant that Johnson couldn't pitch until game three of the Yankees series, two nights earlier. That night Randy threw 117 pitches and struck out ten. On one night's rest, he was back on the hill, this time in relief.

In the Mariner booth, the Niehaus-Cremin battery combined on a perfect pitch. As he so often did, Dave set the scene and let the ballpark do the talking.

And they're gonna go down and get the big guy,
Randy Johnson, and listen to this ovation when
the Cy Young is called in...listen to this...

He was again playing the spaces between the notes. Right along with him, Kevin Cremin gave us the crowd, the swelling ovation, the *sound* of 55,000 rising to their feet, press box announcer Tim Hutlyer in the background saying, "Now pitching for Seattle, number 51, Randy Johnson!" Is it any wonder that hundreds of thousands "remember" being there that day?

The serious baseball fan in Dave knew the historic nature of the staff ace being called in to pitch in relief in the ninth inning of a final game. The experienced broadcaster in him knew the crowd would erupt at the sight of Randy Johnson coming in from the bullpen. That would be a moment when the game would sing its own song and he'd need only bid his audience to listen and have the wisdom to listen with them. It was great radio.

Any questions about whether the big man had anything left in the tank were answered in three tosses.

"Randy came in and blew three fastballs by Wade Boggs," Strange said. "I'm playing third, and I couldn't even see them, hardly. Usually I can pick them up out of my periphery, but I couldn't see them. He was so pumped."

As the game went into extra innings, another extraordinary event occurred as the ace of the Yankee staff, Jack McDowell, also came on in relief. Never before had the aces of two respective staffs faced off in extra innings of a playoff series finale. It was a moment not lost on the players.

David Cone's memories speak to the occasion. "I can't say enough good things about the man who can perform like that when the price is so high," he told Roger Angell. "This was the game I'd come out of, after that base on balls. I'm in the dugout, thinking how I'd let the team down, but when Randy Johnson comes in I stopped being an opponent. What Randy did— that disregard for long-term effects—is what real players do. I was proud of him. He had back trouble the next year and had to go on the DL, and there may be a connection, but you don't think of that at the time. What we knew, watching him, was that he'd already beat us on a four-hitter and here he is back again after only one day of rest, ready to pitch some more, because he was their best. I was in awe, watching.

"Here's a man about to become a free agent who could name his own price anywhere, and he pitches on like that, regardless of the risk to his career. This came on the heels of a bitter strike, when the players had been hammered in public opinion. I think America began to change its mind about players right there. Sitting in the dugout, I applauded him as a fan."

Cone showed his own savvy and commitment that day, throwing 147 pitches. He later said, "I'd have thrown 247 to win that game."

The managers, Buck Showalter and Lou Piniella, had each gone all-in. When Randy Velarde's eleventh-inning single scored Pat Kelly with the go-ahead tally, it appeared the stage had been set for yet another singular moment in Yankee history.

It had instead been set for *the* singular moment in Mariner history, and in Edgar Martinez' fabled year. It had also been set for the most memorable moment in Dave Niehaus' memorable career.

Facing McDowell, Cora led off with a drag bunt down the first-base line, narrowly avoiding Mattingly's tag. Junior sent him to third with a sharp ground ball up the middle. With runners at the corners, Edgar entered the box and dug his customary toe-hold, lead leg turned slightly in, hands high behind his head.

Baseball's individual greatness is derived partly from the fact that it is played without a clock. The game is not constrained by the passage of time. It is, in fact, enhanced by it. Hand in hand with this framework goes the notion that baseball is a game of percentages. For that reason, managers forever employ lefty-versus-righty matchups, intentional walks, sacrifices and a host of maneuvers designed to play what they think are the percentages of any given situation.

As a result, baseball, in a manner unlike any other sport, is so often about potential energy as opposed to kinetic energy. The experienced fan

Daughter Greta, now Mrs. Steven Dunn, dances with her proud father at her wedding, April 30, 1994.

Marilyn and Dave on the deck of their Issaquah home with the Drysdale children—Drew, D.J. and Darren.

Mr. and Mrs. Lou Piniella dine with Mr. and Mrs. Dave Niehaus—their last dinner together.

The author sings the national anthem at the Kingdome in 1989.

Granddaughter Alexa in the Safeco Field booth with Dave.

Dave shares a moment between innings with grandson Steven.

Dave with grandson Zach at the Safeco Field groundbreaking ceremony
with Ken Griffey Jr. in the background.

Granddaughter Audrey visits Dave at the ballpark.

Grandchildren Maddy and Steven share their insights on the game with Dave in the Safeco Field broadcast booth later named for him.

Dave sets up granddaughter Audrey to do some play-by-play.

Dave at the Ford Frick Exhibit in Cooperstown July 26, 2008, standing next to pictures of the broadcasters who preceded him into the Hall of Fame.

The author with Seattle Mariners RBI Club Commissioner Bob Simeone.

Former Mariner Manager Dick Williams gives his induction speech at the 2008 Hall of Fame as lifetime friend, Dave Niehaus, listens on. Williams led three teams to the World Series and was the only manager to have won pennants in both leagues.

"Rich "Goose" Gossage, known primarily as a fire-balling right-handed reliever for the New York Yankees, also entered the Hall of Fame in 2008. Gossage ended his career with the 1994 Seattle Mariners.

The author with the esteemed editor.

Rick Rizzs, singer
Merrilee Rush
(Mrs. Billy Mac),
Kevin Cremin and
the author at a
Seattle Mariners
RBI Club luncheon
honoring Dave Niehaus.

Long-time Mariner executive Al "Moose" Clausen with Dave and Marilyn.

Marilyn Niehaus, Merrilee Rush, Dave Sims and the author in the M's radio booth.

Merrilee Rush, the author and the Mariners' Marianne Wieland.

Rick Rizzs, Greta Niehaus Dunn, Marilyn Niehaus, Merrilee Rush and the author at Safeco Field.

The author with Mariner Producer-Engineer Kevin Cremin.

Dave at his induction
into the Seattle
Mariners Hall of
Fame in 2000.

Dick Enberg and Marilyn Niehaus at Dave's induction into the Hall of Fame.

Ken Griffey Jr. and Marilyn pose with Junior's Hall of Fame plaque.

Marilyn's commitment to the Niehaus family endures with her love for her grandchildren Lexi, Zach, Spencer, Maddy, Steven and Audrey.

Author Billy Mac and Marilyn Niehaus at Rick Rizzs' Toys for Kids Auction, November 2016.

Dave Niehaus' statue at Safeco Field was unveiled on September 16, 2011. Fans are invited to sit next to Dave to have their picture taken.

Steven Niehaus Dunn embraces the bronze likeness of his grandfather.

knows the possibilities inherent in any situation and how they change with every pitch and every strategy employed.

Surveying the field from behind the microphone, Dave Niehaus was fully cognizant of the moment, of its inherent possibilities, its potential outcomes. He was at that moment like any of the greats he'd had the pleasure to describe. He was giving a virtuoso performance on the biggest stage, on his biggest night. That level of awareness and that ability to assess the situation sometimes make a baseball fan prescient—part observer and part prognosticator. Should we be surprised that this man who spent a lifetime in the game would see the events unfold in their possible state just moments before they became reality?

Dave's greatest call would reflect his savvy as well as his skill. It would marry the emerald expanses of his baseball imagination with his well-honed skills of observation. It would be delivered with his uncanny precision of language, his remarkable ability to bring to our ears the full measure of all that was happening at that moment, his ability to deliver not just the "descriptions and accounts" but the full excitement and deeper meaning of the passion inspired by the events.

I was seated that evening down the left-field line, above the bullpen, and could not have had a better vantage point to see the play unfold. McDowell delivered and Edgar hit an absolute bullet of a line drive in the air between short and third. It hooked toward the corner as Gerald Williams, who came on in the late innings for Dion James, gave chase.

First thought: Cora scores, the game is tied. Second thought: it's down the line, not a gapper. Third thought: where's Junior? I looked to second just as Griffey hit the inside of the bag with the perfect seamless stride that launched him toward third. Fourth thought: my God, he's going to score. A quick glance to Williams fielding the ball and another quick glance to third as Griffey, truly running as fast as I had ever seen, again perfectly catches the inside corner of the bag and streaks homeward. A look back to left as Williams launches his throw to the plate and now back to Junior in full gallop. Next thought: Holy #$%* THEY'RE NOT GOING TO GET HIM!

So many things happened in so few moments. Including McDowell's delivery and Leyritz awaiting the throw, fully six of the twelve men in-between the lines were involved in the action. Dave Niehaus' call of that play is every bit as special as the play itself, and when I hear it I am impressed with its completeness, its accuracy and its excitement. It was a moment worthy of his skills and his skills were worthy of the moment.

With both prescience and poise, he classically laid out the myriad possibilities in only a few words. At the moment the smooth, sweet swing of Edgar Martinez turned potential energy kinetic, Dave Niehaus rose to his beloved Mariners' greatest moment with perhaps his greatest call. It was not only the jubilant explosion of nineteen seasons of pent-up frustration, it was the joyous eruption of two decades of unending hope and unyielding faith that this moment would come.

The call would, deservedly, be played again and again. It would fittingly become the most scintillating sound bite in franchise history.

Right now the Mariners are looking for the tie. They would take a fly ball. They would love a base hit into the gap and they could win it with Junior's speed. The stretch and the 0–1 pitch on the way to Edgar Martinez, swung on and LINED DOWN THE LEFT-FIELD LINE FOR A BASE HIT. HERE COMES JOEY, HERE IS JUNIOR TO THIRD BASE, THEY'RE GONNA WAVE HIM IN…THE THROW TO THE PLATE WILL BE…LATE—THE MARINERS ARE GOING TO PLAY FOR THE AMERICAN LEAGUE CHAMPIONSHIP… I DON'T BELIEVE IT! IT JUST CONTINUES…MY OH MY!

Edgar's memory of the play that gave the Mariners the 6–5 victory is understandably quite clear.

"I had struck out against McDowell in the ninth," he said. "I came back to the dugout, down at not coming through. I remember Norm (Charlton) said, 'Stay ready, it's going to be up to you.' And it happened. In the eleventh inning, the chance came back again. I was swinging the bat so well that entire series, I was so confident, even though I had struck out. I wanted another chance. I felt I could get to him. That's how high my confidence was.

"The second pitch was a split-fingered fastball. That was the pitch that I had struck out on previously. The count was 0–1, and I said to myself, 'I have to hit the split.' That's what he had me set up for. He left one up in the zone, and I hit it hard."

As you might expect, the moment is etched in Jay Buhner's memory. "It was totally incredible," he said. "Junior's a fast guy, but the way he cut the corners on the bases on that play, it was amazing. From mid-shortstop to home plate, he was flying."

Dave with his grandson Zach in the Kingdome booth after the M's game five win over the New York Yankees in the 1995 ALDS.

In the ensuing American League Championship Series, the 1995 Seattle Mariners fell to the Cleveland Indians in six games. Certainly there are cities in which such a season would, by definition, be considered a failure. Not this city. Not this season. What happened that October night in the Kingdome reverberated around the baseball cosmos, and more enduringly, within the souls of a new generation of baseball fans in the Pacific Northwest. Seattle has literally never been the same since. Pennant fever does that to you.

In the Mariner locker room, after the concluding game six against the Indians, the players did their best to somehow absorb what they had been through, though surely that required some time. Nearly a half hour after the final out was recorded, one after another, the players began to take notice. A noise, a dull and somewhat distant roar reverberated above them. It was the fans. One by one, some half-dressed, some still in uniform, they appeared in the dugout and walked back onto the field.

Refuse to lose had become refuse to leave.

An extraordinary percentage of the fans had remained in their seats. The same sense of wonder and disbelief and unwillingness to let it all go that permeated the clubhouse was tangible in the stands as well. The line between the fans and the players had blurred completely. It was one of those rare moments the game gives you. The heartbreak of 1994 was now much more than a year ago, it was light years ago. The Pacific Northwest had again fallen in love with baseball and decades later it would be remembered like a first kiss.

Dave Niehaus had signed off some time ago. Yet he remained in his chair in the booth. Who could blame him for savoring this moment? After all, it was he who had played Cupid to these two, the baseball fans of the Pacific Northwest and the grand old game. For nearly three thousand nights, he'd been singing the charms of one to the other, making the match in hopes that one day just such a union could take place.

Norm Charlton was as moved as anyone.

"For me," he recalled, "everything the players did on the field was impressive. But when Cleveland finally beat us, we all went to the locker room, and we were kind of down. Then, someone came in and said, 'Man, you've got to get outside.' We walked back out onto the field, thirty or forty-five minutes after the game. We had just lost, we're going home. We walk out on the field, and all our fans are still there. The stadium is still packed. They're standing—a standing ovation. That was as much a moving moment as when we won 116 games in 2001, with 9/11 and all that, and we carried the flag around the field. I'm very proud to be able to do that, and that was a pretty emotionally moving moment. But I think after we lost and the fans stayed, that's probably the most emotional and the most moving moment I've ever had in baseball. That's probably the one moment that put baseball to stay in Seattle."

The incredible events of 1995 put Seattle Mariners baseball on the map. The '95 M's put Dave Niehaus on the map, in capital letters. He garnered the national exposure and reputation he so richly deserved. His regional status exploded to superstardom. He was no longer just the Northwest's most respected sports broadcaster, he was the most beloved figure in all of Seattle. He was going to have to get used to rock-star status, like it or not.

The only thing that later changed about Dave Niehaus was the seemingly impossible. He enjoyed his work even more. More than once he was quoted, "I still get depressed every time a season ends, because I love the game so much I could watch it 365 days a year." For the first time in memory, nobody in Seattle could wait for baseball to return in the spring.

Dave Niehaus was at the front of the line.

Horsehide in hand, Dave Niehaus takes the mound to throw out the first pitch at Safeco Field as 47,000-plus fans rise to their feet to honor him on July 15, 1999.

Build It and They Will Come: Safeco Field, The House "the Haus" Built

It's unbelievable...I never had an inkling of the love that was out there for me...It has been completely overwhelming.
—Dave Niehaus

THE NEXT SEASON'S EDITION of the Seattle Mariners stormed from the gate, winning twelve of its first sixteen games. Yet, after that blistering start, the Mariners of 1996 just couldn't replicate the magic of the previous season. For quite a while they had the Texas Rangers' number, winning as many games against them as any opponent, especially in their division. In 1996, the Texas Rangers finally had their year.

Despite a ten-game winning streak in mid-September, Lou Piniella's charges dropped six of their final eight to finish four games behind the boys from Arlington. Even worse, Baltimore's 88–74 record guaranteed they, and not the 85–76 Mariners, would be the American League wild card team.

Disappointing as the results were, they were not the worst news the franchise received during the final month of the chase for the AL West crown. The salient memory at the end of the 1996 season would not be the M's fallen pennant hopes. It was their fallen champion in the booth.

The first episode took place Wednesday, August 28. Dave arrived at the ballpark around 2:30 p.m., his usual time. On the way to the ballpark, he'd felt some tightness in his chest, but it subsided. About 4:30, the pain returned, only this time more severe. If anything, he was a gamer, having broadcast his way through countless colds and flus, innumerable nights when the spirit was willing but the flesh was weak. This day was different. He really felt bad.

He called Marilyn and told her he was going to see a doctor. She remembers how he sounded; he was out of breath, his voice nearly gone. Still, he assured her, he would be fine, but he thought it wise to get checked out. He'd be back in the booth for the game.

Dave elected to go to nearby Swedish Hospital to be on the safe side. The truth is, it took some convincing—he was sure he was going to get through the broadcast. As he later told the story, "Forty-five minutes later I was on the operating table." It didn't quite happen that quickly.

At Swedish Hospital, the eminently capable staff in the emergency room diagnosed the severity of the situation. He most certainly wasn't going to be back in the booth that night. After undergoing a variety of tests, including an electrocardiogram, the sixty-one-year-old Niehaus was listed in stable condition and described as "upbeat." He was kept overnight as a precaution, and post-game show host Rich Waltz filled in with Rick Rizzs and Ron Fairly.

It was only the twenty-fourth game in Mariner history Dave had missed, and all his previous absences were for his children's graduations and a couple three-day vacations. Astoundingly, it was the first day of sick leave he had taken in his almost twenty-year stint with the Mariners.

Marilyn was going to the game that evening with her neighbors, the Zieglers. She decided she would have them take her to the ballpark where she'd pick up Dave's car and head for the hospital. She arrived at the stadium to find Dave's car not there. When Dave finally agreed to go to the hospital, he had insisted Rick Rizzs follow in his (Dave's) car, so Dave could drive himself back to the Kingdome.

Suddenly, ground zero in Seattle was the Swedish Hospital switchboard. When Rick and the rest of the crew took to the air that night and let it be known Dave was "under the weather," it wasn't long before somebody managed to ferret out the real skinny. The word spread so quickly that calls came in from Reggie Jackson, umpire Steve Palermo, former broadcast partners Joe Simpson and Chip Caray, as well as veteran announcer Jon Miller, who was, at that time, the Orioles' play-by-play man. Fans called by the dozens.

Thursday, test results indicated signs of coronary heart disease. Dr. Milton English performed a ninety-minute angioplasty to clean out an artery that was reportedly 95% clogged. Marilyn met with the renowned cardiologist who assured her of two things: Dave was going to get better, and, much to her delight, Dr. English added, "We're going to do something about his smoking."

Dave was released Friday morning and, to no one's surprise, immediately announced he would be back in the Kingdome booth that night for the game against the Baltimore Orioles.

As it turned out, he returned to work but would soon land on the DL for the rest of the season.

On Thursday, September 12, the Mariners beat the Kansas City Royals 8–5 for the first of what would be nine wins in a row. It had been a season of struggle, the team never quite finding the consistent groove it had been in at the close of the 1995 campaign. Geographically pinned in the far corner of the Northwest, Seattle annually traveled more miles than any other franchise. It's the grind of living out of a suitcase and countless trips to the airport that wears you down. As Dave always said, "The time in the broadcast booth is the least stressful part."

As Thursday the twelfth became Friday the thirteenth, the team plane was on its way from Kansas City to Minneapolis. Dave simply wasn't feeling well. Since his recent heart procedure, waking up short of breath had become all too familiar. This time, however, he wasn't in his bed at home and his heartbeat was arrhythmic. Upon arrival at about 1:30 a.m., he was taken by ambulance to the downtown Minneapolis Hennepin County Medical Center for evaluation. He was given a treadmill test, which he passed.

"The doctors couldn't find anything wrong, but actually told me it might be a good idea to skip these three games here and go home," he said. Eighteen hours later, he was in the radio booth at the Metrodome preparing for the broadcast.

This time it was Mariner President Chuck Armstrong who intervened. Despite knowing what he was up against, Chuck called the booth and suggested to his long-time friend it might be best for him to forego that night's game. The Saturday edition of *The Seattle Times* reported Dave's reaction: "Chuck asked me to go back as a precaution. I said, 'I will go back and see my cardiologist and I'll see everyone at the Kingdome Monday.'"

Armstrong called Niehaus one of the Mariners' most valuable assets. "We wouldn't ask any of our key players to go out with any kind of health question," he said. "Why risk Dave for a game or two when we want him and need him for years to come? In light of this episode on the plane, it seems most prudent to have him take this time to get things checked out at home."

The following Monday, September 16, Dave was back on the operating table at Swedish Hospital. He underwent a second angioplasty to clear yet another clogged artery. This time he would have to take a respite from the booth.

Once again, the Swedish Hospital switchboard lit up like a Bill Veeck scoreboard. Former players, fellow broadcasters, fans and more fans jammed the lines for the length of his stay. Swedish had never seen anything like it.

Marilyn recalls it vividly. With her typical grace and humility, she told me, "It was only then I began to realize how important he was to everybody."

A number of calls came in from women claiming to be Mrs. Niehaus and asking to be patched through to his room. Mrs. Niehaus was about to get a new moniker. For the duration of his stay, Marilyn would call in as Barbara. She parked in the doctors' lot and entered and exited the hospital through the doctors' dressing area.

Dave, of course, wanted to know when he would be back behind the microphone. It was going to be a while. On September 17, the Mariners announced he would be taking an indefinite leave of absence. In the meantime, the fans began to flood Swedish Hospital with tributes. Someone got the idea of sending Dave an autographed ball with best wishes and the idea took on a life of its own. So many baseballs arrived at Swedish they were collected by the staff and later delivered to Dave in a shopping cart. Dozens became hundreds and hundreds literally became thousands. Each signed by a concerned and adoring fan, they filled one cart and another and still another.

By the end of his stay, some 3,077 "get well" baseballs had been sent by the Mariner faithful. Niehaus was genuinely touched and, after going through them, donated the balls to youth baseball teams around and about Seattle.

Letters poured in, including dozens from family pets—paw prints and all—sending their best wishes.

In his own humble way, Dave Niehaus attributed the outspoken appreciation he received in 1995 to the excitement of the team's first pennant race. This time there was no denying what moved the fans. The concern for him personally, the heartfelt letters and the displays around town were

Dave with shopping carts filled with baseballs sent by well-wishers after his heart attack in 1996.

unmistakable. Even he could no longer deny what so many knew to be true: he was genuinely loved.

"It's unbelievable," he later reflected, "you walk down the street, and people will come up to you and say, 'You look great. It's great to see you.' It does so much for you. I never had an inkling of the love that was out there for me until I had this thing. It has been completely overwhelming."

For the first time in his adult life, he was ready to make some changes. The juicy steaks he enjoyed four times or more a week—except for an occasional fried chicken or deep-fried fish—and the extra ladle of gravy gave way to a healthier diet.

"Whatever I like, I can't eat anymore," he said, "(only) the stuff that tastes terrible. If it tastes good, I can't eat it."

Even more important, it was time to face down his number one demon:

tobacco. He had now gone three weeks without a cigarette for the first time since he was thirteen.

Dave Grosby recalled to me one of the 1995 season's more ironic moments—the night Joe Garagiola was a guest on the radio broadcast as part of his tour of major league parks to promote his campaign against the widespread use of chewing tobacco among players.

"A number of us were in the booth as Garagiola spoke about his efforts and suddenly added, 'Your fine play-by-play announcer, Dave Niehaus, doesn't use tobacco products.' We all nearly exploded in laughter, but Niehaus just nodded with this look of complete innocence on his face as he glanced at us with eyes that said 'not a word from any of you!'"

Smoking nearly three packs a day for more than three decades, Dave and his cigarettes were never far apart. They were, in fact, inseparable. On a car trip to Lake Chelan in eastern Washington, Marilyn once timed the interval between one cigarette being extinguished and the next one being lit. The respite never exceeded one minute. Dave smoked all day, every day, everywhere. Marilyn even served notice about his smoking in bed by moving all of her clothes out of the bedroom walk-in closet and into the one in an adjoining room. Nothing worked.

"Being an inveterate, recidivist and probably doomed captive of the weed," *The Seattle Times* columnist Emmett Watson once wrote, "I smoke whenever I can—in alleys, on back porches, leaning against lamp posts; anyplace. But one good thing came of this rotten habit. I got to know Dave Niehaus quite well."

Dave's affinity for tobacco perhaps was never more evident than the night of Thursday, May 2, 1996.

The Mariners were at home in the Kingdome against the Cleveland Indians. Ken Griffey Jr. led off the home half of the seventh with a line-drive single to left. Edgar Martinez followed with a deep drive into the seats in left-centerfield, narrowing the Tribe's lead to 6–3. Two batters later, when Paul Sorrento singled to right, Cleveland manager Mike Hargrove decided it was time for Orel Hershiser to give way to a fresh arm. He went to the hill, on the way summoning reliever Julian Tavarez.

As the Indians gathered at the mound, like so many others in attendance, I felt the seat beneath me shift. I looked up to see the speakers inside the Dome that hung from lengthy cables were swaying. It was time to get out. The guy at the aisle end of our row three seats away didn't budge. He looked at me and said. "I'm from L.A., this is nothing." My reply was to the point, "In L.A. you don't have ten tons of concrete over your head, let us out."

At the same moment, my friends and I were making our getaway, the press box above the second deck was rumbling as well. Dave Niehaus had lived in L.A., too. In addition to the 1971 quake in Van Nuys, he'd been through two other quakes in southern California. He wasn't taking any chances and was also very much to the point:

"Ladies and gentlemen," he announced, "we're having an earthquake and I'm out of here."

It became part of Mariner lore that Dave Niehaus, no sprinter, beat just about everyone on the lengthy jaunt down the concrete ramps of the Kingdome to the safety of the street below. The next day at the supermarket, Rick Rizzs' butcher even asked him, "How did Niehaus beat me down the ramp?" The untold story was this: Dave made two trips. Dave was the first one out of the booth when the Dome began to bounce. Taking no chances, he sprinted out of his perch above the Kingdome field. Moments later, he was back—for his cigarettes.

Marilyn prayed, if there were some good to come out of her husband's heart attack, it would be an end to his love affair with nicotine. Her prayer was answered.

"To his credit," she said, "he quit—cold turkey. No patches, no anything. He put them down and he never picked another one up."

It was true. For the rest of his days, Dave Niehaus never smoked another cigarette. "It's the hardest thing I've ever done in my life," he said. "I really miss it, but I'll never go back."

Among the most delightful of ironies for Marilyn: now it was Dave who had to remove his clothes from the closet. Finally, he could smell the smoke permeating his wardrobe and he couldn't stand it.

Dave returned to the booth in the Kingdome on Sunday, September 22, not to work, but to see his broadcast colleagues and to be at the park. A few innings into his visit, as he sat next to Kevin Cremin, one of the stadium cameramen trained his lens on the fans' favorite all-time Mariner. The buzz took off around the park like a line drive into the gap. The applause began to swell and voices began to rise. Suddenly, almost as one, the Kingdome crowd came to its feet. As unassuming as ever, Dave looked around the stadium to see what was causing the commotion.

Cremin touched him on the arm. "They're cheering for you, man. It's for you." Players stepped from the dugout, umpires turned and looked to the press box. The mere sighting of this man had brought the game to a halt and the entire crowd to a moment of joyful exultation. Dave Niehaus was back at the park. The baseball world was once again in order.

For the second consecutive year, Dave was named Washington Sportscaster of the Year by the National Sportswriters and Sportscasters Association. The following February, he was ready to go back to work.

As Larry Stone reported, for the first time ever, restaurant hostesses at spring training heard Dave Niehaus ask for the non-smoking section.

"Five months after he had a mild heart attack, Niehaus' new lifestyle is paying off," Larry Stone wrote in *The Seattle Times*. "He looks trim and fit, and says he feels as good as he looks. 'As far as I know, I'm fine,' he said, 'I can't wait. Part of that is because I missed the last seventeen games of last year, and part is because of the kind of club we're going to have. I hate to put them on such a high pedestal, but I think we have a chance to win one hundred ballgames. I think it's going to be a fun, fun year.'"

The 1997 Mariners won ninety games and made the postseason, only to eventually fall to Mike Mussina and the Baltimore Orioles in the ALDS. Meantime, the number one baseball saga in Seattle was being played out off the field.

Dave said this of the years in the Kingdome: "It was laboratory baseball. There were no elements to bother the baseball; no wind, no high sky. But it was never an ugly old lady to me. It will always be a huge part of my life. She was a dowager. When you considered what happened there: it got us a new baseball team in 1977. First time you walked into the Kingdome it was like 'Wow!'"

Although the concrete cavern near Seattle's waterfront, the Kingdome, never truly had been adequate for baseball and long had been the least appealing stadium in the majors, it had served its purpose. In the all-too wet and unpredictable climate of the Pacific Northwest, it had at varying times housed five professional franchises including football, baseball, basketball and both indoor and, ironically, "outdoor" soccer. It had been the site of some memorable rock concerts, college and high school football games, NCAA basketball regionals and Final Fours. Amid rodeos and countless trade shows and exhibitions, it had been home to one-of-a-kind events such as Michael Campbell's "world indoor paper airplane championships."

Ultimately utilitarian in design, concept and execution, it was, as I mentioned earlier, the biggest "basement" in town.

It was a basement so big it could host a baseball team and a football team and a monster truck rally. But it was still a basement. I can tell you from way too much experience, it felt like one, too. Windy wet April or September nights in the comfort of the Dome could be rationalized by the faithful, but those precious twelve to fourteen weekends of summer spent inside the gray bubble were hard to swallow. Like being in a bunker, it was nearly twenty years before there were even any decorations, any bunting or draperies, save for the 1979 MLB All-Star Game.

When I say drab, I mean Johnny Cash would have sung about being confined in there. The Kingdome wasn't just gray, it was San Quentin gray.

There was another memorably depressing quirk about the park: the set of metal doors that exited from the second deck in left-centerfield out onto the outdoor concourses winding down to street level. For the most part, there were never enough fans in the park to warrant those sections being opened. But whether a patron or a member of the staff, every now and then on a gorgeous sunny summer Sunday, someone would open one of those doors. Few things were as depressing as the brilliant sunlight pouring in through those open doors, a painful reminder you had again deigned to spend the treasured summer inside a structure with all the aesthetic niceties of a missile silo.

Let's not forget the acoustics, either. In the days before electronic reverbs, music studios used to bury an eight- to twelve-foot section of concrete pipe below ground with a microphone buried inside that was wired to the recording console. This served as an echo chamber and was used to add that effect to recordings. Imagine if they had been able to bury a five-hundred-foot-diameter concrete soup pot and you have some idea of the acoustic nightmare of the Kingdome. There used to be a room in the stadium that housed dozens of audio delay units, all of which were linked to the various speakers throughout the building in an attempt to somehow synchronize the public address announcements and mollify the rolling echo. To say it didn't work was an "under-under-under-statement-statement-statement."

When the building was full, for seven or eight Seahawk games and six Mariner games (opening night, bat night and a couple Yankee games), the public address system was nearly intelligible. The rest of the time it was the slapback echo chamber of all time. ("Slapback echo" was a term used to

Ken Griffey Jr.,
Dave's grandson
Zach and Dave at
the groundbreaking
for Safeco Field.

describe the audio effect of a reverb setting that caused the sung or spoken word to immediately repeat.)

The national anthems were always a hoot. I can tell you from experience. In those days nobody was all that interested in singing the anthem at Mariner games and filling eighty-one slots a year was a serious challenge. This daunting task was compounded by the fact that few who did sing ever wanted to repeat the experience. In the early years, the crew would roll out a small monitor near the third-base coaching box in the hopeless pretense of the singers being able to hear themselves through that speaker. What inevitably transpired was a singer, who less than a stanza in, would be "cowabungaed" by the tidal wave of echo caroming back from center field with the sound of what they had sung three or four seconds earlier.

There is no counting the number of casualties this caused or the number of times a helpless and befuddled singer awash in echo stopped, started and struggled their way through the sonic nightmare. In my section, there was a nightly bet on whether the singer would make it through *The Star-Spangled Banner* unscathed.

I know. I sang the anthem there many times. As a professional singer and husband of hometown Grammy-nominee Merrilee Rush, I was a regular on the anthem schedule, singing as many as six to eight times a year. In addition to those regularly scheduled appearances, as a season ticket-holder for nearly two decades, I was the safety valve for Mariner Promotions Director Marianne Wieland. Another half-dozen to ten times a year, I'd be in my seat in Section 102 and Marianne would suddenly tap me on the shoulder and ask "Billy, want to do the anthem tonight?"

Trust me, she never had to twist my arm. To sing the anthem at the ballpark is as great a thrill for a singer as any out there. But as many times as I did it, never once did I do it without a conscious effort to shut out the disorienting rebound of my own voice splashing back from the far reaches of the park. "Oh, say can you see, by the...say can you see ..." was what every singer heard in the Kingdome.

And yet the very same feature, the bizarre acoustics of the Dome, made it baseball's greatest park in which to heckle.

Allow a moment's digression here on the fine, ancient and revered art of baseball heckling. First a nod to the great and now almost lost bit player in the great "play" staged nightly at the ballpark—the bench jockey. A bench jockey is a player or coach who rides the opposition or the umpires from the bench. Needling, jabbing away in a never-ending attempt to get under the skin of his target, the bench jockey's time-honored goal is to distract an umpire or player to the point of boiling over.

As a child, I remember witnessing the great PCL bench-jockey, Roger Bowman, train his sights on the estimable umpire Chris Pelekoudas (whose son, Lee, became the Mariners' traveling secretary and moved on to a long career in the front office). The elder Pelekoudas repeatedly stepped out of his crouch as Bowman pecked away. Fans and players alike knew it was only a matter of time before Bowman would be "sent to the showers."

As Chris settled into his crouch, Bowman yelled from the dugout, "Hey, Pelekoudas, you better stand up straight if you wanna sell that cup full of pencils."

Two seconds later, mask off, the ump was four steps toward the dugout pointing to Bowman with one finger in the air. "One more, Bowman, just one more," he warned.

Though born in Chicago, Pelekoudas was Greek through and through, his chiseled Aegean face highlighted by a considerable proboscis. When Pelekoudas returned to his crouch and signaled to the pitcher to resume, the stadium suddenly became uncannily quiet because the crowd was now anticipating the next insult.

Bowman didn't disappoint. Before the hurler could deliver his next offering, Bowman shouted, "Hey Chris, when they were giving out noses, you thought they said hoses and said 'gimme fifty feet!'"

I remember the batter stepping out, grinning, the catcher leaning forward onto his glove doubled up with laughter. Much to everyone's delight, Pelekoudas pointed toward the dugout and raised a thumb in the air as Bowman emerged, the two going jaw-to-jaw before a thoroughly entertained throng at old Sicks' Stadium in Seattle. Such was the art of bench jockeying and heckling. It was never profane. It was always funny. Bowman's biggest crime was making patrons and players alike laugh—an insult not to be borne between the lines.

The Kingdome's acoustics coupled with its lack of patrons meant just about everybody heard just about everything that was yelled. Heck, the left fielder knew what you wanted on your hot dog. Add to all of this the fact that Seattle fans were incredibly docile, not trained in the fine art of East Coast-style barbs. The recipe resulted in every visiting player hearing every taunt that came their way. For those of us who misspent our adult years at the Dome, it was one of the endearing rewards of watching the woeful efforts of the beloved M's.

Our favorite targets were the players who were not just out of shape but nowhere close to it.

"Hey, M*****, the program says 230!"

"Hey. R****** did they chain you to an I-Hop?"

"Hey B***** that's the farthest you've stood from a plate all year!"

Dave Niehaus had a lot of personal experience with heckling. His father, Jack, could be relentless. For some reason, Jack really had it in for Reggie Jackson and truly delighted in giving it to the slugger. When Jack came to Seattle, Dave initially got him front-row seats next to the Mariner dugout. As you might imagine, such proximity made Jack all the more eager, knowing the players could hear him. Dave ultimately had to let Jack know that everybody knew he was "Niehaus' dad" and he needed to go easy. Dave also got him seats a little farther up in the stands.

Unfortunately, the general decline in ballpark civility, quite visibly in places like the Yankee Stadium bleachers, has now made profanity and crudeness all too much a part of the catcalling. The days of good-natured, funny heckling seem numbered. The Kingdome was, in that respect, a

Dave takes a last look at the newly completed Safeco Field shortly before it opened.

throwback. Still this small recompense for spending summers in the Kingdome was not enough to view its demise with more than a passing nostalgia.

The fall of those ceiling tiles from the Kingdome roof in July of 1994 underscored the larger issue of the stadium's days being numbered. The era of corporate suites and luxury boxes rendered the Kingdome obsolete as a revenue model. The streams of income generated by corporate leasing of private enclaves in which clients and customers could be entertained and fed were significant. The NFL and the NBA were ahead of Major League Baseball and the trend was inevitable. The combination of costly repairs and the impossibility of bringing the facility into line with both new ballparks and modernized classics spelled the end for the home of the Mariners and the Seahawks.

For many, there is no question Safeco Field is the "house that Griffey built," for it was Junior's exploits that finally lit the fire in Northwest fans, compelling them not only to come out to see him, but return to see him again and again.

It was Ken Griffey Jr. who inspired even East Coast kids to wear Mariner jerseys with number 24 on them and to check the Seattle box scores to see what heroics he had performed the night before. Because of the three-hour difference between coasts and the demands of newspaper deadlines, West Coast players had long been called "heroes in their own time zone." It was Griffey who finally changed all of that in Seattle. This is not to slight or underestimate the stellar talents alongside whom he played. His special, infectious charisma infused a legion of fans, particularly young fans, for whom he was the "Fresh Prince" of the big leagues.

Sadly, less than a year after Safeco Field opened, Griffey was gone. He would play only the second half of the 1999 season there, a season in which he led the majors with forty-eight home runs. Edgar Martinez and Jay Buhner were left to carry on.

The other primary keeper of the Mariner flame, here before Griffey and still here after him, was Dave Niehaus. There was no question, until Junior's arrival, Dave Niehaus had carried the Mariners for twelve long years, years in which he managed through his brilliant talent and unwavering work ethic to transform the cacophony on the field into a symphony over the airwaves.

Few, if any, broadcasters ever endured as many losing seasons as did Dave Niehaus, or, called as many games for a team no longer in contention. Yet, you never would have known it from his work. Time and again I wandered into the broadcast booth in August and September to find his enthusiasm for the game, the job, and the team unabated by the tally of wins and losses showing in the standings.

There was another salient quality to Dave Niehaus that only those who knew him could know—his genuine humility. This is not to say he wasn't proud of his work, or that he didn't know how good he was at it. In quiet spaces and places far removed from the booth, he might admit privately to his prowess, usually only when prodded and almost only well into a discussion about the game, his situation, or his role in the grand scope of the team, or of baseball in the Northwest.

The franchise that had gotten so little right on so many occasions for so long finally got it right for all time on July 15, 1999, with the opening of Safeco Field.

For many weeks, speculation about who would throw out the first pitch on opening night had swirled around the Mariner offices and fan base. Many names were mentioned, but the Mariner faithful had only one name on their lips. It was repeated countless times and almost always spoken like a prayer, a wish so deeply desired, so passionately and intimately longed for as to be uttered in tones usually reserved for only the most special requests from on high. If you believed in Joe Hardy, if you cherished Roy Hobbs, if the phrase "build it and they will come" meant anything at all to you, then there was one and only one person who deserved this honor, this moment. Not since Edgar Martinez stood in against Jack McDowell had my baseball prayers been as fervent as they were in the stands that night.

Thanks to Tom Hanks, we all know there's no crying in baseball. And we all know that's not true. On Thursday afternoon, October 13, 1960, I raced home from Our Lady of Lourdes School, in south Seattle's Beverly Park district, transistor radio blasting in my ear, hoping to catch the end of what was a spectacular seventh game of the Yankees-Pirates World Series.

As Bill Mazeroski's bottom-of-the-ninth home run sailed over Yogi Berra's head and beyond the left field wall at Forbes Field to give the Bucs a 10–9 win and the Series victory, I found myself jumping around and suddenly, inexplicably crying. I turned to my mother and asked her why. She gently told me sometimes joy is so deep and so far beyond measure, tears are the only way to express it.

It would be almost forty years before baseball again made me feel a joy so deep and so immeasurable that only spontaneous tears could express how deeply I was moved. Just moments before the first pitch on that opening night at Safeco Field, I spotted Dave in a tuxedo on the field near the stands. It was a few moments before press-box announcer Tom Hutyler made the announcement, but by then the sightings were so numerous the crackling energy of anticipation had exploded into realization. It shot through the stands as if lightning had hit the entire stadium at once. Even the hair on your arms stood up. A tumultuous roar enveloped Safeco Field and was echoed in every home and car and bar and gathering place in the great Pacific Northwest. You could barely hear the announcement.

Striding toward the mound, hand raised in salute to the fans, was their champion, their stalwart, their constant and unswerving connection to their now-beloved Mariners. The one who had endured on their behalf, conquered the despair and the doubt, carried them on wide wings of passion, suffered for them and with them through endless miseries, lifted them to unimagined heights. Every night, every inning, he infused them with the joy born of a conscious and abiding love of the sport he described like no other. Their companion, their mentor, their friend—it was he who would take the hill and christen this new vessel of their hopes and dreams. Not one person who knew this man was unmoved at the sight.

Nearly a quarter-century of unerring excellence had gone into this moment. More than a half-continent away, more than a half-century after listening to Stan Musial's heroics on that old Zenith radio on the porch in Princeton, Indiana, Dave Niehaus had himself become "The Man."

Right up to the last moment, Dave Niehaus had no idea he'd be throwing out the first pitch that night at Safeco Field. The Mariners' front office had done an incredible job of keeping it secret. Even his wife, Marilyn, and their children, Andy and Greta, had no idea. As they settled into their seats, fans all around them were asking the same question. "Is Dave going to throw out the first pitch?" They honestly did not know.

A lot of fans have assumed over the years that Dave's first pitch was known to him in advance, because he was wearing a tuxedo. Truth is, he was performing with the Seattle Symphony as part of the opening-night festivities. He wasn't sure what the symphony members would be wearing; he presumed it would be tuxedos, so he wore one himself. Having finished reading the James Earl Jones soliloquy from *Field of Dreams*, Dave waved to the crowd and made his exit. He had only minutes to make the mad dash to the elevator and ascend to the press box in time for the broadcast.

As Dave made his way through the crowd, his old friend and Mariner team president Chuck Armstrong stepped in his way. He put a hand on Dave's shoulder and said, "Wait a minute, you've got one more thing to do." He handed him a baseball. As Chuck summed up the feeling of all concerned, "There was no other choice."

Understandably, Dave Niehaus broke down when Armstrong handed him that baseball. Who wouldn't have, much less one who had given his heart, indeed his whole being, to this franchise? He took a deep breath, wiped the tears aside, and headed for the hill.

His throw from the mound was a little high but every Mariner fan called it a strike. He was asked to autograph the ball and obligingly did so, but somehow it was not given to him. It never was. He confessed to his bride he really wished he'd gotten that ball. But the man from Seattle was still the boy from Princeton and he never said a word. Jack and Delania had raised him to never voice his own wishes at the expense of another and

Dave acknowledges the crowd on opening night at Safeco Field.

despite how precious that ball was, he never asked it be given to him.

During his career, Dave threw out the ceremonial first pitch on four occasions: the third game of the 1995 ALCS, the 1999 opening of Safeco Field, opening day of 2007, when he joined Alvin Davis, Jay Buhner, and Edgar Martinez in the Mariner Hall of Fame, and for the 2008 home opener after the Hall of Fame induction announcement.

His assessment of the four tosses was typically self-effacing.

"I've yet to throw a strike," he laughingly told Larry Stone. "That was ball four. I already have a man on. I'm working from the stretch already."

At last, all was right with the baseball world in Seattle. That is, until the most unimaginable heartbreak befell Seattle and its suddenly booming legion of baseball fans. Despite 48 home runs that summer (leading the AL) and 134 RBI, contentious negotiations between ownership and Ken Griffey Jr. got noticeably worse in the fall of 1999. Griffey demanded a trade and presented the club with a list of only four teams to which they could offer him.

On February 10, 2000, the bombshell dropped. Junior had been dealt to the Cincinnati Reds. He would play but a half-season in Safeco Field. The ballpark on whose creation he had so much impact would then wait a decade to welcome him back as a Mariner. It simply didn't seem possible.

Nonetheless, the 2000 Mariners won ninety-one games. Dave was electric, in the full flower of his creativity. The new ballpark and the resurgent franchise had inspired him to raise his own considerable game even higher. More and more he played with his pitch and his intonation. Pitches below the knee brought out the deep baritone in him as a long, slow "low" would pour forth. He'd call on the tenor part of his range when the pitch danced above the letters. Balls could be "waaaaay" outside or earn a clipped delivery when "*just a bit* off the plate."

Ray Charles, Ella Fitzgerald, Tony Bennett—they all got better as they got older. Their skills sharpened and their instruments still strong, they became more nuanced in their phrasing and their delivery. They used the spaces between the notes; silence was every bit as much their ally as sound. Fifty years removed from Princeton High School, it was again Melody Hour, only this time in the Mariner broadcast booth. The singer from south Indiana was wailing nightly. He practically sang the game. In 2001, his greatest hits collection added yet another selection.

The Mariners of that remarkable season matched baseball's all-time, single-season win total with 116 victories. Edgar Martinez, John Olerud, Bret Boone and Ichiro Suzuki all hit .306 or better with Suzuki leading the way at .350, along the way winning both the American League MVP and Rookie of the Year awards. Martinez, arguably the best designated hitter ever, hit 40 doubles, 23 home runs and drove in 116. Centerfielder Mike Cameron's 25 round-trippers propelled him to 110 RBI. Boone had one of the great offensive seasons by a second baseman in the history of the game. His 37 doubles and 37 homers contributed to an astounding 141 RBI.

The pitching was outstanding with Jamie Moyer's twenty wins leading a staff of five double-digit winners—none of whom lost more than seven games. Kazuhiro Sasaki led all of baseball with forty-five saves. The 2001 season was a year in which the excellence on the field truly matched the excellence in the booth.

A draining, five-game division series against the Indians left the Mariner pitching staff worn and weary. Junk-balling John Halama was due to start game one in the American League Championship Series against the New York Yankees. Despite Halama's successes against New York, manager Lou Piniella decided to move everybody up and pitch his men on three days' rest. The Mariners lost in five games.

In 2001, the Mariners truly caught lightning in a bottle. Riding a combination of career years by a great many on their roster, they tied the major-league record for wins in a season (116) despite having lost their superstars, Griffey and Rodriguez. Ownership had no idea how lucky it had been and it became their belief they should be able to win with what they had. The result: they stood pat during the next two campaigns. Piniella knew what they had was good, but not good enough.

In 2002, the M's won ninety-three games and still the post-season eluded them. As good as their record was, it was only good enough to finish a distant ten games behind the Oakland Athletics. Losing the division crown was nowhere near the biggest loss both Dave and the Mariner faithful were to endure at the end of that campaign

Lou needed some extra pop, in particular from the left side of the plate. Again and again, he lobbied management for the one stick who could provide a timely hit in a key at-bat and make the crucial difference. But the M's ownership group was dominated by a business mindset, not a baseball mindset. By June 4, Piniella's charges had lost ten one-run games. In all, they lost twenty-four games in 2002 by one run. More than a third of those losses were in their own division, three alone to the A's.

When the July 31 trading deadline came and went and ownership refused to step up, it was clear Piniella would step down.

Piniella had carved out seven winning seasons during his decade in the Northwest. Seattle was more than 2,500 miles from his home in Tampa, Florida and his father had taken ill. It was time to go home. With one year left on his contract, the Mariners actually traded him to the then-Devil Rays for outfielder Randy Winn and infielder Antonio Perez, neither of whom had much of an impact on the franchise.

Piniella would have done almost anything to win a World Series in Seattle and would have stayed. But he wasn't going to stay if the organization's

Dave Niehaus, circa 2008.

commitment to winning was not as all-consuming as his own. He was convinced it wasn't the case.

Lou's departure was as hard on Dave Niehaus as it was on anyone. The two men had become good friends, good baseball friends. Theirs was the kind of bond that is forged only between those who give their lives and their careers to the game, who breathe it and sleep it and, above all, cherish it. Their decade together had proved a mutual delight.

Dave even got the M's skipper hooked on crossword puzzles and one of his favorite "Sweet Lou" stories was about Piniella and the daily crossword.

"We had lost a tough game in Boston on a hit-and-run that backfired," Dave said. "We were on our way home, flying across country. I had introduced him to crossword puzzles. So he comes down the aisle of the plane still upset about the game, complaining about how we lost. Then he says (crossword in hand), 'By the way, the clue is 'movie alien,' and it's only two letters.' And I said, 'ET, Lou. ET.' And he says, 'How do you spell that?'"

The rising young managerial star, Bob Melvin, took the reins in 2003, leading the club to another 93-win season. Again, it was not enough to win the division or the wild-card spot in the playoffs. The following year the window closed on the now-veteran team. The M's lost 99 games in 2004, and the losses continued to pile up as Seattle played above .500 only twice more in the decade, winning 88 games in 2007 and 85 in 2009.

Dave's decade-long working friendship with Lou Piniella was never to be repeated as the once-again rudderless franchise employed five different managers over the next six summers. Of the six men who would steer the M's through Dave's last eight years in the booth, Bob Melvin's .481 winning percentage proved the high-water mark.

You'd never have known from Dave Niehaus' broadcasts how frustrating the return of losing baseball had become. Even though his eyesight began to trouble him and he was required to keep a close watch on his health, his passion for the game and for his work never suffered. He also had grandchildren who, by then, were old enough to learn the game from him. His great joy was to teach them how to keep a scorebook and to bring them into the booth during the broadcasts.

After nearly two hundred losses in two years, the 2006 Seattle Mariners went 78–84 under Manager Mike Hargrove and Dave kept hoping. He kept those Marlboros in the rear-view mirror and followed doctor's orders regarding his diet. He and Marilyn earmarked that offseason for some serious rest and relaxation in the form of a long dreamed-of trip overseas. Accordingly, the Niehaus family planned a very special vacation to Europe for that offseason.

A visit to Normandy was planned as one of the highlights of the sabbatical. The excursion took them by bus to the historic beaches on the English Channel. The day was cold and blustery with a biting wind. On the return trip, there was a brief stop for sandwiches, but Dave had no appetite despite it being dinnertime. Marilyn urged him to eat, but the old German stubbornness born of his father kicked in. By the time they got back to Paris, it was late and even colder. They were staying near the Eiffel Tower and although Marilyn wanted to take a cab, Dave insisted on walking. He had no patience for waiting on anything. A block or so from the hotel, he became so ill he could barely walk. He collapsed on the sidewalk. A young couple helped a distraught Marilyn get Dave onto a bench.

They were due to leave for London the next morning to rendezvous with daughter, Greta, and her husband, Steve. After catching his breath, Dave begged her not to call 112 (one of France's many emergency numbers) to give him until the morning. The next day he felt well enough to travel, but upon their arrival in London, Marilyn summoned a physician. The physician summoned an ambulance. Dave had pneumonia.

Matters didn't improve much when they reached the hospital; there were no beds. Dave and Marilyn spent fourteen hours in the emergency ward, waiting for a bed to open up. A patient on a nearby gurney stopped breathing and was attended to only after his daughter began screaming. When a bed finally became available, it was in a general ward—no night stand, no lamp, no phone, but they did give him a sandwich.

Marilyn had reached the limit of her patience and saw to it the next morning that he was transferred to the other wing of the hospital, which was private. She was astounded by the difference in the two facilities housed under the same roof. The private wing was not only well-appointed, it featured a menu of gourmet food and spirits. Dave recovered quickly, rejoining the family for the remainder of the vacation. But Marilyn was going to see to it that he took it easy for the rest of the off-season.

Sometimes the biggest impressions stars make on you is that they don't think of themselves as stars. They simply do what they do, they love it and are exceptionally good at it. Their pride, their identity is wrapped up in their work but not in the fame or the renown.

I once spent a half-hour talking with Sarah Vaughan about boxing in advance of a Hagler-Hearns fight and thirty-plus minutes chatting backstage with Emmylou Harris (who had just cut her trademark hair.) These two ladies represented two of the greatest voices ever in their genres of music and in both cases only when someone called them in to sing did it become clear to me to whom I had been talking. They were each genuine human beings, stunning women and remarkable talents. Like Dave Niehaus, you would never have known they were legends in their professions.

Dave Niehaus had become a treasure to Northwest baseball fans. There was nobody telling him Leo Lassen stories anymore. And yet, his humility about who he was and his feeling of equanimity with the fans is repeated in story after story. Everybody who met him had instantly been given the gift of "their" Dave Niehaus story, precisely because it was so special to meet

Dave hoists the 12th Man flag prior to the Seattle Seahawks game against the Minnesota Vikings at Century Link Field, October 22, 2006.

him and because when you met him it was never "about him." He always made you feel as if he was privileged to meet you.

Ask Craig Geffrey, who managed the team retail operations at the spring training complex in Peoria, Arizona and at Safeco Field. He told me of the night in the mid-2000s, he and a companion attended a Mariner organization dinner at Seattle's cavernous Union Station, an old railroad terminal. With nowhere to sit, Craig asked a couple sitting by themselves if they could join them.

First, realize Dave and Marilyn were so genuinely unassuming that they chose to sit at an empty table far from the spotlight. As dinner progressed, Geffrey and the man who had introduced himself only as "Dave" and his wife as "Marilyn," shared stories about their favorite Mariners and games at Safeco Field. Saying his goodnight later, Craig walked past a front-office co-worker and asked, "Do you know who that guy I was sitting with is?" "You're kidding, aren't you, man?" came the reply. "That's Dave Niehaus!"

Like so many others before and after, Craig Geffrey had met the earnest young man from Indiana. This was the man who didn't need to sit next to the mayor or the owner or the ace of the staff. He was perfectly content to sit next to his wife and someone who, like himself, was a baseball fan.

The 2007 season brought an 88–74 record. Among the highlights was the return of Ken Griffey Jr., a weekend of conflicting emotions for Mariner fans who were eager to see him once again and to express their enduring regard for him and yet, at the same time, heartbroken to see him in a Cincinnati Reds uniform and to be reminded of all that could have been. It was just part of a tumultuous, uneven year, perhaps best exemplified by Mike Hargrove's sudden decision to leave baseball. On July 1, 2007, despite being 45—33 and only four games out of first place, Hargrove abruptly stepped down after a 2–1 win over Toronto at Safeco Field. The litany of names of those occupying the manager's office was beginning to sound like a book from the Old Testament as Hargrove gave way to John McLaren, who gave way to Jim Riggleman, who gave way to Don Wakamatsu, who gave way to Daren Brown.

Through it all, Dave remained publicly upbeat although, privately, he longed for the days when his good buddy Lou Piniella made both the announcer's job and the on-field product a whole lot better.

After that 2007 campaign, Dave's baseball heart was aching once again. The memories of the ride of 1995 and the playoffs of the early 2000s seemed to be fading in conjunction with the prospects of a winning team at Safeco Field. Yet, he always believed, no matter how many times baseball broke your heart, it always healed it again. The game would find a way to make it better. This time it made it all-time better, Hall-of-Fame better. On February 19, 2008, Dave Niehaus celebrated his seventy-third birthday in a most remarkable and truly unforgettable way. Baseball gave him the birthday present of a lifetime.

The phone rang as he was stepping out of the shower. He answered without looking at the caller's number. The gentleman on the other end of the line introduced himself as Dale Petroskey, president of the National Baseball Hall of Fame. He was calling with the news that Dave Niehaus had been chosen as the 2008 recipient of the Ford C. Frick Award, bestowed annually since 1978 to broadcasters for "major contributions to baseball." The Frick takes its name from the late broadcaster, National League president, Commissioner and Hall of Famer who was himself a driving force behind the creation of baseball's Cooperstown in the 1930s.

"It's the most humbling experience, without a doubt, I've had in my life," Niehaus told Kirby Arnold of the Everett *Herald*. "It's the biggest thrill in my life. For us in the broadcasting business, it's our Oscar."

Accordingly, Dave was to be enshrined in the Baseball Hall of Fame in Cooperstown, New York. Where the names Ruth and Cobb and Musial were forever celebrated, the name Niehaus would join their company. Where the careers of Barber and Allen and Caray were held in esteem and honored evermore, the body of work of Dave Niehaus would be equally revered.

There was only one caveat: Dave could not tell anybody until the public announcement was made at approximately 11 a.m. Seattle time. When the hour struck, the Associated Press wires began to whir:

"Long-time Seattle Mariners broadcaster Dave Niehaus is going into the Baseball Hall of Fame. Niehaus is the 2008 winner of the Ford C. Frick Award for broadcast excellence. He will be honored during the Hall of Fame induction ceremony July 27, at Cooperstown, N.Y. The announcement Tuesday came on Niehaus' seventy-third birthday.

Among the first to call was The Kid. Ken Griffey Jr. heard the news and dialed his friend immediately. Dave was quite touched.

Neither of them could know at that moment that, in 2009, Junior would return to Seattle. There was no mistaking the deep and lasting friendship that he had fashioned with Niehaus over the years. Griffey's April 14 "debut" at Safeco Field was a night for Dave to once again break out the prom shoes.

Dave continued to struggle with his health. More than once he told an interviewer, "I'll die in the booth. I've told lots of people that if I die, not if I die, but when I die, I'm sure it's going to be either on an airplane or sitting in a booth and I'll have a heart attack calling a home run." He was even known to add, "When it happens, I want to be cremated and have my ashes put under home plate at Fenway Park in Boston."

He came perilously close to making conjecture a reality. Marilyn and grandson Zak accompanied him on an East Coast swing that included a series at his ultimate shrine, Fenway Park. It was the last road trip she would take with her husband. While in Boston, Dave woke one morning, showered, and, as was his frequent custom, returned to bed to relax, do the crossword puzzle and read the paper.

When Marilyn got up and showered, she thought she heard him yelling from the next room. She went in to check on him but he was quiet. Way too quiet. She called out to him, "David! David!" He didn't respond even when she shook him. She said, "Answer me or I'm calling 911."

Moments later she made the call and nearly a dozen paramedics and emergency medical personnel showed up at their room. They fed Dave some maple syrup and he responded immediately. He had lapsed into diabetic shock. Marilyn knew he needed to go to the hospital, but also was aware that if she suggested it he'd say no. She wisely left it up to the paramedic who gave him no option. They were off to the hospital.

While at the hospital, Marilyn noticed that a policeman had come to the room where Dave was being examined. She inquired of him why he was there. Dave had told the doctor he'd need to get to Fenway Park as quickly as possible, so the doctor called the police department. Fifteen minutes later, Dave, Marilyn and Zak were in a Boston P.D. patrol car whizzing their way to the ballpark where Dave immediately went about his normal routine and called the Mariner-Red Sox game. He was, all else aside, a gamer.

Surreal as it may seem, after the game the threesome walked back to their hotel. Despite falling into a diabetic coma, being rushed to the hospital and shrugging it all off to call a major-league baseball game, he didn't ask for anyone to give him a ride. He could have taken the team bus—but later explained that he didn't want to impose. The man who had given nearly half of his life to this franchise was still too selfless to take someone else's seat on the team bus. His mother had taught him never to impose and he was still heeding her advice.

Dave was good about seeing his doctors but Marilyn noticed that, when he did, he mostly talked baseball with them rather than his health. She remembers that after his prostate surgery at the University of Washington Hospital, one of the doctors approached her. They talked for nearly thirty minutes: "about five minutes about the surgery and another twenty-five about the Mariners." She began to insist her husband talk more about his medical charts than the hitting charts, but Dave instead decided he should now see his doctors by himself.

"That German stubbornness again," sighed Marilyn.

The 2010 season didn't help his blood pressure, either. The Mariners lost more than one hundred games for the fifth time during his tenure in the booth. The franchise had again lost its way and Dave knew there was no quick fix.

Somehow the latest decade had become a replica of the first. An occasional decent campaign was sandwiched among some truly terrible win-loss totals. Dave witnessed a decline in attendance commensurate with the decline of the quality of baseball being played in Seattle.

The Mariners closed out the twentieth century by drawing 3.1 million fans to Safeco Field in 2000, the park's first full year. The 2001 and 2002 editions each spun the turnstiles to the tune of more than 3.5 million paying customers. Both of those years, an average of more than 43,000 per game filled the ballpark. By 2006, that number had dropped to 30,000 per game and only a slight uptick in 2007 prevented a decade of constant erosion of the fan base. In Dave's final year, the drop-off had reached over forty percent.

The Mariners were hanging close to the average AL attendance numbers, but much of that was due to the successful marketing of the beautiful new Safeco Field. By the end of 2013, Mariner attendance was down more than 50% from its 2002 benchmark.

In the inaugural 1977 campaign, the M's drew well but throughout the subsequent history of the franchise, attendance numbers often had been dismal. Certainly the first year was terrific, but the club reached the one million plateau only once over the next seven seasons. It took fifteen years for the team to average more than twenty thousand per game. Thanks to 1995 and the advent of Safeco Field in 1999, the Mariners were one of only a few teams to defy the post-strike declines of the decade following the 1994 lockout.

These numbers tell the story of a franchise in decline, just as the numbers from 1978 to 1990 evidenced a franchise whose brand of baseball wasn't good enough to draw the kind of sustainable big-league attendance numbers required to generate revenues commensurate with keeping a club competitive. That story was, however, misleading—thanks to the man in the Mariner booth.

It is when the turnstile counts are compared side by side with the radio-TV numbers that the impact of Dave Niehaus on major-league baseball in the Northwest can be quantitatively and accurately measured.

During the span of Dave's first three-year contract (1977–1979), attendance fell nearly 40%, but radio ratings went up every year. His second three-year pact saw the trend continue despite a one-year attendance spike in 1982. Still, the radio, and now, television ratings were rock solid and gaining annually. His third deal saw more of the same—half as many fans in the Kingdome as in other parks but radio and television numbers matching all but a few. His initial radio ratings on KVI were frequently double that of local giant, KIRO. When KIRO got the broadcasts, their ratings more than quadrupled.

Jay Buhner told Bob Sherwin of *The Seattle Times* that "Dave Niehaus was more popular than anyone who ever played here. He's a first-class person who loves the game. You can hear the tone of his voice get excited as the game goes along. He keeps you interested during down times, he's not repetitive, he's funny and he makes you feel like you're sitting there with him."

After his career, Buhner became a member of the broadcast team and his deep regard for Dave was apparent when he told me, "Dave was like a father figure to me."

Chuck Armstrong testified to the fact that even members of the front office were among the legion of Dave Niehaus fans.

"If Dave was on radio," Chuck told me, "I'd turn the sound off on the television and I'd listen to him on the radio. If he was on television, then the radio was off. So, I would always want to hear Dave, whichever medium he was broadcasting."

In 1987, after six years with Ken Wilson and three with Rick Rizzs, Dave Niehaus had achieved something extraordinary. He was not just the voice of the franchise. Lack of winning teams, lack of a superstar player and the constant turnover of the players such as Tom Paciorek, who did connect with the fans, made the Mariners a team without a face. It may not have had a face, but it sure as hell had a voice. That voice soon became the face as well. In every survey taken, the most recognizable name associated with the team was Dave Niehaus.

Dave had become the man most trusted by Mariner fans and most admired. As the team's television package prospered in the 1990s, another trend developed. The radio numbers were first-rate when he began the game on the wires. In the fifth inning, when he moved over a booth to do television, the numbers went with him. The spike in listeners was traceable, real and the numbers concrete.

Alvin Davis, the first Rookie of the Year and number one presence on the field, will tell you. He was the most popular man in uniform but the second-most popular man in the stadium. Second-baseman Harold Reynolds knew it, too. The fans loved Harold but they especially loved Dave. When the Junior Griffey era dawned, it marked the first time a Mariner player's popularity was equal to that of Dave's. Yet even Junior was not the guy who had been coming into our homes for nearly a dozen years.

The trend continued throughout Niehaus' remarkable career in Seattle. His ratings never flagged. His presence and the level of trust between himself and the fans had a discernable effect on the club's survival. Through a confluence of circumstances, including first tenuous then unpopular ownership, mediocre teams and a genuinely unpleasant stadium, the job Dave Niehaus did in the booth stood in direct contrast to the atmosphere in which it was done. From 1977 to 1989 when Ken Griffey Jr. arrived, Seattle's baseball superstar was Dave Niehaus.

It is neither hyperbole nor hagiography to suggest he carried the franchise its first eleven years. He was the constant, the conduit. Every night, that whiskey-tenored baritone welcomed us, as we slid comfortably into our seat, once again eager to hear Dave guide us through the night's action. We trusted him, we knew he knew the game and we knew he'd tell us the truth even when the truth wasn't what we hoped to hear. And when we heard it, he consoled us and made us understand why he loved the game despite it all and why we should, too. The end result was tangible: his love for the game instilled in us a love of our own.

The financial impact was considerable as well. Niehaus' presence made radio advertising revenues markedly more valuable. His presence on TV enabled the Mariners to lure sponsors for both sections of the broadcast.

Advertisers were always surprised that when their ad said "Tell 'em Dave Niehaus sent you," he did, they went, and they indeed told 'em.

In one of baseball's lesser media markets, he became worth the kind of contracts given to some of the brightest lights in the business. His salary became commensurate with many of the top-echelon broadcasters in baseball and certainly at the top of the scale in the Pacific Northwest. You can easily make the case that he was at least Mariner co-MVP for thirty-four solid years.

Dave was more than just a baseball announcer, he was, quite literally, an apostle for this game he loved so dearly. His mellifluous baritone not only reached into people's homes, it reached into their hearts. It touched them in a way they never thought possible and fostered in them a connection to the game at the same visceral level that he himself was connected. There are countless stories of ordinary people to whom he introduced the game, people whose lives became truly enriched by the game.

Diana Rodriguez is one of those people, one of those stories.

"One summer day as I was punching the buttons from station to station, trying to find something to listen to on the radio, I heard this voice. And the voice had a quality to it that made me leave it on the station and pay attention. It was a smoky, gravelly voice and it was describing a ballpark somewhere back East. He described a beautiful warm sunny day and that the grass was green and almost glorious. I kept on listening. It was Dave Niehaus.

"Now at that time, I was not a baseball fan. I had been to a couple of games in the Kingdome, but it never grabbed me.

"But there was something about Dave describing the pitch, the hit, the fielding that made me want to listen. He painted a picture of the game. I could visualize what was happening on field. I could hear the hum of the crowd and almost smell the cotton candy and popcorn. Also there was something comforting about Dave's voice, like he was an older uncle, or grandfather who had stories to tell. He told those stories so well that I wanted to hear them.

"I began to listen to games on the radio, as I did not have a TV and was not able to watch them. I came to love baseball because of him. I bought a TV and started to watch the games. I started going to baseball games on a regular basis because of him. During the first half the '90s, I averaged thirty to forty games a year. I read books about baseball, started to study the Baseball Encyclopedia, so I could be all nerdy about obscure facts and statistics that no one else in the world cared about except other nerds like me.

"Some of the happiest times of my life happened at baseball games. Being there for great games, great company and sense of community. I was there for game five against the Yankees, one of my best memories, sitting in section 317, row 10, seats 1 and 2 with my friend Pat Elmer. When Griffey slid across home plate, grown men next to me burst into tears. I had never experienced that kind of emotion or joy before for a sport. When they lost against the Indians for the ACLS, my friend Hazel and I cried along with Joey and everyone else in the Dome. When I went to work the next day, my co-worker Dennis and I hugged and broke into tears. I have cheered and suffered with the M's for over two decades. I still root for them every spring with that expectation that "hope springs eternal" and that this could be the year. I love that baseball is timeless and is what is good about America. To me the happiest place on earth, whether we win or lose, is Safeco Field.

"I have Dave to thank for that."

Dave Niehaus succeeded in making himself the very man he had hoped to be. He was, like his inspiration Harry Caray, a nightly guest in the homes of the fans—and a most welcome one. He was a Hall of Famer. He was a husband, a father, a grandfather, who owed almost all of it to the game he loved.

J Michael Kenyon told me, "In nearly seventy years of hanging around the game and going to ballgames, I never knew anyone who had more fun doing it than Dave, nor anyone who made it seem any more delightful for everyone around him. In the three-plus decades I was around David Arnold Niehaus, I cannot, for the life of me, remember an instance when there was a baseball game in prospect, either one just played, or about to be played, or maybe even to be played the next day, that he wasn't almost literally glowing at the prospect.

"If anyone on earth was ever happier than the Noose while baseball was going on, I would be gob-smacked. That he was able to spend a half century 'pronouncing' baseball is ample proof to me that, whatever else one can say about this life, there was at least one time when everything happened just as it should have for at least one very happy Hoosier."

Yet, to be sure, his lifelong attachment to the game was but the second-greatest love story of his life. Baseball gave him his vocation and brought him both fame and wealth far beyond the dreams of his Indiana boyhood. But it was the enduring love he fashioned with Marilyn that brought him the stability and the security that was not always to be found in a life filled with suitcases and plane tickets, two months at spring training and eighty-one away games a year.

Their lifelong love brought him his children and his grandchildren. Her devotion to their family kept his world intact, regardless of whether he was in Boston or Toronto or Oakland or Kansas City. She was there with him from that night in southern California in 1961, until that night in the Northwest in November of 2010.

He continued regular visits to his cardiologist as much out of his own concern as Marilyn's insistence he keep an eye on his health and listen to the doctors. Just days before he died, he consulted with Dr. English, but simply did not wish to undergo open-heart surgery.

November 10, 2010, was a sunny day, unusually so for the season, so Dave Niehaus prepared to engage in his favorite off-season activity. He readied some ribs for the barbecue. Marilyn went downstairs to watch television. After a while, realizing she didn't hear him moving about, Marilyn went upstairs to check on him. Through her kitchen window she saw him, face down on the deck. She summoned 911, went outside and rolled Dave over. She began compressing his chest. The paramedics arrived and, moments later, the full weight of the moment became clear when she was told a chaplain was on the way.

Dave had suffered a fatal heart attack and was pronounced dead at his home.

In part due to the dispatches sent by police and firefighters and monitored on scanners, the news flashed across the city and the region. The Mariner switchboard was flooded with calls, radio and television stations besieged by the distraught and disbelieving.

Fittingly, Safeco Field became the site of spontaneous tribute. Droves of fans brought whatever they could to pay tribute, whatever newspaper clipping or photo or program they possessed that connected them with Dave. The sidewalks outside the stadium became a makeshift cathedral. The loss was tangible, the grief inconsolable. Flowers adorned the ad hoc altar alongside offerings of salami, loaves of rye bread and jars of mustard.

Two days later, the gates were opened to allow fans inside to pass by home plate where Dave's photo was placed next to a wreath of white roses and a replica of his Hall of Fame plaque. More than 3,600 filed through the turnstiles to pay their respects.

On November 13, Rick Rizzs bravely hosted a more official gathering at Safeco Field and a similar number of fans attended despite the wet and cold weather. Marilyn and her family were there to thank each and every one. Edgar Martinez, Dan Wilson and Jay Buhner each spoke. Buhner wore white shoes.

The street outside the ballpark was renamed Dave Niehaus Way. The 2011 Mariners wore commemorative patches on their uniform. The radio and televisions suites became the Dave Niehaus Broadcast Center.

Opening night, April 8, 2011, was the first M's game played after Dave's passing. The pre-game tribute deeply moved the more than forty-five thousand fans in attendance as well as the television and radio audiences. A nearly fifteen-minute ceremony preceded the game and featured two moments that remain etched in the collective baseball memory of the Pacific Northwest. The first was the moment the cloth draped across the top of the broadcast booth was removed to reveal "Dave Niehaus 1977–2010" emblazoned beneath.

Despite their heavy hearts, the sell-out throng rose as one when Dave's picture appeared on the video screen in centerfield. The ovation thundered its way through the SoDo District and rumbled its way across the Puget Sound as countless Mariner fans in their homes and bars and restaurants across the city rose with them.

And when it seemed there was no greater threshold to reach, the explosion of heartfelt emotion surged anew, even higher. For there on the mound, horsehide in hand, stood the grocer's daughter from Salt Lake City, the indomitable Marilyn Niehaus, whose love for her husband and for the franchise had now come full circle. Eleven members of her family at her side, she waved to the crowd and threw out the first pitch. And like that first pitch thrown more than a decade earlier by her husband, every Mariner fan called it a strike.

Dave giving his national Baseball Hall of Fame acceptance speech, July 27, 2008.

Knockin' on Heaven's Door: Back in Cooperstown, This Time for Good

My first day at Cooperstown. It's like going to Disneyland except
you don't have to pay for the rides. I can't wait to get there.
—Dave Niehaus

AS IS THE CASE WITH ALL INDUCTEES, David was staying at the Otesaga Resort Hotel in Cooperstown. Until recently, Dave Niehaus had never been to Cooperstown. On May 24, 2008, he appeared there at a "Faces of the Game" symposium on broadcasting. Also on the agenda was the advance, get-acquainted meeting with Hall of Fame officials to go over the logistical nuts and bolts of the induction ceremony and the events surrounding it. Just weeks before the event, he spoke of it with great anticipation.

"To be at the Jerusalem of baseball," he said, "the Holy Land of baseball—Cooperstown—is going to be one of the most spectacular things in my life."

As you might expect, the preparation was important to Dave. He very much looked forward to his introduction to the curators and to the people charged with overseeing the July event. The truth, however, was that it all paled in comparison with his first chance to see the Hall itself. He described walking through the front door and into the apse that houses the entry exhibit as "like walking into a cathedral."

Imagine this man who had spent more than a half-century in service to the game, walking into its most hallowed halls. The panoply of sights

Welcome to Cooperstown, New York.

Dave soaks up the atmosphere in the dugout of Doubleday Field in Cooperstown, home of the annual Hall of Fame Classic.

and sounds before him mixing with the cascade of memories and anecdotes pouring through his brain had to have made for one of his most thrilling moments. Everywhere he turned were the reminders of the men whose exploits he had both admired and broadcast to the world.

There was no bad baseball at Cooperstown, only excellence and accomplishment. The very best were represented here and he was now to be among them.

He sought out the plaques of Stan Musial and Gil Hodges and Walker Cooper and Jackie Robinson, "Pee Wee" Reese and Duke Snider, Don Drysdale and Nolan Ryan.

He recounted the weekend trip to Frank Lee of *The Grand Salami* magazine.

"Curt Smith, the author," Dave said, "who has written a couple of books on baseball broadcasters, invited me way before I had ever known about winning the award...they picked me up at my hotel and drove me up there, a four-hour trip, and I got a private tour with the curator of the museum. I can sincerely say—with the exception of my marriage, the birth of my children and my grandchildren—it was the most exciting day of my life. It was an epiphany.

"I'm sure it's incredible for any baseball fan to go to the Hall, but not everybody gets to go down into the catacombs of the Hall and put on special gloves and handle artifacts like Ted Williams' bat, which he used his last time he was at the plate when he hit a home run and walked off the field at Fenway Park. It was a fascinating day, one of the most fascinating days of my life. I really just scratched the surface. I really didn't get to see that much of the Hall. But I found out a lot of interesting things about it. One of the most attended exhibits, one of the most popular exhibits at the Hall of Fame, is the one on the women's old professional baseball league.

"You know, when you enter the actual Hall—where the plaques are located—it's like entering a sanctuary; it reminds you of a church. And if you're a baseball fan, it's so hallowed that you almost speak in whispers. It's almost like being at St. Peter's Basilica in Rome."

Now, but a few weeks removed from that initial visit to the shrine, he was back. This time he would never leave. This time his name would be inscribed alongside Allen and Barber and those who followed. His name would be forever joined with the man whose voice had inspired him to find his own, Harry Caray. A place among the immortals, a seat at the table with Miller Huggins and the Babe, elbow room at the bar with Ty Cobb and Mickey Mantle, a spot on the Pullman with Satchel Paige and Christy Mathewson was now his. There is no underestimating the wonder of it all for the boy from Princeton, Indiana.

Dave Grosby and his wife, Bonnie, made the trek to Cooperstown. As it happened, they pulled up to the Hall of Fame on Friday evening just as Dave Niehaus was walking out of the building. The Groz recalls, "His eyes literally danced as he spoke of talking to Ron Santo and Ernie Banks, even Stan Musial at the breakfast buffet, jokingly telling him to get out of the way. He was floating. It was the happiest expression I have ever seen on an adult's face, ever."

Thursday evening and Friday morning as he visited the museum and strolled the hotel, he saw the likes of Bob Gibson and Reggie Jackson.

"It's fantasy land, baby," he quipped.

On Friday afternoon, Dave attended the ceremony honoring the late Buck O'Neil at which a life-size statue of Buck was unveiled. The monument graced the new exhibit honoring the winners of the newly established "Buck O'Neil Lifetime Achievement Award." Buck had been named the first winner, and members of his family were in attendance along with Hall of Famers Lou Brock, Bob Feller, Bob Gibson, Reggie Jackson, Ferguson Jenkins, Joe Morgan, Billy Williams, and Dave Winfield.

Buck had been very special to Dave Niehaus. Every year, during one of the Mariner road trips to Kansas City, the voluable Buck had been a guest on the radio pre-game show. It was an annual delight scores of listeners looked forward to each season.

July 27 was a beautiful Sunday, sixty-five degrees and sunny, a perfect day for baseball. The "Veteran Spieler" awoke early and, as he dressed, his thoughts were centered primarily on his wife and family.

The ceremony began as the Hall welcomed the 2008 inductees and their families and friends. It was a truly prestigious gathering. Fifty-six of the sixty-four living Hall of Famers were in attendance, and new Hall President Jeff Idelson described it as the largest gathering of Hall of Famers ever in one place. Hall of Fame pitcher Tom Seaver gave the introduction.

As Dave took the microphone, he paused for a moment, collecting himself. This remarkable journey had begun so long ago and seemingly so far away and the emotion of it all swept over him.

Dave holds Babe Ruth's #3 jersey while on a private tour of the archives at the Baseball Hall of Fame.

He did what he had always done. He went directly to that part of himself that had remained constant from Lowell Elementary in Princeton to Bloomington, from Mt. Rushmore to the Big Apple, to Anaheim and eventually Seattle. He went to the one place he had never left in a lifetime of comings and goings. He went home. And just as he had every night for decades when he went to the ballpark, he took us with him.

Dave could have chosen to take us to Fenway Park or old Memorial Stadium in Baltimore, to Yankee Stadium or the Big A. He could have chosen to take us to Sportsman's Park or Crosley Field, to Dodger Stadium or Safeco Field. He took us instead to 625 North West Street.

He could have taken us to any one of countless sunny summer days. He chose instead to carry us back to one sultry summer evening. He could have taken us to a host of afternoons amid a throng of thousands. He chose instead to take us to a single evening on a simple front porch with his Dad, his Mom and the voice of Harry Caray.

He stepped up to the plate that day in upstate New York and with a simple, sweet swing took us all around the bases with him and brought us, too, back home. The crowd listened intently as he spoke:

"Come with me now to the front porch of 625 North West Street, Princeton, Indiana, in 1946, on a hot, sultry July evening just like today, about 8:30 at night and an eleven-year old boy is chasing lightening bugs and capturing them in a mason jar that had holes punched into it with an ice pick. Every once in a while, he would squish one between his thumb and forefinger just to see the glow. Now, come on now, you know you've done that, too.

"Dad is sitting on a porch with a cold slice of watermelon on one knee and a hot ear of buttered corn on the other with a cold beverage sitting on the ground. And suddenly, from the old Zenith floor model radio in the living room comes this voice screaming, 'It might be, it could be, it is,' and the young boy jumps about three or four inches off the ground with each halting phrase. Magic is happening in St. Louis, Missouri, Stan Musial hit another home run about a zillion miles away and a career has germinated that ends up here in Cooperstown today."

Seated next to each other, wiping the tears from their eyes, the two men who had been at his side more than any others throughout his career shared a smile. Were you to ask Rick Rizzs or Kevin Cremin to list Dave's pre-eminent skills as a baseball broadcaster, they would sooner than later list his ability to tell a story.

As Rick put it to me, "The reason he connected with the fans was that he was such a great storyteller—all the great ones got that from the guys they grew up listening to. He enjoyed painting the pictures, putting people in the front row at the ballpark, making everybody see the game as he saw it. With that comes the knowledge that you're the conduit, the connection."

His trademark was his ability to do so while seamlessly weaving it into the call of the action. Kevin remembers it well: "No one could tell a story and do play-by-play without missing any of the play and never missing a beat in the story like Dave—it was a textbook example of how to weave a story into an at-bat…that Midwestern thing—he was able to do that. And it's a lost art, I think, because it's a radio art."

And here was their friend and colleague, Dave Niehaus, in the biggest at-bat of his career, telling a story. Never failing to miss the action, never abandoning the central narrative of his induction, he told us a story just as he had so often in the thousands and thousands of major league games he had broadcast. Just this once, it was not "one of his stories," it was "his story." It was the one that spoke volumes about his life and his career and the triumph of his achievement. Where he had come from was who he was, who he had always been, and whom he would be remembered as.

And, as always, his thoughts, his spirit and his gratitude were with his wife, Marilyn, and his family:

"Your first thoughts on a day like this go out to your most dearly beloved ones. A summer evening in 1963, I had a date with a beautiful girl. I was going to take her to Dodger Stadium to see again Stan Musial make his final appearance in Los Angeles. I took her to dinner first, asked her to marry me and never made it to the game.

"And here she sits, forty-five years later. I wouldn't be here without you, Marilyn. You gave me two sons and a daughter and they have given me six fabulous grandchildren. How lucky can a man be?"

His thoughts then turned to the pursuit for which he had so passionately given his life's work:

"To quote A. Bartlett Giamatti, 'The real activity was done with the radio, and not the seeing, all falsifying television, was the playing of the game in the only place it will last, the enclosed green field of the mind.' Radio plays with the mind, it gives you a mental workout and delusions of grandeur, that's what Harry Caray did to me.

"My dad took me to my first big-league game at Sportsman's Park in St. Louis probably, I don't know, 1947, '48, and quite frankly, I was never so disappointed in my life. Caray had put these guys on such a pedestal, I just knew it was a Parthenon that I was going to, not a ballpark. You know what, years later, I know I was right on both counts."

And in the simplest Midwestern description of the effect it had on him, he continued:

"Once you're bitten by the baseball bug, it never goes away, and that's what happened with me."

Dave would go on that afternoon to recognize the colleagues, players, managers, and owners who had played such pivotal and supporting roles in his career. Typically, he did so without a hint of his own importance or any reference to the hours of dedication and effort that had gone into his work. It was all about his gratitude, it was all about his teammates. And this man whose every broadcast was filled with soaring descriptions, fittingly chose to end his remarks with the simplest and most direct of conclusions, one that was emblematic of both his humility and his gratitude:

"And finally, I know there are several bigger names who have preceded me in winning this award. There will be several bigger names after me to win this award. But no one will ever be more appreciative."

There wasn't a dry eye in the entire Seattle Mariner universe.

Dave recalled, "I turned around, and Sandy Koufax was there. He (Koufax) said, 'That was just great. That was fabulous.' And I know he meant it. I didn't know he was seated right behind me. Talk about a Hall of Fame kiss, man. Wow. There he was. I said, 'Thanks a lot, Sandy,' That's when I almost cried."

Since 1995, baseball fans of the Pacific Northwest had wondered if they could ever again feel the pride and emotion they felt when Edgar Martinez doubled off Jack McDowell in game five of the ALDS against New York, wondered if they'd ever again feel the thrill they felt when Griffey rounded

Dave and sports-radio host Dave "the Groz" Grosby at the Hall of Fame ceremony.

The Niehaus family in Cooperstown, from left: Matt, Dave, Andy and Greta.

third and Sammy Perlozzo waved him in. They felt it this day and it was Dave Niehaus carrying the mail again.

This time it was he who was being waved home.

Back in Toronto under the watchful eye of his original Mariner broadcaster partner, Ken Wilson, the Mariners were in the process of giving David the Induction Day tribute of beating the Blue Jays, 7–5. The most forlorn of modern baseball franchises had, now and forever, a Hall of Famer. It was the first time in the long and celebrated history of the game that a team's broadcaster had been enshrined in Cooperstown before any of its longtime players. It could not have been more fitting.

Every year at Cooperstown, on Sunday night of Hall of Fame weekend, the newly inducted members are welcomed to a truly exclusive dinner. Closed to the press and the public, only current and past inductees are permitted to attend. It usually goes well into the night and one can only imagine how much it means to the newest members. (Dave would have quoted his old friend Lefty Phillips—"This is the Coupe de Ville.")

No one would have questioned Dave staying through the evening's festivities and taking the next day off. And yet, at 7:45 p.m., he left the dinner to be driven to Albany so he could catch the morning flight to Dallas and arrive in time to be in the booth for Monday night's game against the

Texas Rangers. The man from Princeton felt his obligation to the franchise and the fans was more important. There could be no clearer demonstration of his regard for his work, for his sense of honor and for his commitment to the game.

"These are the people who put me in the Hall of Fame," he said. "There are three generations of people who have listened to me. That's who I owe this award to."

In a poll conducted by the *Seattle Post-Intelligencer*, fans were asked to determine their favorite Mariner of all time. There were some stellar candidates and good choices, from Alvin Davis to Jay Buhner to Edgar Martinez, from Randy Johnson to Ken Griffey Jr. The landslide winner was Dave Niehaus. The one Mariner who hadn't a single at-bat or a solitary strikeout, whose name was never carried by a manager to home plate before a game, never on the lineup card and never in the program, was the one who was held dearest by the fans. The one Mariner who never wore a number was number one in the hearts of those who followed this franchise.

Dave would eventually have a number. In honor of the initial year of the franchise and his first year in the Mariner booth, number 77 was assigned to Dave Niehaus. It is emblematic of his profound effect on the game and this organization that you can, to this day, go to the Seattle Mariners team store and buy a jersey commemorating their broadcaster. Think about it. How many teams in baseball offer a replica jersey and have a number retired honoring their man behind the microphone?

Dave walks the red carpet in Cooperstown.

At a spring training game in Arizona in March of 2013, I spotted a woman wearing a number 77 Niehaus jersey and asked her to tell me why she was wearing it. She was Nancy Blazee from Edmonds, Washington. She had won tickets to opening night in 1977 and she told me, "(I wear it) because he was the greatest Mariner of them all.

"He was family, every night," she said. "When we were at the park, we'd look up to the booth to catch a glimpse of Dave, because sometimes he'd stand up between innings and look out at the crowd. And he always looked out at us, he never looked down on us, because we were family, too, his baseball family."

There is a patch available for the Niehaus jersey, an emblem of a microphone that adorns the plaque on the press box at Safeco Field that honors him.

"I've ordered my microphone patch," Blazee said, pointing to the upper left portion on the front of the jersey. "I'm going to sew it here, so that every time I sing the national anthem at the game, when I put my hand over my heart, I'll think of Dave."

Baseball, family, country—Dave Niehaus in three words.

There is a truly lifelike statue of Dave Niehaus that, appropriately enough, sits in the stands in right field. Fans nightly visit him in droves. Created by Chicago-based Lou Cella of the Rotblatt-Amrany Studio of Fine Art, it was unveiled September 16, 2011. It depicts Dave at the desk, headphones on, broadcasting a game. The scorebook in front of him is open to game five of the 1995 playoff series against the Yankees, arguably the greatest moment and one of the greatest calls of his career. The Mariners assign attendants there nightly to order the flow of traffic and take photographs for the legions that revere him.

On Opening Night in 2013, I asked a young man why he sported number 77 on his back. Though only twenty-six and born nine years into Dave's tenure with the M's, Henry Yarsinske told me: "He was my summer. I remember how happy he was. Even when it was a blowout, he made you happy you were listening. I grew up with Dave in the kitchen."

Yarsinske paused as he looked at the statue and gathered himself. He softly added, "Me and my Mom and Dave."

We were both quiet for a moment. Henry was back in his mom's kitchen and I was back at 625 North West Street.

When you have stood in front of a Picasso or a Miro or a Pollock, you never see a painting the same way again. When in the solitude of a late evening, you have listened to Ella Fitzgerald wail, you are forever bewitched, bothered and bewildered. Theirs was an art that was fashioned in the moment, the sweet yet savory brew born of preparation and spontaneity, of learned fundamentals and a passion for the extemporaneous. Such was the art of Dave Niehaus. He was that good.

A great many broadcasters have days off built into their contracts. Until his last few years, Dave was never one of them. As his children grew older and grandchildren arrived, Dave decided he wanted to give his family more of his time during the summers. Still, his annual travel schedule was impressive. At the time of his death in 2010, Dave Niehaus had been the lead broadcaster for the Seattle Mariners for thirty-four seasons. During that span, the team played 5,385 games. Dave was in the booth for 5,284 of them. Consider his seven years with California and more than forty Cactus League springs and Dave probably called well over 7,500 games.

He never brought anything less than his best to the booth—every day, every game, every broadcast.

Author Curt Smith, in his *Voices of the Game: The First Full-Scale Overview of Baseball Broadcasting, 1921 to the Present*, called Dave "one of the great play-by-play men." Smith said, "He's got voice, personality, detail and humor, and a great home-run call; what more can you ask for? He's a great showman, and baseball is entertainment. He knows how to keep an audience. He, more than anyone, kept baseball alive in Seattle."

What he brought to his work during spring training was as priceless and as imaginative as what he did during the regular season. In those broadcasts, his ever-resilient, ever-hopeful eye cast on the campaign ahead, he was an annual reminder of the hope and the promise that came with spring. The waning of winter brought the day that pitchers and catchers reported, the arrival of roster players and the first pitch of the preseason. Baseball was back.

In 1994, during a spring training broadcast, a bird decided to take up a perch on the ledge of the broadcasting booth in Peoria, Arizona. As it did, Dave was speaking of the Cactus League sunshine and the Seattle weather back home:

"It's eighty-two degrees here in southern Arizona and not a cloud in the sky and back home in Seattle, it's overcast and raining and forty-five degrees." At that moment, the bird began to chirp. Dave was quiet, allowing Kevin Cremin's microphones to pick up the bird's contribution. He turned to sidekick Chip Caray and said, "You hear that?" The bird warbled again. "You hear that bird?" As if on cue, the feathered friend sang out once more.

"Fans, what better reminder could there be that the season of renewal is upon us, that opening day is just around the corner."

On the evening of his passing, the awful news spread rapidly. The community was stunned and shaken, the loss palpable and too difficult to digest. The public outpouring of grief and affection in Seattle was unprecedented. Fans filled the sidewalks in front of Safeco Field, lined up for hours to attend his memorial, and flags across the state flew at half-mast. To this day, there remains a sense of disbelief that we have heard his last broadcast—that now there is a silence where once there was a roar.

For those who listened to him, there will never be a season during which he is not with us. There will never be a summer that doesn't make us ache to hear him once again. He is part and parcel of our heartfelt connection to the game and he never will be forgotten.

There will be an afternoon sometime in the distant future when an aging, veteran baseball fan sits by his grandchildren at the ballpark, tells them of the blue darter and the frozen rope and recalls the voice that first spoke those words to him over the airwaves. And he will speak his name.

There will be an evening when a long-time fan sits in the quiet of his living room with only the radio for a companion. A hard-throwing reliever will leave one over the middle of the plate, and some young slugger will send that baseball soaring toward its new home in the bleachers. That fan's thoughts will momentarily wander within and across that "enclosed green field of the mind." A long-remembered soundtrack will play, complete with the static of memory's transmission, complete with the sound of the distant crowd gathered long ago, complete with the rising voice of the young man from Princeton, Indiana.

Once again a pitch will be swung on and belted, back to the track, to the wall, and it will *fly, fly away.*

APPENDIX

Awards won by Dave Niehaus

Named one of *The Seattle Times* Top 10 Most Influential People of the
   Twentieth Century in the Pacific Northwest
Named Washington state broadcaster of the year in 1995, 1996, 1997,
   and 2004 by the Washington State Association of Broadcasters
Honored in 1997 by the Washington State House of Representatives for
   "contributions to the quality of life in the Pacific Northwest"
Named a game-play announcer for the Nintendo 64 product,
   Ken Griffey Jr.'s Slugfest, 1999
Named to the Mariners Hall of Fame, 2000
Inducted into the Puget Sound Sports Hall of Fame, 2003
One World Award from the Washington Council of the Blind, 2004
Named to Washington State Sports Hall of Fame, 2005
Seattle Seafair parade grand marshal, 2007
Won the Ford C. Frick Award, Baseball Hall of Fame, 2008

Mariner Broadcasters

Ken Brett (1986)
Nellie Briles (1985)
Jay Buhner (2002–2005,
   2011–2012)
Chip Caray (1993–1997)
Ron Fairly (1993–2006, 2011–2012)
Bill Freehan (1979–1980)
Greg Gumbel (1991)
Dave Henderson (1997–2006,
   2011–2012)
Ken Levine (1992–1994,
   2011–2012)
Dave Niehaus (1977–2010)
Tom Paciorek (2001)
Amaury Pi-Gonzalez (Spanish,
   2003–2006)

Don Poier (1981)
Billy Sample (1992)
Joe Simpson (1987–1991)
Wes Stock (1982–1983)
Dave Valle (1997–2006,
   2011–2012)
Dan Wilson (2011–2012)
Ken Wilson (1977–1982,
   2011–2012)
Rick Rizzs (1983–1991, 1995–)
Dave Sims (2007–)
Mike Blowers (2007–)
Aaron Goldsmith (2013–)
Julio Cruz (Spanish, 2002–)
Alex Rivera (Spanish, 2007–)

BIBLIOGRAPHY

Charles C. Alexander, *Breaking the Slump: Baseball in the Depression Era*. New York: Columbia University Press, 2002

David Andriesen, "Niehaus Has His Day in Sun," *Seattle Post-Intelligencer*, July 27, 2008

John Hickey, "Day Dedicated to Dave," *Seattle Post-Intelligencer*, August 3, 2008

———. "Niehaus' Ode to Spring: Play Ball!" *Seattle Post-Intelligencer*, April 6, 2008

Kirby Arnold, "Hall of Fame for Mariners Announcer Dave Niehaus," the *Everett Herald*, February 20, 2008

———. "Mariners to Rotate Announcers," *Everett Herald*, January 20, 2011

Gene Autry, *Gene Autry and the Lost Dogie*. Racine, Wisconsin: Whitman Publishing, 1953

Geoff Baker, "Remembering M's Voice," *The Seattle Times*, December 12, 2010

Jennifer Bjorhus, Bob Sherwin, "Niehaus Plans To Return To Booth Tonight," *The Seattle Times*, August 30, 1996

John Blanchette, "My Oh My Niehaus Gets His Call" *Spokane Spokesman-Review*, February 20, 2008

Fred Brack, *Evergreen State Magazine*, May-June 1986

Jerry Brewer, "Touching Tribute for Niehaus," *The Seattle Times*, April 9, 2011

Jack Broom, "Play-By-Play Guy Plays Down Role—But M's Success Puts Niehaus in Limelight," *The Seattle Times*, October 1, 1995

Enrique Cerna, *Conversations*, interviews with Dave Niehaus, KCTS, channel 9

Bob Condotta, "End of One Era, Start of Another—Ten Years After the Kingdome Tiles Fell," *The Seattle Times*, July 19, 2004

Chris Donnelly, *Baseball's Greatest Series: Yankees, Mariners, and the 1995 Matchup That Changed History*. Rutgers University: Rivergate Books, 2010

Glenn Drosendahl interview with Marilyn Niehaus, November 11, 2011, historylink.com

Shannon Drayer, "Marilyn Niehaus shares memories of Dave as the Niehaus sculpture is unveiled," mynorthwest.com, September 16, 2011

Doug Feldman, *Dizzy and the Gas House Gang: The St. Louis Cardinals and Depression-Era Baseball*. Jefferson, N.C.: McFarland & Co., 2000

Mike Gastineau & Art Thiel, *The Great Book of Seattle Sports Lists*. Philadelphia: Running Press, 2009

Bob Finnigan, "Farewell to Camp Runamuck—M's Have Fond Memories of 16 Springs at Diablo," *The Seattle Times*, April 3, 1992

_____. "Niehaus in Hospital," *The Seattle Times*, September 13, 1996

_____. "M's Pitch $100m Deal to Griffey," *The Seattle Times*, April 5, 1999

_____. "What Else? Griffey Has a Big Blast—Junior's 450-Foot Slam Is Grand," *The Seattle Times*, March 5, 1994

_____. *The Grand Salami*, Volume 2, Issue 2, May 1997

Teddy Greenstein, *Chicago Tribune*, June 15, 2007

John Hickey, "Day Dedicated to Dave," *Seattle Post-Intelligencer*, August 3, 2008

Roger Kahn, *The Boys of Summer*, NY: Harper Perennial Modern Classics, 2006

Steve Kelley, "Year Will Be Remembered For M's Magic—2001, a Time Like No Other," *The Seattle Times*, December 30, 2001

J Michael Kenyon, *Seattle Post-Intelligencer*, May 25, 1979

Larry LaRue, "Oh My: M's Voice Goes Silent," *The News Tribune*, November 11, 2010

Frank Lee, *The Grand Salami*, August 2008

Blaine Newnham, "Niehaus Kept Baseball Alive In Seattle," *The Seattle Times*, May 7, 2000

_____. "Talks Needed Now To Keep M's In Seattle Past 1987," *The Seattle Times*, February 22, 1987

_____. "The Soul, the Voice, of the M's," *The Seattle Times*, October 22, 1996

David Postman, "House Honors Niehaus' Contribution to Northwest," *The Seattle Times*, April 9, 1997

Albert T. Powers, *The Business of Baseball*. Jefferson, N.C.: McFarland & Co, 2003

Dan Raley, *How Seattle Became a Big-League Sports Town: From George Wilson to Russell Wilson*. Seattle: Fairgreen Publishing, LLC, 2015

Dan Raley, *Pitchers of Beer: The Story of the Seattle Rainiers.* Lincoln, Nebraska: University of Nebraska Press, 2012

Andy Rathbun, "Fans Say Goodbye: Several Thousand Pay Their Respects to Dave Niehaus," *Seattle Post-Intelligencer,* November 13, 2010

Dick Rockne, "Niehaus Flies, Flies Away—M's Broadcaster Plays It Safe During Quake," *The Seattle Times,* May 4, 1996

Michael Rozak, *Inside Sports,* August 1986

Bob Sherwin, "Fans Voice Love for Niehaus" *The Seattle Times,* May 9, 2000

——. "Niehaus Back, but Put Away the Salami, Grandma," *The Seattle Times,* August 31, 1996

Bob Sherwin, Bob Finnigan, "Niehaus Resting After Second Angioplasty," *The Seattle Times,* September 17, 1996

Pamela Sitt, "My First Job: Dave Niehaus," *The Seattle Times,* September 7, 2003

Curt Smith, *"Voices of the Game: The First Full-Scale Overview of Baseball Broadcasting, 1921 to the Present."* Barnes & Noble, 1987

Larry Stone, "Calling the Shots—the Art of Baseball," *The Seattle Times,* June 4, 2006

——. "Gorman Was Positive Force in the Early Days for Mariners," *The Seattle Times,* April 3, 2011

——. "Mariners Broadcaster Dave Niehaus Dies," *The Seattle Times,* November 10, 2010

——. "M's Storyteller Will Live Forever with this Statue," *The Seattle Times,* September 17, 2011

——. "My Oh My Forever," *The Seattle Times,* July 27, 2008

——. "Niehaus Delivers in the Clutch," *The Seattle Times,* July 28, 2008

——. "Niehaus Feels Call of the Hall," *The Seattle Times,* July 23, 2008

——. "Niehaus Remembers His Hero—Broadcaster Spent Youth Listening to Caray on Radio," *The Seattle Times,* February 20, 1998

——. "Niehaus the Voice of Summer in Seattle," *The Seattle Times,* March 14, 2007

——. "Refuse To Lose 1995: The Magical Season," *The Seattle Times,* March 31, 2005

——. "Strike Zone Still Elusive For M's Hall Of Famer," *The Seattle Times,* April 2, 2008

Art Thiel, *Out of Left Field: How the Mariners Made Baseball Fly in Seattle*. Seattle: Sasquatch Books, 2003

Emmett Watson, "Mariner Baseball Broadcaster Glad Just to be on Base," *The Seattle Times*, March 10, 1991

———. "Mariner 'Voice' Dave Niehaus Confers Stability on the Franchise," *The Seattle Times*, September 14, 1999

———. *The Seattle Times*, August, 1985

———. "Minor League Presidents," mlb.com

———. "An Unbelievable Experience—Baseball Hall of Fame," *The Seattle Times*, July 26, 2008

———. "A Storyteller of the Old School," *The Seattle Times*, June 1, 2003

———. "Greatest Gift—on His 73rd Birthday, Niehaus Gets Hall of Fame Call," *The Seattle Times*, February 20, 2008

———. "Griffey Memories—From Teammates to Announcers, Here Are Some of Their Favorites Special Section Mariners Baseball '09," *The Seattle Times*, April 5, 2009

———. "Levine to Join Niehaus in Booth," *The Seattle Times*, February 19, 1992

———. "Mariner Announcer Niehaus Hospitalized—Tests 'Came up Clean' after Chest Pain," *The Seattle Times*, August 29, 1996

———. "Mariners Sign Niehaus for 3 Years," *The Seattle Times*, December 7, 1991

———. "Niehaus Out Again," *The Seattle Times*, September 14, 1996

———. "Radio Interest Gives M's Positive Vibes—Team Can Expect Substantial Boost as Stations Bid for Broadcast Rights," *The Seattle Times*, March 24, 1997

———. "Remembering M's voice—Dave Niehaus 1935–2010, a Celebration of Life Saturday at Safeco Field," *The Seattle Times*, December 12, 2010

———. "Rizzs Says, 'Goodbye, M's'—Detroit Tigers Hire Mariner Announcer," *The Seattle Times*, November 21, 1991

———. "Six Seattle Icons Join Hall Of Fame—Northwest," *The Seattle Times*, January 7, 2004

———. "State Sports Hall Names Inductees—Northwest," *The Seattle Times*, April 21, 2005

INDEX

A Celebration of Life for Dave Niehaus

Safeco Field • November 17, 2010

Emcee
Rick Rizzs

Speakers
Andy Niehaus
Greta Niehaus Dunn
Ken Levine
Alvin Davis
Dan Wilson
Jay Buhner
Ken Griffey Jr.

*The Niehaus family has suggested that those who wish
to make a donation in Dave's memory consider the following:*

American Heart Association (www.americanheart.org)
American Diabetes Association (www.diabetes.org)
Food Allergy & Anaphylaxis Network (www.foodallergy.org)

ABOUT THE AUTHOR

BILLY MAC, a friend of Dave Niehaus, grew up in New Orleans where he was educated at Jesuit High School and Tulane University. Billy is a life-long entertainer, singer, songwriter, and piano player.

As a season-ticket holder for two decades, he was privileged to have been acquainted through the years with many Mariner coaches, players, front-office personnel, and baseball writers and broadcasters. He is a member of the Seattle Mariners RBI Club, a group of civic and business leaders who have supported the team tirelessly since 1979.

Billy and his wife, Grammy®-nominated singer Merrilee Rush, live on a small farm east of Seattle.